TRANSFORMING POWER
The Politics of Electricity Planning

AYNSLEY KELLOW

Griffith University

CAMBRIDGE
UNIVERSITY PRESS

For Julie

HD
9697
A3
A85
1996

Published by the Press Syndicate of the University of Cambridge
The Pitt Building, Trumpington Street, Cambridge CB2 1RP, UK
40 West 20th Street, New York, NY 10011–4211, USA
10 Stamford Road, Oakleigh, Melbourne 3166, Australia

Printed in Hong Kong by Colorcraft

National Library of Australia cataloguing-in-publication data

Kellow, Aynsley J. (Aynsley John), 1951–.
Transforming power: the politics of electricity planning.
Bibliography.
Includes index.
1. Electric utilities – Australia. 2. Electric utilities –
Canada. 3. Electric utilities – New Zealand. 4. Energy
policy – Australia. 5. Energy policy – Canada. 6. Energy
policy – New Zealand. I. Title.
333.7932

Library of Congress cataloguing-in-publication data

Kellow, Aynsley J. (Aynsley John), 1951–.
Transforming power: The politics of electricity planning / Aynsley Kellow.
p.   cm.
Includes bibliographical references and index.
1. Electric industries – Australia. 2. Electric industries –
Canada. 3. Electric industries – New Zealand. 4. Energy policy –
Australia. 5. Energy policy – Canada. 6. Energy policy – New
Zealand. I. Title.
HD9697.A3A85 1995
333.79'32–dc20   95–16932

A catalogue record for this book is available from the British Library.

ISBN 0 521 47122 2 Hardback

Contents

Tables and maps

Acknowledgements

The publisher would like to thank the sources for extracts quoted on the following pages: pp. 15 and 17, reprinted from Plummer/Ortega/ Guptia, *Strategic Management and Planning for Electric Utilities* ® 1985 by permission of Prentice-Hall Inc., Englewood Cliffs, NJ; p. 18, reprinted from Formaini, *The Myth of Scientific Public Policy* by permission of Transaction Publishers © 1990, all rights reserved; p. 23, reprinted from Joskow and Schmalensee, *Markets for Power: An Analysis of Electric Utility Deregulation* MIT Press © 1983; pp. 28 and 30, reprinted from Fischer, *Technocracy and the Politics of Expertise* pp. 45 and 31 © 1990 by permission of Sage Publications, Inc.; pp. 32 and 33, reprinted from Noll, *Regulatory Policy and the Social Sciences* © 1985 the Regents of the University of California; pp. 144, 145 and 148, reprinted from *Report on Electricity Supply and Demand Beyond the Mid-1990s* by permission of the Parliament of Victoria; p. 165, reprinted from *Short Term Demand Management Options* (Crown Copyright Material) by permission of the Government Printer of the State of Victoria, first published by The Law Printer, PO Box 292, South Melbourne, 3205 (this document is not an official copy of Crown Copyright material and the State of Victoria accepts no responsibility for its accuracy). Every effort has been made to trace the original source material contained in this book. Where the attempt has been unsuccessful, the publishers would be pleased to hear from the copyright holders to rectify any omission.

Preface

This study grew out of a longstanding interest in electricity planning that goes back to the struggles over Lake Manapouri and Upper Clutha River in New Zealand, which aroused my interest when a student at the University of Otago. While I had long been interested in politics, these cases did as much as anything to convince me that there was more to politics than elections and politicians – that what was at stake and what happened between elections was equally, perhaps more, important. The conflict over hydroelectric development in the South Island of New Zealand, therefore, had a lot to do with my focusing on the study of public policy and, to that extent, this book involves revisiting my intellectual roots.

These cases demonstrated that the options available to politicians and public alike were themselves the result of choices made more deeply within the structures of government, and called attention to the need to look at underlying planning processes rather than just at the politics surrounding the construction of a single power scheme. They also raised questions about the accountability of those making such decisions – questions fundamental to democratic governance in an age of increasing technological sophistication. The book also owes much to four years spent at the Centre for Environmental Studies at the University of Tasmania at the peak of the fight to save the Franklin River from hydro-electric development. There the earlier loss of Lake Pedder presented some remarkable parallels with the history of conflict over electric power development in New Zealand. Again, the politics of this case focused attention on the underlying planning processes deeply embedded in Tasmanian society and politics, and fundamental to the economy of the state.

While I had gathered some material on the Clyde Dam while at Otago, the research for the book began in earnest while at Tasmania. I was supported by several small research grants from the university, which allowed travel back to New Zealand to examine planning processes. Work continued when I moved to Deakin University and was assisted by grants that permitted the travel to Canada without which the broader comparative perspective would not have been possible. The project was not supported by the Australian Research Council. This turned out to be a blessing in disguise as the faster progress such support would have permitted would have resulted in the study getting the Ontario situation entirely wrong as it would have been completed just as Ontario Hydro underwent its remarkable transformation. The project was assisted by a consultancy to the Electricity Development Strategy Consultative Panel in Victoria. Finally, the completion of the book was supported by Griffith University during a period study leave split between Clemson University in South Carolina and the Australian National University, where I was visiting fellow and sabbatical fellow in the Reshaping Australian Institutions project in the Research School of Social Sciences, attached to the Federalism Research Centre.

Aside from these institutional debts, I owe much to individuals. Dr Marvin Shaffer, Marvin Shaffer & Associates, White Rock, BC, had worked on the Site C case, and his visit to Australia in 1985 aroused my interest in developments there. And, while the work relies mostly on documentary sources rather than interviews with participants, the Canadian case would not have been possible without the active assistance of several individuals – Marvin Shaffer among them – who shared their insights and provided key documents. In particular, I would like to thank: Ken Peterson, then Director of Planning, BC Hydro; Thom Thompson, Manager, Government and Public Affairs, BC Hydro; Jack Edwards, Manager, External Relations, BC Hydro; John Grunau, Senior Policy Analyst, Policy Development, BC Hydro and formerly with the BC Utilities Commission; John G. McIntyre, Chairman and CEO, BC Utilities Commission; Chris Sanderson, Lawson Lundell Lawson & McIntosh, Vancouver; Philip D. Carter, Director, Energy Policy Branch, Ministry of Energy, Mines and Petroleum Resources, Victoria, BC; and Dr R. Kenneth Carty, Department of Political Science, University of British Columbia.

There is an equally long list of people in Ontario who made several visits there more productive than would otherwise have been possible: Dave Abbott, Corporate Relations Planning and Research Department at Ontario Hydro; Amir Shalaby, Jim Kirby, Mike Agrell and David Anderson in System Planning Division at Ontario Hydro; and Dr Roger Higgin, Ontario Energy Board.

My visits to Ontario were assisted greatly by Dr Robert J. Williams, Department of Political Science, University of Waterloo. Not only did Bob provide me with assistance of an academic nature but also on countless occasions Bob and his wife Nola provided me with hospitality. Bob's colleagues at Waterloo provided both hospitality to a stranger and numerous insights into Ontario politics, especially Terry Downey on uranium mining and Neil Freeman on the history of Ontario Hydro.

I owe debts to many others. Tony Wood guided my first, faltering steps at researching the New Zealand material. The late Dick Jones, John Todd and the graduate students at the Centre for Environmental Studies at the University of Tasmania provided succour, comfort and encouragement. Also at Tasmania, Bob Rutherford and Mark Trethewey taught me most of what I know of the economics of electricity generation and planning, and Ralph Chapman and Bruce Davis taught me a similar amount about politics in Tasmania. Visitors to Tasmania, including Thomas Johansson, Cliff Hooker, Bill Russell, James Ridgeway and Ivo Rens, all contributed directly or indirectly with insights into all manner of things from energy 'backcasting' to Nicolas Georgescu-Roegen's marriage of thermo-dynamics and economics.

The development of the project was assisted by criticisms of a paper given there, at the Thurmond Institute at Clemson University, South Carolina, and other conversations with Jim Hite and Jim London. Special thanks are due to Brian Galligan at the Federalism Research Centre at the Australian National University for an interest that extends far beyond my time there as visiting fellow; to John Power, Chair of the Victorian Electricity Planning Consultative Panel; Jane Marceau for suggesting Mazmanian and Nienaber's study of the US Army Corps of Engineers to me; and Suelette Dreyfus for sharing insights into Victoria. Ted Lowi has long provided a theoretical spring I have tapped, and several conversa-tions with him have contributed to the theoretical perspective that underpins this study. Aubrey Chandica assisted greatly by preparing the maps.

Julie Husin has throughout kept me up to the task, tolerated my absences and (perhaps most importantly) kept me smiling.

Finally, it should be pointed out that the focus here is on the *politics* of electricity planning. While this is the work of a political scientist, it does deal with matters of substance that belong to the realm of economics or engineering. (After all, since it employs a theoretical perspective that argues that the substance of policy has consequences for politics, it could hardly do otherwise.) Every attempt has been made, however, to try to make the substantive issues comprehensible to my fellow political scientists while trying to do justice to the other disciplines. For those who might wish to test my pursuit of the latter (and for those who might be more interested in the policy issues themselves), I have included full references for the technical and economic literature on which I have based my understanding. For those interested in the politics who might be confused by the technical terms, a glossary is provided.

Finally, it should be noted that, at the time of writing, the institutional arrangements for electricity planning is a constantly shifting field. Every endeavour has been made to ensure that the material is accurate as of the end of 1993, but readers should note that much has happened since – especially in Victoria, where a massive privatisation program is under way. Much remains to be written about these changes and their impact on the conservation programs and planning techniques that are the focus of this book.

Aynsley Kellow

Introduction

If the theme of this book were to be expressed in a single question, it would be something like this: How can societies construct new sets of social institutions flexible enough to adjust both to the uncertainties of the postmodern age and to the new global, national and local concerns for environmental protection?

Its subject matter is somewhat narrower (and more modest) than that, but the question is one to which the present study – of electricity planning by public utilities in three nations – can provide some answers. To be quite specific, the study looks at the way electricity utilities have adapted to the risk and uncertainty pervading their worlds since at least 1973 when the first energy crisis brought discontinuity to what had previously been a stable planning environment. In a sense it is a comparative study of institutional innovation because it takes a state of the art planning technique – *least-cost utility planning – as an exemplar and, in a series of case studies, examines whether utilities adopted it (or similar approaches), if so, how readily and if not, why not. It seeks to identify the reasons for each of these responses.

The work attempts to appeal to two sets of readers. First, it seeks to interest those who work either in electric utilities or in government agencies who must deal with the issues of electricity planning and its relationship to matters of institutional design. At a more academic level, the issues the case studies raise about the relationship between society and technologically sophisticated areas of human activity involve some questions central to political science. Like many pieces of policy analytic writing, therefore, the book contains material that spans the practical and the theoretical realms.

* Words in bold are explained in the glossary.

1

The study was driven more by an interest in the policy issues than any grand theoretical scheme, and the theme of modernism and post-modernism was resisted for a while, but eventually it proved too seductive. Electricity planning, generation and supply is inescapably bound up with modernism. Economies of scale encouraged the formation of large organisations to undertake the activity. These economies of scale meant that electricity has long been regarded as a natural monopoly, which encouraged the establishment of public ownership in many countries and the regulation of public utilities in places (such as much of the United States) where that was anathema. The need for standardisation of voltage and frequency and the need for planning over long time horizons reinforced both the need for government involvement and the reliance of governments on technical experts. The technology encouraged centralisation. Since high levels of electricity consumption came to be considered as integral to any modern industrial society, and since demand seemed to increase endlessly (desirably so, if demand was inextricably bound up with economic growth), electricity planning became emblematic of the modern age: seemingly depoliticised, and undertaken by technical experts.

While the 'end of ideology' might have been problematic in other areas of modern society, there seemed little doubt that it ended in the electricity industry once the basic questions of ownership and regulation had been settled. The electrical utilities that generate and supply this product are themselves archetypical of modernity; they are organisations that possess many of the characteristics of Weber's ideal type of bureaucratic organisation, which is central to modern society. Electric transmission lines came to stand as symbols of modern society. And electricity forecasting and planning became leading examples of the central role played by science and technology as legitimating ideologies in modern societies. Forecasting was conducted on the positivistic, natural science assumptions favoured both by engineers and by the economists who craved natural science respectability, overlooking the fact that it was an activity undertaken in a self-reactive policy context in which the outcome being forecast could be affected not just by other agents in society but also, where forecasting and planning occurred in the same agency, by the forecaster.[1] Indeed, since the forecast outcome could have positive or negative consequences for the forecasting organisation, there was a real risk that the forecast itself could become a powerful tool in attempts by the forecasting agency to maximise its advantage.

In many respects, the kind of organisation adopted by the electrical utilities during their development phase can also be seen as modernist, not just in the sense that form follows function but also in their emphasis on bureaucracy and 'Fordism', or mechanistic structures of control built on a 'fully rationalised base of divided and deskilled labour'.[2] Private electrical utilities were often run along business lines by people with business skills, but at lower levels they relied on the expertise of engineers; in public utilities, control tended to be given over to the engineers almost completely, so both were modernist in the sense that, as Clegg put it, 'Employment [is] based on specialised training and formal certification of competence, acquired prior to gaining the job'.[3]

While there are limits to the utility of such a term, the modernist label is appropriate for electrical utilities, embodying as they do the very spirit of modern industrial society. Their product is totally standardised, and it relies on the exercise of technical rationality. This combination of technical rationality and the integration provided by common professional training made electrical utilities very powerful organisations capable not only of supremacy within their own policy arena but also of considerable influence in other arenas such as economic development.

Modernism can be seen as positivistic, technocentric and rationalistic, and was identified with the belief in linear progress, absolute truths, the rational planning of ideal social orders and the standardisation of both knowledge and production.[4] On the other hand, Harvey has identified the most startling feature of postmodernism as its total acceptance of ephemerality, fragmentation, discontinuity and the chaotic.[5] The traditional electric utility – with its economies of scale, standardised product, technical–scientific rationality and related positivistic planning – can thus be seen as being representative of Fordist modernity. Risk-adapted utilities are bound to stress economies of scope (diversity), decentralisation and flexibility. Whether this adds up to Harvey's 'flexible postmodernity'[6] is not certain, but neither is it central to our argument, which (more modestly) is simply that utilities have had to adapt to the uncertainties of what we could call the postmodern age.

The very strength of the utilities became their weakness. Donald Schon has pointed out that all institutions are to some extent monuments to past problems.[7] Public electrical utilities became monuments to expansionist electricity planning, supported by prodevelopment politics, which militated against searching political scrutiny because politicians wanted to be able to deliver the benefits the construction and operation of an expanded electricity system would bring to their constituents. These imperatives often meant that concerns for the natural environment (in the form of air and water quality or wild and natural rivers with hydroelectric potential) and with the social disruption power projects could bring were often given short shrift in decisionmaking.[8] The strategic location of utilities allowed them to brush such concerns aside, and it also allowed them to push for expansion long after it ceased to be

necessary or desirable. Utilities came to suffer from what Langdon
Winner has termed 'reverse adaptation', or the selection of ends to suit
the available means.[9] Many utilities yielded to the temptation to forecast
ever-expanding demand because it served the goals of organisational
maintenance or expansion. It was not just that demand forecasts were
self-fulfilling prophesies; it was also often the case that utilities' expansion plans represented self-prophesying fulfilments of bureaucratic
ambition. When demand failed to match these expectations from the
mid 1970s many utilities ran into problems, having expensive overcapacity that they found difficult to sell. This outcome was not solely
confined to utilities in public ownership, but it did have some severe
financial consequences for investor-owned utilities, and some utilities
defaulted on debt.[10]

These uncertainties in the electricity demand equation sheeted home
to utilities what the period of 'endless' expansion had masked: that there
were sizeable uncertainties in the planning and forecasting of electricity,
especially since these activities took place over a long time frame.
Further, the uncertainties had increased not just because of the effects
of energy price shocks but also because simultaneous demands for
environmental assessment and planning had extended still further the
lead time for power station construction. As the construction of excess
capacity demonstrated only too clearly, this uncertainty was reflected in
very real costs that had long been masked by the ability of utilities to
market the output from any excess capacity.

New planning approaches were developed to deal with these
uncertainties. Least-cost utility planning (or LCUP, which is explained
further in chapter 1) employed advances in information-processing
technology to develop interactive models to identify the lowest-cost
development program under a wide range of demand scenarios.
Demand-side management (DSM, sometimes referred to as demand
management, or DM) and non-conventional sources of supply came into
greater prominence under the LCUP approach not just because of any
social or environmental advantages these technologies might have been
deemed to have but also because they could be brought on line with very
short lead times and thus provided *economic* advantages for utilities in
reducing the costs of uncertainty.

The costs of excess capacity were felt in most countries, but there is no
better example of the problem than France. Electricité de France (EdF)
is a publicly owned utility formed in 1946. It took control of a few
municipal companies and some nationalised industries that generated
electricity for their own requirements.[11] EdF adopted a nuclear expansion program from the late 1960s, which resulted in considerable excess
capacity after the mid 1980s, despite an aggressive promotion of elec-

tricity consumption after 1970.[12] As a result it had to suspend nuclear investments and attempt to find export markets elsewhere in Europe.[13] Indeed, in the face of a stagnating economy, low demand growth and a heavy commitment to nuclear energy, 'electricity forecasting was virtually turned into an electricity sales program, and EdF has received the order to strengthen its domestic sales "pitch" and to extend its commercial strategy to the international arena'.[14]

Electricity planning in France has been described as demonstrating 'technocratic elitism'.[15] It had relied on projections from past demand as a means of forecasting, an approach that had proved successful during the period when electricity was achieving market penetration, because demand was growing as fast as supply could increase. The rule of thumb in the postwar years was a doubling of demand every ten years. But then things began to go awry, and forecasts of future demand became self-fulfilling prophesies. Baumgartner and Midttun have described the problem thus:

> The moment potential demand caught up with actual supply, the forecasts were in danger of being proved wrong. But then EdF learned that it could use pricing and sales policies to produce the demand that its method had predicted and which, with unchanged policy stances, would not have materialised.[16]

Things got worse after the oil crisis in 1973 because the French state took the deliberate decision to address its balance of trade and exchange rate crisis (and to restore its lost industrial grandeur) by making a heavy commitment to nuclear generation. This policy led beyond self-fulfilling forecasting to reverse adaptation, because the commitment to the nuclear path has meant that conservation options have been overlooked and planning has become a search for customers to use the capacity of generating plant already planned or under construction, even if those customers were outside France.

This result came about because of the administrative centralism of the French state planning system and the integration achieved by the state planners sharing a common background as graduates of the élite engineering schools.[17] While the Ministry of Finance approved EdF's plans, and the Planning Bureau mediated between these agencies and other energy suppliers, 'the quarrel remains entirely within the family of graduates from the élite engineering schools'.[18] The role of these *grandes écoles* in providing institutional integration is a point to which we shall return in chapter 1.

The situation in the United States has been in marked contrast to that in France. The US Public Utilities Regulatory Policies Act of 1978 encouraged deregulation and competition in the electricity industry. By the early 1990s non-utility power producers were providing 38 000 **MW** to national supply, or about 5 per cent of the national total. A further 60 000 MW was under construction or in various stages of development. What this meant was that, at the margin, most new generating capacity in the US was being provided by independent power producers.[19] In addition, encouraged by innovative state regulatory commissions, many utilities were investing heavily in conservation. Forecasting appears to have been more reactive in the United States, seemingly as a result of the absence of centralism, with instead a 'market-like' arena with competing sources of expertise.[20] We shall return to the situation in the United States in chapter 1 when discussing the role of institutions in electricity planning in greater theoretical depth, but the important point to note here is that the considerably brighter picture in the United States appears to have more to do with the presence of alternative sources of advice and creative policy intervention than with the presence of private ownership.

Yet private ownership is often seen as a panacea for problems in the electricity sector. The electricity sector in the United Kingdom underwent radical restructuring as part of the Thatcherite reforms. The assets and liabilities of the former Central Electricity Generating Board were transferred to four new companies: National Power Company, PowerGen, Nuclear Electric and the National Grid Holding Company. National Power and PowerGen were then floated as public companies, but Nuclear Electric had an uneconomic asset base, and it was continued in public ownership. The area boards that had undertaken distribution were established as companies on a regional basis and assumed ownership of the National Grid Holding Company, regulated by a Director-General of Electricity Supply with power to issue licences for transmission and distribution under the Electricity Act.[21]

However, one can question whether such a structure is necessarily more likely to produce better planning. The presence of private utilities with free access to the transmission grid was not able to prevent significant problems in the United States, nor did it necessarily lead to the adoption of new approaches to planning and conservation. One problem, for example, is that the perspectives of private utilities, private consumers and society on such questions as the value of conservation do not necessarily coincide, a point to which we shall return in chapter 1.

All of this suggests that there is a need for new sets of institutions if the new approaches to electricity planning, which offer so much by way of both economic savings and minimisation of environmental problems such as global warming, are to be adopted. Some of these changes will be in the nature of utilities themselves as organisations, but we can also expect that changes in the broader institutions involved will also be required. At the organisational level, risk-adapted utilities open to supply from cogenerators and other non-utility generators, and to demand-side management, are likely to be very different from the old-style modernist organisations.

If the old electrical utilities can be seen as modernist, the responsive utilities can be seen as approximating the postmodern, as defined by Clegg:

> Where modernist organisation was rigid, postmodernist organisation is flexible. Where modernist consumption was premised on mass forms, postmodernist consumption is premised on niches. Where modernist organisation was premised on technological determinism, postmodernist organisation is premised on technological choices made possible through 'de-dedicated' microelectronic equipment.[22]

While there is a degree of resonance between the responsive electrical utility and Clegg's attributes of the postmodern organisation, however, the extent to which the former have resulted from 'technological choices made possible through "de-dedicated" microelectronic equipment' is debatable. While microelectronics has made possible some advances in electricity generation and load management, the stimulus for change has come primarily from a consideration of the growing costs of very much *dedicated* electric equipment used in the past in an age of increasing uncertainty and the need, therefore, for less dedicated inflexibility in electric power system planning. The technology has made flexibility possible, but the economics of uncertainty has made it more compelling; there is a need, therefore, to be wary of explanations based on a view of technological determinism.

Our purpose here, then, is to examine the forecasting and planning processes in a number of electrical utilities and the way these utilities have responded to the uncertainties of what we might call the post-modern era with a view to identifying some of the institutional factors leading to reverse adaptation and those conducive to the reform of these utilities into organisations adapted both to uncertainty and to related environmental concerns such as global warming.

The method of inquiry followed is that of a series of comparative case studies of electricity planning in a number of political jurisdictions. The case studies have been selected for reasons related both to the institutional themes explored and to the logic of comparison. The rationale for following this method and the basis for case selection can best be explained by reference to one of the institutional themes explored: federalism.

Federalism is one institutional factor that might be significant, and which we shall explore, because it has been argued that interstate competition to attract resource development can have pernicious consequences, with states bidding down social returns (including the acceptance of greater environmental damage) in order to obtain the benefits of development. The Canadian staples theorist Garth Stevenson put forward this view concerning the effects of interstate competition on resource development,[23] and it became entrenched as orthodoxy about resource politics in Australia during the 1980s. It seemed to strike a particular resonance with the so-called resources boom in Australia in the late 1970s and early 1980s, a period of considerable investment in resource projects, which were mostly energy-based and which stemmed from international restructuring in the wake of rises in the price of oil. The scramble by the states for a share of the 'bonanza' (which turned out to be at least partly fools' gold) was most evident with the relocation of aluminium smelting capacity to Australia and the related electricity construction projects.[24]

There have, however, been some dissenting voices. Galligan has pointed out that Stevenson's pessimistic view, which rests on horizontal competition between the states to attract resource development, ignores the potential benefits of vertical competition between State and Federal Governments, which could drive up the social returns from resource developments.[25] In a comparative review of state minerals and energy policies Galligan, O'Faircheallaigh and Kellow[26] found only qualified support for the Stevenson thesis and little evidence of low returns in the important export coal industry, for example. This is but one question that might be illuminated by the present study, but it is one that suggests a basis for its scope.

If we are to explore the features of the political system that are conducive to adaptiveness on the part of electric utilities, there is a need for research to be comparative rather than simply confined to one nation. In Australia the tendency has been not to examine comparable unitary nations and thus examine the effects of federalism (by making federalism the independent variable) but to try to find other 'experiments' in federalism to see whether different arrangements are possible or preferable. The comparison is made easier if it is made between two former British colonies because the countries share many traditions, institutions and aspects of political culture. For this reason Australian scholars of federalism have often seen Canada as a suitable candidate for comparison.[27]

In restricting comparative research to Australia and Canada there is a danger, however, of ignoring the dictates of sound comparative methodology. If we are interested in the effects of federalism another federal system is almost the last place we should look in order to make valid generalisations. The comparison we should make if we wish to make theoretical generalisations about the effects of federalism is between federal nations and unitary nations that are similar in as many other respects as possible. For this reason we should expect that there would be an abundance of research comparing federal Australia with its unitary neighbour, New Zealand, not just because of proximity but also because of the high degree of similarity between the two.

The methodological underpinnings of comparative politics are essentially the same as those underlying the study of public policy by the case study method. Both these areas of scholarly endeavour are confronted by the same methodological problems: (1) there is a relatively small number of suitable cases available for study; and (2) the number of variables that must be explained (at least potentially) is extremely large. The problem can be stated succinctly as 'small n, many variables'. Research in the social sciences usually relies on the availability of ample cases and a limited number of variables, so that there is no difficulty in finding enough cases in which the independent variable is either present or absent, and in which all other variables are essentially constant. Therefore, when changes in the dependent variable appear to be associated with changes in the independent variable, we can make relatively reliable assumptions about causal relationships between independent and dependent variables. With the study of comparative politics and the study of public policy the requirements for a large number of cases and a small number of variables are seldom met.[28]

The way this methodological problem is best addressed in both cases is by focusing the analysis on cases in which there is as much similarity as possible of the variables that are not under consideration but variation of the features in which we are interested. Thus, if we are interested in the effects of affluence on voting behaviour, we examine voting behaviour in affluent and poor societies; if we are interested in the effects of federalism on the policy process, we compare the functioning of the policy process in federal and similar non-federal systems. The methodological dictates are different, therefore, depending on whether we are interested in studying the effects of federalism or studying how different federal systems cope with different problems. The latter point suggests that the comparison of similar federal systems is entirely proper, but the former suggests that comparisons between Canada and Australia have been methodologically unsound if they have sought to make generalisations about the consequences of federalism.

Of course, social science research does not often proceed on the basis of such neat comparisons. There are always problems in finding directly comparable cases, as each case has its own historical idiosyncrasies, and the best intentions of the researcher can come undone. For example, Ontario Hydro was selected for the present study as a Canadian case of an unchanging utility; instead, it became a study of a utility undergoing changes perhaps more significant than any other case selected! There is also much insight to be gained from studying a single case in some depth. Inevitably, each case study is to a greater or lesser extent unique, and the approach here is (as much as possible) to let each case speak for itself rather than force it into some preconceived mould.[29] But if we cannot step into the same river twice, we can at least try to immerse ourselves in similar streams of issues and thus seek insights into points of similarity and difference.

For these reasons the present study looks at institutional factors and electricity planning in New Zealand as well as two Australian states and two Canadian provinces. As well as identifying the significant points of difference on which the study is based, it is also necessary to identify the important similarities between the countries in which the cases are located. All share a similar history as former British colonies. The British factor has given all a parliamentary system of government within a constitutional monarchy, but their colonial heritage has also helped to produce some common features of political economy, with a more activist state and a resultant tendency to prodevelopment politics.[30] This pattern resulted from the difficulties of capital formation in colonial economies, with the repatriation, rather than reinvestment, of profits and the immense size of the tasks necessary to develop the colonies relative to the size of their existing economies, and has been labelled 'colonial socialism'. It is a pattern also found in former colonies not part of the British Empire such as Argentina and Brazil,[31] and it is this factor (rather than some British proclivity for public ownership) that explains the absence of private ownership of electrical utilities in the cases studied, although in some colonies (such as those in South America) established by nations with a strong statist tradition, the nature of the state in the colonising nation is undoubtedly also a factor.

There are, however, some differences, which will be seen to have had significant consequences for the reform of electricity planning. Most of these differences will emerge from the cases themselves, but one merits special mention: the use of regulatory commissions in Canada. As will be seen, the regulatory process has played an important part in bringing about reform in British Columbia and has had a lesser role to play in Ontario. There is no comparable institution in either of the Australian cases or in New Zealand.[32] The adoption of such regulatory institutions in the Canadian provinces is undoubtedly a case of contagion from across the border in the United States, where there is a long history of the regulation public utilities in public or private ownership. The difference is especially significant because both New Zealand and several Australian states are going down the path of privatisation or 'corporatisation' of their electric utilities (following the United Kingdom) but without necessarily establishing similar regulatory frameworks. And yet, as a

World Bank study has pointed out, 'The first step in regulatory reform of the sector is to articulate clearly the objectives of reform and to focus on greater transparency and public accountability in governing energy-sector institutions'.[33]

It is at least possible that the new privately owned utilities (or corporatised ones, which are to behave as if privately owned) might be just as prone to inflexibility and environmental insensitivity as the old, unreconstructed publicly owned utilities without the discipline, and above all the public accountability, that a strict regulatory regime can impose. Again, this has been recognised by the World Bank:

> Greater openness through a more transparent regulatory process can also have significant long-run environmental benefits. Currently in many countries there is no intervention point within the command-and-control form of regulating monopoly power sectors where nongovernmental environmental concerns can be articulated. With a more open regulatory body, consumers, investors, and environmentalists can all be heard in setting policies regarding the investment program, pricing, access to service, reliability of service, energy conservation, plant location, and environmental issues.[34]

It is not self-evident that consumers, investors and environmentalists are better off in the absence of regulation simply because the utilities are operating on a profit motive, and in areas such as conservation of resources and environmental factors it is likely that they will be worse off.

Bearing all this in mind, the approach followed here is to examine a number of case studies of electricity planning. The first two, Tasmania and New Zealand, are primarily cases that demonstrate the nature of past adaptation to expansion (and, incidentally, to environmental degradation). They are not intended to demonstrate the reform process but rather the persistence of old, ill-adapted institutions in the face of changed circumstances. Both have undergone subsequent reform, but in Tasmania it has been the result of planning going so far astray that the need for reform was undeniable. In New Zealand the rationale for reform was part of a wider drive to place public enterprises on a more commercial footing rather than being specifically focused on the electricity sector. Then follow two chapters that demonstrate the process of change in two Canadian utilities: British Columbia Hydro and Ontario Hydro. Ontario Hydro had originally been selected because it was widely regarded as a juggernaut, an 'electric empire' whose expansion could not be curbed.[35] Typical of the way reality can confound the researcher, the utility began to change substantially while the research was in progress, delaying the project, and it too became a study of change rather than stasis.

The final case study is one of attempts to reform electricity institutions in the Australian state of Victoria. It had been selected initially because it appeared in the mid 1980s to be an innovative state, and it too has changed in terms of 'what it is a case of'. The relative lack of reform now dominates that case, and it is more now a study of factors limiting change. There is some method in the order in which the cases are presented because each will shed some light on the key issues at stake, firstly those institutional factors associated with old approaches to planning, then the processes of change and finally (in the Victorian case) the contending factors that limited progress towards reform.

I shall conclude by trying to draw some observations from the case studies, but first it is necessary to consider in greater depth some theoretical perspectives relevant to the study. This introduction has indicated that the book deals with the phenomenon of the reverse adaptation of institutions responsible for electricity planning and the reform of these institutions so that they are better suited to the uncertainties of the postmodern era. Before we examine the detail of the case studies we must gain a better understanding of some theoretical perspectives that can illuminate these issues. These concern the economics of electricity supply and least-cost utility planning, the nature of utilities as organisations and the politics surrounding publicly owned electrical utilities. Some of these points have been touched on here, but some must be argued for in greater depth. This task is addressed in chapter 1.

CHAPTER 1

Institutions and electricity planning

There are few more powerful symbols of modern industrial society than the high-voltage electrical **transmission** lines that bring electricity from the power stations where it is generated to the urban consumers, individual and industrial alike. Modern society is, above all, an *electrical* society such is its dependence on this rather peculiar energy source, which cannot be stored but which can be put to a multitude of uses.

The nature of the product itself meant that societies had to place great reliance on the technical expertise of engineers so that there has long been a tension between their professional opinions regarding safety and security of supply and the demands of economic rationality.[1] The technical characteristics of electricity generation and supply meant that there were considerable economies of scale such that electricity was long regarded as the classical example of a natural monopoly. This in turn meant that societies had to deal with this economic problem and usually did so by one of two means: regulation or public ownership.[2] Private ownership with regulation was often – although not always – the path followed in the United States, but the response of both Britain and most of its other former colonies was eventually to go down the path of public ownership. While this choice of policy sometimes reflected the views on public ownership of democratic socialist parties, it often resulted from governments (regardless of political persuasion) assuming responsibility for failed private undertakings, and often it was necessary to facilitate mining or other industrial development.

Where public ownership was the path followed the organisation of the electricity supply was largely seen as a technical matter to which politicians had little to contribute despite the fact that – thanks to the early association with the needs of industry – electricity development often became a tool of industrial development more generally. Often this

13

technical independence was manifested in the establishment of independent electricity commissions from which political controls were largely removed. Often, however, the independence was simply *de facto* with the utilities existing as government departments subject to ministerial responsibility but enjoying considerable freedom because of the lack of technical expertise on the part of the political masters and their general support for expansionist policies because of the benefits, such as jobs, that they brought.

Either way, many societies were seen to have created political Frankensteins, like that fictional monster, harnessing electricity but beyond control.[3] This seeming absence of control was not apparent while growth and expansion were sought by utilities, governments and societies alike. But from the 1970s onwards societies' needs changed. Energy became more expensive, and the thermodynamic impossibility of limitless expansion finally came to be signalled in the marketplace – with a little help from the Organisation of Petroleum Exporting Countries. Citizens came to question some of the costs of expansion that utilities had been able to ignore in the past; costs reflected in acid rain, the destruction of wild rivers and the risk of nuclear contamination and global warming. These factors introduced considerable uncertainty into the planning of utilities where once there had been the certainty of limitless expansion. The problem was that the imperatives of growth were deeply embedded in the social institutions that had evolved around the supply of electricity. By *institutions* here I mean not just the formal organisations that govern electricity supply but also the attitudes, rights, norms, laws and assumptions that surround them.[4] (Markets and marriage are both institutions that are not manifest in formal organisation.)

This book is an examination of this institutional adaptation to past certainty and the reform of electricity institutions to ensure that they are adapted to the uncertain circumstances of the 1990s. It is in essence a study of institutional innovation with the innovation being the risk-sensitive approach to electricity planning known as least-cost utility planning. LCUP and the similar approach called integrated resource planning (IRP) promise considerable advantages for planners, but the case for their advantages is not beyond controversy. Their potential is not at issue here. What is important is that LCUP represents a move away from the deterministic planning of the past, and the adoption of LCUP can be taken as a proxy for reform.

This chapter seeks to deal with some theory relevant to this task. It looks first at some economic theory relevant to electricity planning and summarises the technique of LCUP. It then considers some explanations of bias in organisations that might lead them to becoming reverse-adapted; this involves (among other things) a consideration of what can be termed the politics of technology as well as economic theories of bureaucratic behaviour. Finally, it seeks to provide a perspective to link these themes with others (including the politics of development and the effect of competitive federalism) in a theoretically interesting way. Let us turn, then, to examine the nature of LCUP.

Economics of electricity planning and LCUP

Electricity planning involves the very difficult task of estimating future demand fifteen years or more into the future and then committing large amounts of capital to provide the generating capacity to meet that demand. Few undertakings involve such long planning horizons.[5]

The special challenge of planning for electricity generation results from the very long lead time for constructing new capacity, and this factor makes planning errors an ever-present possibility. There was little problem with uncertainty when the electricity industry was becoming established and capturing market share as any errors were usually failures to provide enough capacity for a demand that was growing extremely rapidly. The fact that the electricity undertakings of many countries were placed under some form of public ownership because of natural monopoly considerations meant that the historical need to expand to meet demand was reinforced by the bureaucratic bias towards output maximisation thanks to political constraints requiring zero profits. This bias was exacerbated by the presence of two professional groups in the electrical utilities: 'the engineers and the accountants, particularly the engineers who see increased output as a monument to their professionalism'.[6] In addition, many public utilities were required by law to meet new needs as they arose, particularly under programs such as those of rural electrification.

Institutional arrangements geared to expansion ran into problems with the onset of the energy crises of the 1970s and the emergence of environmental concern. The situation has been summarised thus:

> It took the [oil] embargo – a calamitous, unpredictable event in terms of long range planning – to close the awareness gap created by inaccurate information concerning the true cost of capital, construction, and fuel. Demand dropped precipitously on the heels of fuel costs that tripled, even for coal-based utilities. Suddenly the lag was reversed. Construction programs and reserve margins were out of synchronisation with reduced demands on utility systems. Clearly, the dislocations in the utility business were beyond the scope of corrective measures under the control of utility managers. The utility crisis has been a public crisis ever since.[7]

Output maximisation was achieved by devices such as encouraging consumption by setting tariffs below economic costs, especially for large industrial users with highly elastic demand (often aluminium smelters), who would be cross-subsidised from those small consumers with relatively inelastic demand.[8] This was all masked by rapid demand growth during the era of market penetration for electricity, but institutional arrangements based on assumptions that demand was insatiable and exponential growth would go on forever were allowed to grow up. But the future is uncertain, and electricity is not exempt from the laws of economics, and electric utilities, with their long lead times, were vulnerable to demand growth below that forecast with the result that they can be saddled with costly overcapacity. This problem caused utility bond defaults in the United States in the uncertain energy market after the oil price shocks of the 1970s.[9]

In a nutshell, the economies of scale in the industry, which had been moving towards bigger and bigger generating units, came to a shuddering halt. In part, this was due to what Richard Hirsh has called 'technological stasis',[10] but the deceleration was made all the more sudden because the need for environmental clearances extended lead times and resulted in increased uncertainty costs for large units.

And yet techniques became available for accounting for uncertainty in the planning exercise by using probabilistic rather than deterministic approaches to the demand/supply equation. The cheapest means of meeting the expected load was no longer always the most efficient use of resources, and the assumption that the electricity demanded should always be supplied became questionable. Rather than providing **reserve margins** by means of excess capacity, plant such as combustion turbines could sometimes be justified (despite their high cost, if needed) on the grounds that they could be installed at very short notice and could cover capacity shortfalls if required much more cheaply than providing additional capacity by conventional means. Other devices such as **site banking**, energy conservation and extending the life of old plant all have a place in this approach.

It has not just been the disparity between the amount of electricity forecast and the amount actually consumed that has confounded electrical utilities since the 1970s. The uncertainty over electricity markets has been exacerbated by non-market concerns. The addition of environmental regulation extended lead times and accentuated the costs of uncertainty. The move to larger, more efficient generating units also meant more 'lumpy' or large additions to capacity, which increased the risk of error in ways often ignored by utilities unused to surprises in the application of their forecasts. Moreover, concerns over the use of nuclear energy and the combustion of fossil fuels and their effect on greenhouse gases has brought the whole rationale behind expansionist electric power policies under increasing scrutiny.

Probabilistic simulation techniques were originally formulated in a classic paper in 1972.[11] Least-cost utility planning emerged in practical application in the late 1970s in the Pacific north-west of the United States, which experienced some serious planning errors in building new nuclear capacity. This region had been exposed to the catastrophic consequences of overestimating demand and, as we shall see later, this response is typical of the way organisations respond to uncertainty. We will now examine precisely how LCUP differs from traditional approaches to electricity planning.

In the past electricity planning was strongly positivistic, and consisted of preparing a projection of demand and then preparing a development plan, which would meet the median growth forecast at the lowest cost (measured in present-value terms, discounting cost streams at an appropriate rate). Such an approach did not necessarily result in least-cost electricity planning, however, because there was no certainty that the median forecast would occur. Planning to meet the median forecast could involve constructing high fixed-cost plant, which had very little flexibility (in economic terms) if the forecast was astray. There was an ever-present risk that error would occur, and any error would thus carry with it uncertainty costs, measured in the cost of the capital plant that represented overcapacity or the lost revenue from the inability to supply electricity if demand ran above forecast levels.

Part of the problem with electrical utilities in the post-1973 period was that they were extremely well adapted to the period of continual growth that had prevailed since their establishment. Any overcapacity could inevitably be sold with little delay and therefore little cost. Moreover, in many countries postwar austerity had brought with it shortages of construction resources at a time when demand really took off. Therefore, in many places, the 1950s and 1960s had been times of power cuts and restrictions which helped to build support for growth inside and outside utilities. Utilities thus reached their apotheosis with the assumption that they could sell all the electricity they could generate embedded within them.

Nevertheless, it is questionable whether they were ever really predicting the future or simply planning for a certain kind of future under the guise of pseudosophisticated forecasting techniques, which Herman Daly argued were about equivalent to oracles divining the future from the entrails of chickens.[12] We considered this problem in the introduction and saw specifically how it afflicted electricity planning in France. The general problem can be summarised thus:

> One unintended consequence of two decades of uninterrupted growth was the illusion engendered in utility managers that forecasters, in fact, were predicting the future. Needless to say, the future has firmly reestablished its fundamental inscrutability, but the illusion died hard.[13]

On the most charitable interpretation, the predictions of the fore-casters can be seen as self-fulfilling. Christopher Hood has pointed to this problem with social institutions such as stock markets, which differ from, say, betting markets where 'the amount of money staked on a horse is only a symptom, never a cause, of its probable success'.[14] But, in addition to the prospect that predictions of the effects of social processes might be their own causes, there is also the possibility with highly technical matters that those with expertise might find that some means suit their particular bureaucratic ends better than others and will use their command of the heights of knowledge to ensure that those means are selected. We will return to this point later in considering the role of organisations in the electricity planning process.

This points to a fundamental problem with traditional electricity planning: it was a process dominated by engineers who generally had no social science training and who were ignorant of the fact that their forecasts could themselves alter the future and thus become self-fulfilling or self-confounding. The 'Oedipus effect' in social forecasting relates to this possibility that the actions taken by human actors in response to a forecast might alter the future.[15] This is why Daly's point about prediction becoming planning has such force (and his reference to the oracles so apposite). This judgment is in fact harsh on the engineers because social science itself (particularly economics) during this period tended to be blissfully ignorant of the inevitably subjective nature of social inquiry in its desire to be objective, like the 'hard' sciences.

The whole question of risk and uncertainty in electricity planning brings the debate between objective and subjective social science into focus. As Robert Formaini has put it:

> objectivists believe that reality is totally outside of human consciousness, although human reason can be a very accurate guide to that reality. Sub-jectivists argue that reality is not simply a collection of objects, standing apart from human consciousness, but a mixture of those objects and subjective perceptions of them. Whether one takes the objectivist or subjectivist position dramatically affects one's perceptions of risk. Objectivists theorise that risk is integral to the objects that are the focus of analysis. Conversely, subjectivists theorise that risk is the outcome of an interaction between human perceptions and the objects being examined.[16]

Traditional planning must therefore be seen as no less a planning process or the deliberate choice of particular societal outcomes simply because it began with an 'objective' forecast. The combination of accept-ance of this forecast, a utility preparedness to err on the side of building overcapacity and the political imperatives towards development have contributed to a process that electricity-intensive industry (such as aluminium smelting) has been able to exploit, socialising its own uncertainty costs in the process. It should be noted that it is possible to incorporate this view into a wider critique of capitalism,[17] although it is not necessary to do so for our purposes here. We shall presently examine the nature of these organisational and political imperatives towards growth and overcapacity (and thus against more flexible planning), but let us first look at precisely what LCUP entails as an alternative to traditional electricity planning.

The response necessitated by the rise in uncertainty in electricity planning is to maintain flexibility. 'For most utilities this presents a dilemma since the most economical plants require construction lead times of from 6 to 12 years and are capital intensive.'[18] Many public utilities have absorbed the costs of uncertainty by overcapitalising and by continuing as if nothing much has changed and passing the costs of their planning errors on to consumers, often with government consent or complicity. This is easier to achieve with non-regulated public utilities than with regulated private utility companies, but the latter have not been immune. More efficient ways of coping with uncertainty include direct load control, refurbishment of existing plants to extend their life and reinforcing transmission lines to provide for more flexible generation patterns. Other techniques include site banking, demand management and selecting more flexible fuel types and plant sizes.

Site banking is a technique for reducing the lead time for new capacity. It consists of conducting detailed design work, obtaining environmental clearances and possibly undertaking some initial site preparation works well in advance of a power station being needed. The station can thus be built and commissioned in a much shorter lead time if and when it is actually needed. Site banking costs money, but it reduces the costs of uncertainty and is often cheaper than covering the uncertainty in a demand forecast by actually commissioning plant.[19]

Demand management can include 'demarketing', or inducing (even paying) customers not to consume (that is, to conserve).[20] It can also entail improving plant utilisation to lower unit costs by encouraging **peak clipping**, **valley filling** or **load shifting** to smooth the daily and seasonal load fluctuations. The lead time on these 'negawatts' (to use Amory Lovins' term) is usually much less than that of conventional new capacity, but many utilities have also found negawatts to be cheaper than new megawatts, even ignoring their contribution to lowering uncertainty costs.

Another option is to offer discounts to large consumers in exchange for interruptibility, a measure often taken where there is a large interruptible load such as an aluminium smelter.[21] **Combustion turbine** plant can be installed at very short notice and is very cheap in terms of capital cost so it can be used in expansion plans to cover uncertainty; such plant might never be used or might be used only until more conventional plant is commissioned.[22] Traditional planning has usually relegated combustion turbines to a role meeting daily peaks rather than covering risk because of their high fuel costs, and has not considered that the economies of scale of larger units must be traded off against the higher uncertainty costs associated with them. And if conventional thermal generating capacity is needed, smaller generating units can again reduce lead times – by three to five months per 100 MW decrease in unit size.[23]

This trade-off between economies of scale and greater uncertainty costs points to a general problem that underscores the essential difference between LCUP and traditional planning: it is that many of these responses to the costs of uncertainty go against some significant trends in generation costs when uncertainty does not exist. There are considerable economies of scale associated with large generating units – if the planner could be certain that future demand will be as forecast. Otherwise, larger units will simply add to uncertainty costs by making the mistakes larger. Engineers insulated from uncertainty costs will opt for larger units with their lower capital costs per megawatt of installed capacity and their higher thermal efficiencies. They will also see combustion turbine plant only as a means of meeting peak demand, because of its high fuel costs, oblivious to the point that it might be the cheapest way of covering uncertainties in the load forecast. What utilities needed (and some developed) was a planning process that made the uncertainty costs explicit and then helped to identify which mix of the above measures will meet probable load growth scenarios for the least total cost – an approach that became known as least-cost utility planning.

The key to this approach lies in the fact that forecasters have often assigned probabilities to different possible forecasts of demand. The essence of LCUP is to subject different development plans (involving different mixes of demand-side management, site banking, new capacity and so on) to an analysis that estimates their cost under different load growth scenarios and then weights the cost for each scenario according to the probability attached to each scenario. Thus, if there are three load forecasts with probabilities of 0.3, 0.4 and 0.3, and the total present-value system cost of one development plan under each scenario is (respectively) $1200m, $1000m and $900m, the weighted cost of this option is $1030m ($360m + $400m + $270m). This is slightly higher than the $1000m estimate we would derive from an analysis that looked only at the costs of meeting the most probable load forecast; the difference represents the cost of uncertainty. The LCUP approach involves identifying the development plan that yields the lowest weighted cost, thus taking into account the uncertainty that exists in planning over the long term and making these costs explicit as well as paying them, rather than gambling that the most likely outcome will result. It requires a considerable retreat from hubris on the part of forecasters and, by admitting to the possibility of error, could diminish the authority accruing to those who lay claim to such expertise.

What is significant is that this probabilistic approach can yield preferred development plans that would not be selected if the 'most probable' or median growth approach were taken. Thus, a mix that had costs under the three demand growth scenarios of $1000m, $1200m and $900m respectively would have a present-value cost of $990m weighted to incorporate uncertainty – $40m cheaper than the development plan designed to meet most cheaply only the most probable demand forecast, even though the present-value cost of that development plan under the 'most likely' demand growth scenario is $200m (20 per cent) more than the first plan.[24]

The LCUP approach is even more complex than traditional planning, which might help to explain why politicians have rarely imposed it on utilities, but, in a nutshell, it entails trying to minimise all costs (including uncertainty costs) by means of the specific incorporation of risk rather than planning as if knowledge of future demand were certain and displacing the costs of uncertainty into the future. It might be criticised as still being positivistic, but by admitting to the possibility – indeed the probability – of error, it acknowledges the self-reactive nature of such forecasting and planning. The possible advantages of LCUP can be seen when it is considered that the size of the uncertainty in demand fifteen years into the future in the Australian state of New South Wales in the mid 1980s was about equivalent to the output of a power station with a capital cost of $2 billion.[25]

Having examined LCUP, let us now consider why utilities might be slow to adopt planning techniques that might help minimise mistakes of such potential enormity. Here we shall look both at theories that seek to explain utility behaviour and at the experience of the United States, where utilities have led the way in adopting the new approaches to planning.

Organisational bias in electricity planning

In order to understand the past behaviour of utilities and why utilities might be slow to adopt the LCUP approach to planning, it is useful first to look at some economic theory about electricity planning. Every attempt will be made to present this material as clearly as possible, but some readers will doubtless find it obscure. For those lacking the patience, the drift of the following paragraphs can be summarised thus: the absence of a profit incentive encourages publicly owned utilities to invest in excess capacity. Once we have done this we will consider another theoretical perspective on institutions that can contribute to our understanding. Of particular interest will be the significance of technical complexity since it creates some very significant issues for democratic governance.

Two economic theories have been advanced to describe electric utility equipment selection decisions. The first is, rather straightforwardly, that the utility will minimise the costs of meeting demand. Clearly, it will do so in order to maximise profits if it is not subject to regulation or is subject to price regulation – that is, regulation that specifies the price it may charge with no reference to the amount of capital invested. If, however, the utility is subject to regulation that limits it to a particular rate of return on capital, it will seek to maximise profits subject to this constraint by 'gold-plating' its plant.[26] Thus, it will spend more on capital rather than pursue less capital-intensive but perhaps more labour-intensive plant design options, even when the latter are more efficient. Thus a utility would build a plant with a higher thermal efficiency than would be necessary if it were choosing a plant designed to minimise costs. According to this theory – known as the **Averch–Johnson hypothesis** after its creators[27] – under rate-of-return regulation, 'for a given quantity of electricity produced the mix of equipment used would be more capital intensive than under cost minimisation'.[28]

This hypothesis has consequences for the planning activity of utilities because one would expect that there would be more than just gold-plating as a result. Rather than just the capital-intensiveness of each piece of plant being affected, the mix of types of plant will be altered in the capital-intensive direction. Thus there will be more hydroelectric, nuclear or coal facilities built than oil or gas power stations.

It is not immediately obvious how this theory would apply to a utility that is publicly owned but not subject to regulation by an independent regulatory commission – that is, where prices are simply set by the government on the recommendation of the utility. The answer depends on the nature of the government–utility relationship. If the government sets tight prices which will be tough for the utility to meet, it is likely that the utility will follow a cost minimisation strategy. If, however, the government tends simply to rubber-stamp the rises sought by the utility, and the utility is – as is often the case – forbidden from making a profit, gold-plating is likely to occur, because a zero rate of return under these circumstances is likely to outweigh the ineffective price regulation. That is to say, a zero profit constraint is still a rate of return constraint. Any likely profits must then be absorbed in additional costs of one sort or another, and further capital expansion is a means of ensuring this result – one that happily coincides with goals of bureaucratic expansion.

Therefore, it is not just the Averch–Johnson effect that tends to produce overcapacity but also a coincidence of Averch–Johnson behaviour with bureaucratic tendencies towards organisational growth, which in itself is likely to feature more prominently as an organisational goal – explicit or tacit – when the utility is subject to a zero profit constraint. Organisations tend to seek growth because it means more rapid promotion and greater financial rewards than does shrinkage or stasis.[29] While these tendencies are usually held to be present in all organisations, they are usually worse in public sector organisations, which are not driven by the pursuit of profit. According to public choice theory, there are reasons why the tendency towards gold-plating might be accentuated in publicly owned utilities. Bureaucrats will increase their pecuniary and non-pecuniary streams of income by increasing staff, capital and budget.[30] Thus public managers will relocate activities from the future to the present and, by increasing output sales, increase the size of the firm. Additionally, however, the stream of benefits received by public utility managers are less closely related to future profitability than their private sector counterparts since they are unable to fully capitalise gains that will accrue in the future. Hence public (rather than private) utility managers will attach lower value to future gains compared to present gains and have an incentive to increase present gains at the expense of the future. This is to say that they will adopt a lower discount rate in making decisions than will their private counterparts. As a result, 'dams will be bigger and investments more capital consuming than would otherwise be the case'.[31] Again, this will count against LCUP with its emphasis on the cost of idle capital.

It should also be noted, however, that the costs to the utility of undercapacity are usually greater than those of overcapacity.[32] This bias in favour of overcapacity is exacerbated when the cost of capital to the utility is subsidised – as it often has been in Australia and New Zealand – by the provision of government loan funds to utilities or semigovernment borrowings at less than market rates of interest, thanks to the government guarantee provided to the utility. The perceived risks of under- and overcapacity for electricity planners are usually, therefore, asymmetrical.

The consequences of this subsidisation of capital and other inputs into public electricity generation have been described thus:

> There is ... an important set of efficiency issues that results from the lower costs that public power authorities incur by virtue of their access to public resources (hydro capacity), subsidised capital (rural cooperatives and municipals), government guaranteed loans (TVA), and exemptions from income taxes and property taxes ... This provides an implicit subsidy for electricity and will induce consumers to consume more electricity relative to other goods and services. Such subsidies obviously conflict with energy conservation goals.[33]

It should not be concluded from this that the economics of regulated electric utility behaviour are unilaterally conducive to decisions antithetical to environmental concerns. Murphy and Soyster, finding support for the Averch–Johnson hypothesis, have concluded from their study of regulated utilities in the United States that 'more capital-intensive technologies are chosen. More coal plants with scrubbers are built, and more retrofitting of existing coal plants occurs as regulation tightens'.[34] This result comes at the expense of building gas or oil plant; the desirability of which depends on how one views the thermodynamic appropriateness of using these higher-quality fuels for electricity generation as well as considerations such as the sulphur content of them all. Nevertheless, the important point to recognise here is that public utilities are still likely to demonstrate Averch–Johnson behaviour if they operate under a zero profit constraint because this amounts to rate-of-return regulation, even if the rate of return is capped at zero, and that this tendency is reinforced by the bureaucratic growth imperative.

The introduction of risk-sensitive planning appears to have started in private utilities in the United States where the organisational growth imperative was tempered by the profit motive.[35] However, it should be noted that it took creative regulatory intervention to bring about the introduction of LCUP and the vigorous promotion of demand-side management, which forms part of that approach. LCUP had its practical origins in the Northwest Power Planning Council, which involved the states of Oregon, Washington, Idaho and Montana and was established in 1981 by federal legislation.[36] This body was established as the result of planning problems that were to result in a default on bonds in 1983 by the Washington Public Power Supply System. WPPSS had a heavy commitment to nuclear construction when markets for its capacity evaporated.[37] It had been encouraged to build five nuclear plants by the regional transmission agency, the Bonneville Power Administration, which had been created in 1937 to transmit and market power from the Bonneville Dam on the Columbia River.[38] The BPA had been vigorous in attempting to attract industry by promoting the sale of low-price electricity to the aluminium industry and, to a lesser extent, to the pulp and paper industry.[39] The Northwest Planning Council was established as a counter to the BPA, although the BPA must concur with its plans, and it is responsible for implementing them and has final responsibility for planning, with no mechanism provided for reconciling differences.[40]

The act establishing the Northwest Planning Council required the planners to give conservation options a 10 per cent economic bonus to reflect the environmental and social aspects of conservation not re-flected in market prices. This was an explicit recognition that the perspectives of utility planners and society did not coincide. There were considerable advantages in pursuing conservation options in terms of reducing both uncertainty costs (since the lead time of conservation was short) and absolute costs. The average cost of energy saved identified in the 1986 plan was a very competitive 2.4 c/kWh, with the aim being to cut demand by 3700 MW (14 per cent) by 2006.[41]

One obstacle to utilities tapping into such negawatts, however, was the fact that – just as the perspectives of society and planners do not coincide – the perception of such opportunities for the private consumers who need to make the savings did not coincide with the social benefits.[42] Private individuals tend to discount the stream of future benefits of conservation more highly than does society and so are reluctant to spend on conservation. For this reason policies are often needed to encourage the adoption of conservation. They might take the form of marketing campaigns, but there is often a need to resort to financial inducements. Hence, utilities covered by the Northwest Planning Council spent more than $800m on conservation programs between 1980 and 1986.[43]

By 1989 sixteen American states had adopted LCUP.[44] A survey indicated that, in 1985, seventy-six utilities spent $582m on conservation programs and $135m on load management.[45] This activity was largely concentrated in only seven utilities in Florida, New England and California (plus the Tennessee Valley Authority), and appears to be the result of what has been termed 'regulatory interventionism' on the part of utilities commissions prepared to adjust rates so as not to penalise utilities for achieving conservation.[46] The conventional rate-making procedures in the United States have tended to reward utilities for increasing sales, because rates are set periodically, but short-run marginal revenues almost always exceed short-run production costs so profits are maximised by promoting sales.[47]

Another important factor in recent changes in the United States also had its origin in federal legislation. The Public Utility Regulatory Policies Act of 1978 (PURPA) required utilities to purchase electricity from qualifying cogenerators and small power producers at a price equal to the **avoided cost** for the utility.[48] As such additions to capacity typically have shorter lead times than large conventional generation projects, they have played their part in reducing uncertainty costs but, again, they have often provided cheaper cost alternatives to new plant.

The response in the United States is typical of the way institutions respond to uncertainty. One can contrast the recent past with earlier, more stable times by noting that: 'A greater element of uncertainty now creeps in, though it can be limited in principle by sufficiently sophisticated prediction or anticipation'.[49] Yet any technological innovation depends on institutional factors for its adoption and requires institutional innovation that goes beyond the level of the organisation. The

United States experience shows how the issues under examination here transcend questions of ownership and organisational structure, although we need an understanding of how broader institutions interact with organisational factors. We have looked above at two economic factors likely to affect such innovation, but there are others.

The need to adapt to rapid change, which has been characterised as being 'like learning to hit a moving target',[50] is by no means unique to electrical utilities in the postmodern era. Adaptivity has become a commonly stressed value in contemporary governance, and: 'One could almost speak of a "cult of adaptivity" which clearly to some extent is a reaction to an earlier cult of long-range planning'.[51] But, while 'unforeseen changes which cause large, carefully-planned projects to fall flat on their faces are a classic administrative banana-skin', such changes 'become more costly the more (literally) concrete the wrong predictions are'.[52] Most electricity projects are very concrete indeed, and few more so than massive hydroelectric dams.

However, what is important is not the absolute rate of change in the environment but the pace of change in the environment relative to the rate of adaptation by political institutions. This is why the lead time problem in electricity planning is so crucial. Again, while electrical utilities are not unique in this respect (it takes eight to ten years to plan and build a major hospital), the lead time for adding new major power stations, including environmental clearances, is more than ten years and often as high as fifteen, which means that utilities are very much at the extreme when compared with other human undertakings. The potential for a kind of organisational arthritis to slow responsiveness while the world changes is thus particularly important because the long lead time means that maladaptation can occur with slower rates of change in the organisation's environment. As I have argued above, utilities can shape the future by their decisions, but those decisions can make less and less sense as time marches on.

All these problems are exacerbated when we add another ingredient present in electrical utilities: a high degree of technical specialisation. This diminishes accountability because elected politicians and the public can rarely understand the issues at stake, and we often speak of **technocracy** under such circumstances. But if all organisations are monuments to past problems, they are also embodiments of past means to deal with those problems, and they will prefer to maintain the *status quo* if at all possible. A new problem requiring a new approach, or a new means of solving an old problem, will threaten those whose position depends on the old means. Thus Elliott and Elliott have argued that technocracy often involves a 'tendency to subordinate *ends* to *means*'.[53] As we have seen, Langdon Winner has called this 'reverse adaptation'.[54]

Reverse adaptation appears to result from a coincidence of professional norms and abilities and self-interest. It can affect not just the
electrical utility as a whole but also subunits within it. Thus,
'Transmission engineers find reasons to build new power lines ... [and]
power plant operators favour expenditures that will make generating
plants easier to operate'.[55] But neither is reverse adaptation unique to
electricity planning. The following observation has been made of the
Manhattan project to build the atom bomb:

> The American bomb project was launched by men who sincerely believed they
> were in a race with Hitler. When it became clear that Hitler was not building a
> bomb, the Americans found a new target in the Japanese and convinced
> themselves there was no alternative to bombing Hiroshima and Nagasaki. Four
> years later, when the Soviet Union exploded its first atomic bomb, the
> Americans felt they had to stay ahead in the arms race.[56]

In the case of the Manhattan project, we can also see at play a
phenomenon that reinforces reverse adaptation: the tendency for past
commitments to shape future choice and money spent in the past to
serve as the justification for future decisions. Economists warn us against
this phenomenon in their decisionmaking advice; they tell us that we
should ignore sunk costs, let bygones be bygones and not cry over spilt
milk. In reality, however, there are forces that encourage us to do just
that. We can point here to Leon Festinger's concept of cognitive dissonance, which refers to the ability of individuals to explain away evidence
that challenges deeply held beliefs and assumptions.[57] Thus reverse-
adapted utilities will persist with standard operating procedures long
after they have ceased to be appropriate. Deviations from demand
forecasts will be rationalised so as not to threaten expansion programs.[58]
Humans are often reluctant to admit to their errors, and adversarial
political processes, whereby opposing political parties are forever looking
to exploit mistakes, do nothing to encourage policymakers to own up to
theirs. The experience of 'whistleblowers' also suggests that owning up
to the mistakes of others is not encouraged by social institutions.

Politics and electricity planning

The discussion thus far has sought to provide some insight into electricity
planning – both traditional planning and the type that reflects the final
demise of certainty in modern societies – and the factors that might contribute to the failure of utilities to adapt to these changed circumstances.
I shall now locate these specific concerns in some wider perspectives in
political science and provide a conceptual framework with which to make
sense of the persistence or change of institutions for electricity planning
revealed in the case studies that follow.

Many of the issues raised thus far relate to questions of technocracy, central to almost any broad concern with the politics of the modern (or postmodern) age. One problem that pervades modern society is what Herbert Marcuse called the 'one-dimensional' nature of the technocratic consciousness which seems to dominate its governance.[59] It has been summed up thus:

> Fundamental to technocratic consciousness, it is best understood as a failure to identify and maintain a clear distinction between two basic modes of reason, one technical and the other normative.[60]

Jurgen Habermas argues that each of these modes of reason relates to a distinct sphere of human activity: technical reason to the sphere of economic production; normative reason to the social sphere, including family, culture, religion and politics.[61] The sphere of economic production is dominated by concerns of how things work while the social realm is 'normatively constructed through mutually established intersubjective understandings between the members of a community or social group'.[62] While there are now serious critiques of the objectivist basis of this technocratic consciousness, the fact remains that (valid or not) objectivism has prevailed over subjectivism in the discourse of modern government.[63] The social realm had taken precedence over the technical throughout most of history, but the relationship between the two was gradually reversed with the dramatic rise of modernism with its emphasis on industrial and material progress and a resultant adulation of technology. As a result humans were treated as means for the achievement of economic or technological ends, and any debate over ends was displaced by debates over means; in other words, reverse adaptation occurred.

Consequently ordinary citizens have been disenfranchised and some of the more important fundamental assumptions embedded in our institutions have been isolated from political debate. As Fischer puts it, 'As technical issues overshadow all others, attention increasingly turns to complex debate among experts'.[64] Thus debates take place about which electricity technology should be used, or which site should be selected, but rarely do debates occur over the values embedded in the institutions and technologies around the margins of which these arguments swirl, like turbulent air, affecting progress, but rarely affecting direction.

> Lacking experts in ethics, morals, and general human decency (in the sense that we recognise technical experts), we acknowledge no privileged methodological rules capable of deciding the normative issues that confront us. For this reason, such discussions are merely written off as 'just matters of opinion'.[65]

Again, the story of the American bomb project lends support to this view because the decisions of the scientists were frequently distorted by personal ambition and institutional self-interest; just as often, they ignored the broader questions of humanity, the cumulative dangers of a runaway arms race and the unregulated expansion of nuclear power ... Those who sought to slow the momentum ... were told they were not 'expert' enough to understand the extent of the problem – and they could not learn any more about it because the details were top secret.[66]

These tendencies are captured – and indeed celebrated – by the dominant model of the policy process. Incrementalism, drawing heavily on notions of Popperian piecemeal social engineering for its epistemological force, eschews debates over ends and focuses on debates over (or, perhaps more accurately, agreement on) means.[67] That it is both an appealing prescriptive model and widely accepted as an accurate descriptive model in Western democracies underlines the resonance it has with modernism.

Incrementalism involves the adoption of policies that differ only marginally from the *status quo* on the basis of very little analysis of alternatives and is at its most powerful as an account of policymaking in the highly pluralistic United States, where the separation of powers makes agreement on goals so unlikely that a winning coalition in support of any policy measure can only be built if the search for consensus focuses on means rather than potentially divisive ends. Thus defence procurement, with its cornucopia of contracts benefiting specific localities, was often the driving force behind defence policy in the United States. But while the greater centralisation of authority in the British system of government and other prime ministerial systems diminishes the tendency to incremental policymaking, there are features of the bureaucratic system that reinforce this tendency for the ends embedded in options to go unquestioned. It has been argued that three elements of British administrative decorum have a pernicious effect on forecasting practices: a very careful definition of roles, impersonality and administrative tidiness.[68] Because of the requirement for impersonality only forecasts that come from an organisation rather than an individual can be accepted, and – thanks to the other two principles – only those organisations with a clearly established interest and status will qualify as legitimate sources of forecasts, and the fewer of these there are the better.

Thus these administrative principles – 'so much prized that they are sometimes uncritically equated with good administration' – act so as to restrict the flow of information, restrict individual initiative or the questioning of the organisational line, and provide no check on professional or bureaucratic bias, so that 'it may happen ... that the only authorised and acknowledged sources of expert advice are interested parties to a decision, or are strongly predisposed to a particular course of action'.[69]

This reliance on one source of expertise is highly dangerous, particularly for forecasting and planning. One view is that, above a certain very low level, expertise and accuracy of forecasts are unrelated, and indeed accuracy might even drop after a certain level.[70] But, as we saw earlier, such errors can work to the advantage of some sectors of society, such as energy-intensive industries, which can consume surplus power and 'correct' the planning error. Again, this draws attention to the relationship between the professionals performing the planning and the wider society.

According to one view, a close relationship has long existed between engineers and capitalism, arguing that mechanical devices and scientific methods were introduced into the workshop in order to assure complete control over the production process.[71] 'However firmly ... [engineers] convinced themselves that they served the interests of society as a whole, they in reality served only the dominant class in society ...'[72] This, however, is but one of four models of technocracy. Elliott and Elliott have pointed out that, in addition to this 'servants of power' model of technocracy, there are three other ways of interpreting the phenomenon: as 'benevolent technocracy', as rule by a self-interested élite and according to an 'autonomous technology' model.[73]

We do not, for our purposes here, need to choose one of these models over the others. All that is necessary is to note that this study of electricity planning can be located within a broader study of technocracy and that this raises some interesting questions about the relationship between technically oriented institutions. Fischer has listed these questions as:

> Can we build participatory institutions that establish and mediate procedural and discursive relationships between élite decision makers and the public? Can we design political structures at the organisational and community levels of a technological society that can, in turn, be authentically linked up with top-level decision processes? Is it, in short, possible to establish a public community capable of engendering a political conversation between the rulers and the ruled?[74]

To structure our examination of these issues we need some conceptual tools with which to make sense of the role of technical expertise within the agencies we intend to study and to account for the reforms of LCUP in a theoretically interesting way. We also need to be able to account for or relate such a conceptual framework to some of the other political dynamics we might expect to be at work, such as the effects of federalism and other imperatives that might favour expansion. The important point here is to relate these changes in a theoretically significant fashion to other regime changes so that the electrical utilities can be seen in the context of the larger functions of the state.

Theodore J. Lowi has developed an approach that can provide this linkage. Lowi links the content of public policy with regime structure in such a way as to tie the policy changes we have identified as being involved in the move towards flexibility to the nature of agencies themselves. In short, he argues that policy changes of this kind will require changes to the kind of bureaucratic agency involved in the policy arena. He argues, in short, that agency structure depends on the kind of policy for which the agency is responsible. We might add that, should the changes not occur, the desired policy shift is likely to be transitory because the old agency structure is likely to snap the policy back into the old pattern, like a molecule temporarily bent into a different configuration. Lowi's basic argument is that, where 'politics' includes the nature of bureaucratic agencies, policy determines politics.[75] He distinguishes four types of policy, but we are concerned here with only two of them: distributive policies and regulatory policies.

Lowi's argument has developed somewhat over a thirty-year maturation period. In its earlier formulations it has widely been interpreted (by this author among many[76]) as resting on distinctions between the nature of costs and benefits inherent in any policy. Thus, distributive policies can be seen as providing private benefits at public expense. The impact of such policies on the political system is to involve the beneficiaries (since the narrowly concentrated benefits are enough to overcome economic disincentives to organise) while not exciting opposition from those who bear the costs. As the costs are dispersed over the whole of society (all consumers or all taxpayers) they are small enough for each so as not to excite political opposition. Often the costs are dispersed not only in space but also in time – by borrowing or by impacts on the future natural environment. Any opponents who do emerge can be 'bought off' by disaggregating the benefits so as to include them, and their share of the benefit (however small) will be large enough to outweigh their share of the costs. Thus a hydroelectric dam provides jobs to workers and lucrative contracts to industry. Its costs are borne by future consumers of electricity and those for whom posterity is diminished by the loss of a naturally flowing river. Particularly in the time before environmental concern, such projects were very attractive politically.

Regulatory policies involve the imposition of negative sanctions or costs at the same time as benefits are provided. They require a degree of consistency from one case to the next, and this element is usually provided by rules and precedents. Thus policies that make explicit choices between electricity generation and the environment (or electricity generation and energy conservation, or electricity generation and other productive uses of capital) are regulatory. They are likely to excite participation both from likely losers and from likely winners, and will be much more conflictual.

It should be noted that Lowi later explicitly formulates his typology in a different manner, using distinctions between whether the policy operates on individual conduct or the environment of conduct, and between whether the policy involves primary rules (obligations or costs) or secondary rules (benefits, powers or privileges). Lowi uses these two distinctions as the axes of the four-celled matrix setting out his typology. The other two cells are filled with redistributive policy and constituent policy; the latter a category that has proved rather troublesome. While there remain some problems with this approach, there are advantages in the terminology of the latter-day Lowi.

The latter analysis based on the individual conduct/environment of impact distinction and the primary/secondary rule distinction represents an advance over an approach based solely on the distribution of costs and benefits because it can account for policies with no obvious economic impact. The latter analysis can subsume the costs/benefits approach so that policies categorised on these grounds can be seen as having characteristics that are subsets of the latter categories. Property rights must, after all, be established first by governments before markets can operate, and whether goods are deemed public or private is determined crucially (and fundamentally) by exclusion, usually achieved by the use of coercion by the state.

Distributive agencies are able to operate as if they had unlimited resources, and there are no integrative rules of conduct, only rules designating facilities. They can take each decision or facility and treat it as distinct from all others as there are few criteria or precedents that tie decisions together. In the United States log-rolling sees a number of pork-barrel projects brought together and given common authorisation in a public works statute 'composed of dozens of individual authorisations to build, design, or inquire into proposals for specific, named projects. The only connection among the projects and proposals is the agency authorised to take the actions'.[77] Opposition can be bought off by adding further projects, particularly by the use of commitments to conduct further studies on proposals that could become later authorisations. There are no rules or standards for comparing agency decisions that might inhibit this flexibility to disaggregate decisions into separate units.

The problems for such agencies are how they behave with any consistency at all in the absence of rules and how they manage to achieve any internal coordination when the various subunits have no 'rule book' to guide them. Lowi suggests that the answer lies in professionalism:

> Common schooling, common texts, common 'cookbook' formulas, equations, techniques, and computer programs help give these personnel the same premises, so that when confronted with the same problem they are likely to make the same decision despite the absence of policy guidelines.[78]

The importance of professional training in providing coordination and integration in an organisation was the focus of Herbert Kaufman's book, *The Forest Ranger.*[79]

Regulatory agencies, on the other hand, operate in an environment governed by rules and precedent. They are expected to implement policies that involve explicit choices between interests with a degree of consistency. It is the presence of this application of rules rather than the necessity of technical expertise that Lowi sees as significant. After all, he points out, building a road (a distributive policy) is no more technical than designing and managing a social security system.[80] With regulatory agencies

> interpretations of rules of conduct are passed along as operating rules of the agency officials, incorporating their reading of the statute with their understanding of legislative intent, court rulings, or executive orders. Other operating rules come from previous cases.[81]

Thus the key is not whether the organisation is still staffed primarily by technical specialists but the fact that technical specialisation is not likely to serve as the basis for integration in such agencies. The senior personnel in such agencies 'are more likely to be experts on process and procedure than on substance'.[82] Regulatory agencies are likely, therefore, to be dominated by lawyers (or other process specialists) and distributive agencies by engineers (or other subject specialists).

Roberts and Bluhm, in their study of electrical utilities, also found this difference to be significant. They suggest that organisations managed by lawyers will act quite differently from those managed by engineers.[83] Theirs is essentially a study of utilities as business organisations, however, and they fail to consider that there might be institutional reasons why some agencies might have lawyers at the top and others have engineers.

Public electrical utilities in an expansionary era can be seen clearly as distributive agencies; they are involved in promoting individual public works projects, with costs and coercion displaced elsewhere in time and space. The costs are displaced on to consumers or taxpayers in future and, significantly, on to the environment in the form of air or water pollution or destruction of wilderness or amenity. In contrast to the immediate and tangible benefits, the costs are, in Downs's terms, remote in time, space and comprehensibility.[84] The risk-adapted and environmentally sensitive public electrical utility, on the other hand, must seek to balance costs between investment in electrical generating capacity and other public investments, and between such investments and investment in techniques and approaches such as demand-side management and purchases from independent power producers. Moreover, it must incorporate environmental considerations into its calculus.

Regulatory policies, Lowi maintains, require that administrators know the rules and share interpretations about when and how to apply them.[85]

The need for consistency and fairness between cases makes administrative precedent important. Such agencies will be rule-bound and less dependent on professionalism for coordination and integration. While these rules and norms are often imposed from outside the utility, the utility must begin to act on them if it is to act successfully (assuming it cannot subvert them). And while the rules are relatively new, there are few precedents to guide the utility, but the fact remains that the change from a development phase to LCUP involves a shift from distributive to regulatory policy, and the consequent changes in the agency must be seen as a shift from distributive to regulatory agency.

If the move towards flexible electricity planning requires a shift from distributive to regulatory policy, and a concomitant shift from distributive to regulatory agencies, Lowi's analysis suggests that we should expect some observable changes in the structure of the utilities. We would expect the changed agencies to have more specialised work units but to have less reliance on professional specialisation of individual staff. There should be less decentralisation and greater centralisation of authority as reliance on professional norms for coordination is supplanted by rules and procedures. We would expect more lateral entry into the upper ranks of the organisation and more of the senior personnel to be professionally trained.[86]

There has been little research exploring the relevance of Lowi's approach to public policy on electricity, and the one example deals with the general political aspects of Lowi's earlier work rather than the more specifically bureaucratic aspects of the later Lowi.[87] Riley, in a study of power development in Manitoba, Saskatchewan and Alberta, found that a strong determinant of power policy was the fuel source available in the province in question.[88] This resulted from the distributive aspects of electric power development, particularly the fact that the political benefits of such developments are enhanced if expenditure on construction materials, labour and fuel is concentrated within the state or province making the decisions. In a 1976 study McColl found a similar pattern in the Australian states. Distributive politics triumphed over economics in a number of power station investment decisions.[89]

This points to a link between the 'arenas of power' approach of Lowi and the phenomenon of reverse adaptation noted in the discussion of technocracy above. The distributive nature of expansionary electricity planning and development serves as a powerful institutional reinforcement of the tendency of technocrats to adapt ends to available means because the utilities themselves represent bureaucratic means of a particular kind that owe their existence to past distributive policymaking exhibiting state or provincial preferences. The distributive nature of policy in the expansionary era of electricity planning simultaneously gives power to the technical expert and institutional succour to the maintenance or expansion of the distributive electricity planning agency. Recall our earlier discussion of electricity planning in France: the common professional training of the planners in the *grandes écoles* was crucial there in leading to reverse adaptedness. Lowi's approach focuses attention on precisely this factor, but it also points to the way this approach can account for the influence of competitive federalism on electricity planning because under such a system the benefits of construction and operation of a growing electricity system accrue at the state level while the costs tend to be dispersed nationally.

It should not be assumed automatically that all electricity policy was distributive in nature during the development phase of the industry. There are plenty of examples of regulatory-type conflict, but one from Britain is particularly illustrative. There, repeated attempts to adopt Caledonian Power Bills to authorise hydroelectric generation in Inverness-shire (to promote a carbide industry in Scotland) in the 1920s and 1930s were defeated in parliament by landlord and mining interests.[90] Electricity planning is not, therefore, inherently distributive, particularly when it is in private hands, but it becomes more so when placed under public ownership. The introduction of uncertainty into the planning equation of utilities, together with the emergence of environmental concern – and its institutionalisation in government – can be seen as having transformed electricity planning into a regulatory policy type (similar in nature to the Caledonian Power Bills) because environmental policy now requires the consistent application of rules and guidelines imposed by governments in order to balance interests in cheap electricity and power plant construction against those of conservation, environmental protection, independent power producers, cogenerators and so on.

The prospects for applying an arenas of power approach to electricity planning look promising, therefore, notwithstanding the negative conclusions of Uslaner about the utility of typologies in general in his study of United States energy policy.[91] Uslaner rather misses Lowi's point by assuming that there is an identifiable policy called 'energy policy' with uniform characteristics that are theoretically relevant. Lowi would argue that it is unsatisfactory to try 'to distinguish among policies according to subject matter'. Using another example, Lowi argued that '"marriage policy" is not a meaningful category'.[92] As we have seen above, 'electricity policy' (as a subset of energy policy) might have distributive or regulatory characteristics. To treat it as a unified, undifferentiated whole is to overlook the very phenomena that are significant here.

For similar reasons, this study will not follow closely what might otherwise serve as the basis for useful comparison: Roberts and Bluhm's excellent study of the organisational factors conducive to 'positive responsiveness' in electrical utilities to environmental regulation.[93] Roberts and Bluhm have much to contribute in a number of ways to our present purpose, particularly on the influence of external regulation, the role of professionals and so on, and numerous references are made to their work, which has been an important stimulus for this study. Their focus, however, is on organisations rather than institutions. They make no attempt to give equal weight in their study to the factors external to the utilities and, in particular, do not consider that the nature of the policies pursued might be responsible for the changes they study.

Conclusion

This chapter has sought to make some theoretical sense of the issues that are the subject of this study. It has sought to explain the LCUP approach to electricity planning and to point out how it differs from the positivist approaches to forecasting and planning, which were dominant during the modernist or expansionary phase of electrical utilities.

It has also sought, however, to provide a coherent way of understanding the role of technical expertise and political institutions (broadly conceived) in bringing about an adherence to the old planning approaches long after they ceased to be appropriate. A version of Lowi's arenas of power schema appears to provide not only an understanding of the political support for the 'modernist' approach to planning but also a bridge to the question of organisational structure, particularly the role of technical expertise in the process. In developing my conceptual framework I have used as my empirical point of reference a brief examination of the way institutional factors facilitated the introduction of LCUP in the United States. In so doing insight has been gained into 'institutional best practice' so that the cases that follow can be placed in some larger (international) frame of reference.

I will proceed through the case studies, therefore, looking for signs of the adoption of LCUP and related demand-side management and granting of access to non-utility generators, and asking whether they have been related to a shift of electricity planning from a distributive arena to a regulatory one. The regulation need not be formal, by a regulatory commission, but by the imposition of new obligations that transform the rules of the game for utilities.

CHAPTER 2

Tasmania:
The means justify the ends

The first case study provides a good insight into the reverse adaptation of an electric utility. In the late 1970s and early 1980s a utility that had, as the result of active government support for more than fifty years, become a dam-building company and the primary agent of development in the Australian state of Tasmania ran into concerted opposition. The opposition came over the proposal to build a dam in a wilderness area, but the opponents also exposed a planning process that essentially involved the derivation of a demand forecast to justify the power scheme.

In October 1979 the Hydro Electric Commission of Tasmania (HEC) presented to the State Government a report recommending construction of a dam (the Gordon Below Franklin) on the Gordon River below its confluence with the Franklin River in the remote south-west wilderness area of the state.[1] It was to be the first dam in an 'Integrated Development' program, to be followed by a second dam on the Franklin, through which would be diverted the waters of the King River, thus increasing the yield of both power stations.

This proposed dam was to divide opinion, both in Tasmania and on mainland Australia, and expose the inability of Tasmania's political institutions to resolve such conflicts. It led to the forced resignation of one minister, the toppling of the state's Premier by his party and the eventual loss of government by the Australian Labor Party. The resulting campaign to save the Franklin River came to dominate the political agenda in the state and, for a time, the Australian Commonwealth. The controversy was resolved ultimately not at the state level but by the Commonwealth Government in an action that survived a challenge from Tasmania in the High Court and in the process confirmed an extension of Commonwealth power over environmental issues.

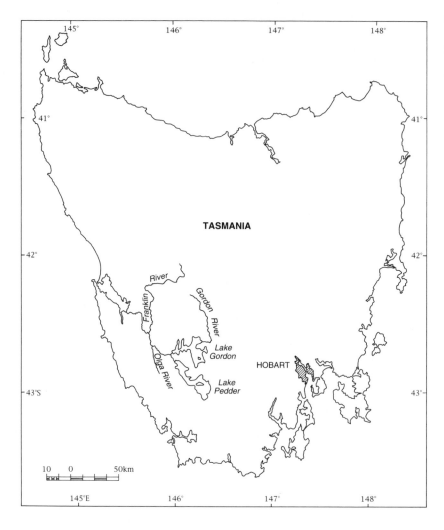

The depth of the conflict at the state level was a reflection of the extent to which the imperatives of growth in electricity consumption and the resultant construction of hydroelectric schemes had become embedded in the state's political institutions. Historically, the HEC had enjoyed unquestioned support for its dam-building program. These projects quite literally had opened up some areas of the state to civilisation and had become synonymous with the development of the local economy – and thus with the well-being of the populace. But Tasmania is a place of great natural beauty, and its south-west is an area almost untouched in any significant way by human interference. The HEC's plans to develop its hydroelectric potential aroused opposition on an unprecedented scale, and the opponents were driven, in their desire to protect the south-west, to question the institutions and processes that lay behind the proposals. Ultimately, the HEC was changed radically, although the change resulted more from the predictions of the conservationists about future power demand being proved correct than from a recognition that a different course for the state was desirable.

The struggle to save the Franklin demonstrates clearly the nature of reverse adaptation in electric utilities, and this is our primary interest here rather than the process of reform, which occurred in the late 1980s and early 1990s. By that time there was such a surplus of electricity in the state that the need to reform the utility was apparent even to those who had been its staunchest supporters during the Franklin conflict. The HEC had, in effect, become a dam-building company. Its major activities were related to new power development; when any justification for further development evaporated, there was no choice but to run down the considerable construction workforce and restructure the utility into what was effectively an electricity production and distribution company.

The Gordon Below Franklin project was the result of thirty years planning activity by the HEC. Initial survey work in the south-west had been commenced in 1948–49 so, by the time the report was released in 1979, the HEC was quite sure that it knew what should be done, and the proposal thus had considerable momentum behind it. The Chief Commissioner in 1979, J. R. Ashton, had been involved in the initial survey work in the south-west as a young engineer.[2] By 1979 history had begun to turn against the HEC. A bitter conflict had been waged over the Gordon Stage 1 project in the late 1960s and early 1970s, and many conservationists who were veterans of this campaign were ready to give the Gordon Below Franklin proposal a hostile and sceptical reception. This earlier scheme had involved the inundation of beautiful Lake Pedder, regarded by many as the jewel of the south-west.[3]

Even this initial conflict over the exploitation of the south-west wilderness had its roots in earlier times, however. For example, the faith in the ability of cheap hydroelectric power to provide economic riches for a marginal state with a marginal economy (which underlay both these controversies) dated back at least to the 1930s. This policy (known as 'hydroindustrialisation') underpinned the perceived necessity for all power development projects in Tasmania because two-thirds of electricity generated was sold to energy-intensive industries, principally pulp and paper production and metallurgical processing (aluminium, ferromanganese and zinc).[4] In order to understand the reverse adaptation of the HEC that led to the Franklin struggle we must look at the way hydroindustrialisation had become the gospel of development in a state with few economic advantages. First, however, we shall examine the main features of the conflict over the Gordon Below Franklin because the facts of the case both provide the context for the later discussion of planning processes and indicate the strength of the political forces at play in Tasmania.

A brief case history[5]

The Hydro Electric Commission of Tasmania is a semiautonomous public corporation that traditionally has enjoyed a large degree of independence. The HEC was deliberately distanced from the political process by its enabling statute so that, while the State Government guaranteed its debt, it had little control over the HEC's day-to-day affairs.[6] The HEC had to obtain parliamentary approval for new construction projects, which meant both houses of parliament. (Tasmania has a Legislative Council, which was not organised on party lines, as well as a lower house, the House of Assembly.) This meant that the government, having command of only the lower house, was never really totally in control of the HEC. The Minister in Charge of the Hydro Electric Commission was answerable to parliament for its actions, but the HEC was immune from ministerial direction. Moreover, the HEC enjoyed widespread popular support, having come to be regarded as the most important agent of economic development, both by attracting industry with cheap electricity and by providing jobs in the construction of power schemes.

Nevertheless, the HEC ran into opposition in the late 1970s when it sought parliamentary approval for the Gordon Below Franklin scheme. The Gordon Stage 1 project had generated considerable controversy in the early 1970s when the pro-wilderness forces also formed a nationwide lobby group, the Lake Pedder Action Group, to press for intervention by the Commonwealth Government. The Tasmanian Government was unresponsive to the demands of the conservationists and the Commonwealth became their last hope, but it lacked effective constitutional power to protect Lake Pedder in the face of the HEC and the State Government.[7] Although Lake Pedder was lost, electricity planning in Tasmania became politicised for the first time, and the Pedder experience produced a determination in the conservationists' camp in the late 1970s that further HEC plans for the south-west would not succeed. The Wilderness Society, the most important group in the later struggle, was formed in 1975 after the Pedder battle.

While the Gordon Below Franklin scheme, with a proposed annual energy output of 172 **MWav**,[8] was small by world standards, it was significant in the Tasmanian context because total demand in the state was then slightly less than 1000 MWav. The HEC report recommending it as part of an 'Integrated Development' program canvassed a number of alternative proposals, the most important being a coal-fired thermal station of 2×200 MW configuration and the so-called 'Separate' hydro-electric development (which involved a dam on the Gordon River above its confluence with the Olga River, to be followed by a dam and power station on the King River through which the waters of the Franklin would subsequently be diverted). The report, which also examined electricity demand and the social and environmental impacts of the main contending schemes, represented an improvement over previous HEC reports, largely because the Premier, Doug Lowe, had told the HEC in 1978 that it should not regard approval for its preferred scheme as certain and that it would have to provide a strong case for it.

The Premier established a Coordination Committee on Future Power Development to consider the public response to the HEC document, which, he hoped, would then be considered by a joint select committee of both houses of state parliament. Another report from the National Parks and Wildlife Service at this time recommended the declaration of a wild rivers national park in the area affected by both hydroelectric proposals. Development and conservation interests were thus set on collision course.

One impediment to Lowe's attempts to resolve the conflict was the independent status of the HEC. The Lowe Government had sought to deal with this obstacle in 1978 by attempting to place the HEC under ministerial control; the HEC opposed this move and was supported by the Legislative Council. Without the support of the Legislative Council for an amendment to its statute all Lowe could do was to establish an Energy Advisory Council in October 1978 and a Directorate of Energy within the Premier's Department in February 1979. Even then, the HEC resented this loss of its monopoly position as a source of policy advice, but grudgingly accepted the directorate's existence.

In May 1980 the Coordination Committee released its report in which it recommended construction of a thermal station, followed subse-quently by the Gordon Above Olga, which had formed the first part of the non-preferred Separate Development. Both conservation groups and pro-hydro groups made submissions to the Coordinating Committee but, as it became apparent that the HEC might not get its own way, the pro-hydro interests began to organise on an unprecedented scale. In April 1980, at the instigation of the Tasmanian Chamber of Industries, the HEC's thirteen major bulk consumers formed a group to seek support for the HEC's preferred option. Soon after the release of the Coordinating Committee's report a group representing HEC employees, the Hydro Employees Action Team (HEAT), was formed to protect the jobs of those employed in hydro construction. HEAT enjoyed at least the tacit approval of the HEC because employees were forbidden by law from making any public statements concerning HEC affairs without the consent of the Commissioner. Also formed was a group called the Association of Consumers of Electricity, which included among its members the former HEC Commissioner, Sir Alan Knight, and former Premier Eric Reece.

The government also came under increasing pressure from the unions within the Labor Party. At a meeting of the ALP State Council on 5 and 6 July, just before Cabinet considered the matter, there was an unsuccessful attempt to bind the government to the Gordon Below Franklin scheme.[9]

The support for the HEC, therefore, included the industrial consumers who benefited from any surplus of electricity and unions whose members relied on hydro construction for employment. This alignment of capital and labour is not unusual with 'pork barrel' or distributive policies, but this issue grew to affect the whole of Tasmanian society, and it sorely tested the adequacy of the state's political institutions, which were structured on disciplined, responsible parties based on the traditional conflict between Capital and Labour.[10]

Cabinet met to consider the issue on 8 July 1980, and Lowe outlined the following five options to the meeting:[11]

1 The Integrated Development recommended by the HEC
2 The Gordon Below Franklin followed by smaller hydro schemes outside the catchment of the Gordon and Franklin Rivers
3 A thermal/hydro development program consisting of a 1×200 MW station followed by the Gordon Above Olga and then smaller hydro as the need arose
4 An all-thermal development program
5 The Gordon Above Olga followed by smaller hydro schemes outside the south-west wilderness area.

Options 1 (integrated development) and 4 (all thermal) were ruled out at an early stage, and an HEC briefing persuaded the Cabinet that the coal-fired thermal option (3) was unlikely to be economically viable compared with hydro options. Employment was ultimately the deciding factor, which was understandable given that much of the pressure on the government was coming from trade union sources. When the HEC admitted that the Gordon Above Olga would provide more jobs during construction than would the Gordon Below Franklin, Lowe believed he had found the necessary compromise to ensure employment while limiting damage to the south-west wilderness.

The Cabinet adopted a package of proposals, which included construction of the Gordon Above Olga, an energy conservation strategy, development of the coal industry (including conversion of the Bell Bay oil-fired power station to coal), a review of electricity pricing policy and establishment of a wild rivers national park on boundaries that would allow construction of the Gordon Above Olga.

The Wilderness Society initially regarded these proposals favourably, but soon decided to hold firm against any further hydroelectric development in the south-west. The HEC stated that it would operate within the constraints to ensure the best possible result, but the constraints on the HEC were minimal, and it still regarded the 'best possible result' as being approval for the construction of the Gordon Below Franklin. The Chief Commissioner of the HEC, Russell Ashton, regarded it as both proper and his duty to lobby the upper house to persuade it to correct the government's 'mistake'.

The Legislative Council had appointed a select committee to consider the issue, and the HEC provided it and the public with much information and argument in favour of its preferred option, including (during October 1980) material that took no account of the government's decision to review pricing policies as a possible means to slow demand growth. The HEC continued to base its analyses on load forecasts that took no account of the government's conservation and coal substitution policies, and even made claims that there would be difficulties in finding finance for the Olga scheme.

Lowe's relationship with Commissioner Ashton by this stage had deteriorated considerably. The HEC was lobbying the Legislative Council without even the courtesy of giving the Premier prior notification of its activities. Even more ominous was the fact that the Liberal Party opposition was beginning to exploit the widening gap between the government and the HEC, using the power of the Legislative Council and opposition to the government scheme among the non-Labor majority of 'independent' members, many of whom had past Liberal Party affiliations.[12] Lowe often found that material unknown to him or only just presented to the government was in the hands of the opponents of the government's policy.

The bill authorising the Gordon Above Olga scheme was introduced to parliament on 13 November 1980, and it was quickly passed by the government-controlled House of Assembly. An opinion poll taken at this time revealed that 56 per cent of the population supported the government's decision while only 30 per cent were opposed, but this finding had little effect on the Legislative Council. The report of the Legislative Council select committee favoured the Gordon Below Franklin and the council amended the bill, substituting details of the Franklin scheme for the Olga scheme in the schedule to the bill.[13] This amendment was carried, and the resulting deadlock could not be resolved by the ensuing conference of managers of the two houses, which remained deadlocked for all of 1981.

The government began to crack under the strain created by this impasse. Lowe faced continued opposition from trade union elements in the Labor Party (particularly metals and construction unions) and, encouraged by this, Harry Holgate challenged unsuccessfully for the leadership in June 1981. The pressure on Lowe's leadership continued at the State Council meeting of the ALP on 4 July when the parliamentary party was virtually instructed by the party machine to resolve the issue by means of a referendum. On 16 September the government decided (although now only by the narrow margin of twelve votes to ten) both to adhere to its earlier decision to build the Olga scheme and preserve the Franklin River and that the matter should be decided by a referendum.

While the parliamentary Labor Party had not envisaged that a 'No Dams' option would be included on the ballot paper, Lowe told a press conference that he believed that, when Cabinet decided the precise form of the ballot, it would be a genuine exercise in democracy and a 'No Dams' option would be included. Holgate and others in the faction opposed to Lowe (which included the HEC unions) claimed that this was a misrepresentation of the parliamentary Labor Party decision, and a Cabinet meeting the next day decided that there would not be a 'No Dams' option. This decision led to a successful leadership challenge on 11 November 1981 when Lowe was replaced by Holgate. Lowe resigned from the Labor Party and sat on the cross-benches in parliament as an independent. He was followed the next week by the government whip. This action cost the Holgate Government its majority in the House of Assembly, and it was subsequently defeated and forced to the polls after losing a confidence motion.

The referendum, without a 'No Dams' option, was held on 12 December 1981. Only three members of Cabinet campaigned for the Olga scheme with any conviction. The HEC and its allies mounted a strong campaign for the Franklin dam, and the Wilderness Society urged voters to write 'No Dams' on their ballot papers. Of the votes cast in the referendum, 47 per cent were for the Gordon Below Franklin, 8 per cent for the Olga and an incredible 45 per cent were informal (33 per cent were marked 'No Dams').[14]

In an election on 26 May 1982 the Liberal opposition was swept to power in a landslide after promising to authorise the Gordon Below Franklin.[15] There was by this stage no difference between the two parties – both promised to build the dam – but the Labor Party had by now lost all credibility. Conservative pro-dams working-class voters combined with traditional Liberal voters to return the first Liberal Government ever to govern in Tasmania in its own right.[16] On its election, the Gray Liberal Government secured legislation authorising the Franklin dam.

The conservation groups mounted a blockade against the construction of the dam over the Christmas–New Year period of 1982–83, and eventually the Hawke Labor Government was elected at the national level in the 5 March poll, having promised to halt the dam. The Commonwealth Government legislated to stop construction of the dam, and the validity of its legislation was upheld in a High Court decision handed down on 1 July 1983. Although it was not legally obliged to do so, the Commonwealth subsequently provided Tasmania with compensation totalling about $290 million, which included funding for the construction of two hydroelectric projects, the King River and Henty-Anthony schemes, which would provide employment for the workers displaced by the cancellation of the Gordon Below Franklin and capacity to meet future demand. The Commonwealth was not prepared to accept the HEC's demand forecast uncritically and promised simply to provide a similar subsidy for capacity beyond the King and Henty-Anthony should demand growth require it.

In the event, demand growth fell far short of HEC expectations to the extent that the Gordon Below Franklin – had it been commissioned in 1990 as planned – would have been a costly white elephant. This situation resulted from the demise of the policy of hydroindustrialisation, which had driven industry policy in the state for fifty years, and had resulted in electricity planning by the HEC becoming a process of reverse adaptation. We now turn to this process.

Hydroindustrialisation and electricity planning in Tasmania

Out-migration plagued the Tasmanian economy after the transportation of convicts to the penal colony (known then as Van Diemen's Land) in the 1850s ended at the same time as gold was discovered in Victoria, and thousands of freed convicts and other Tasmanians left to seek their fortunes. Depopulation was halted temporarily by a mining boom in the north-west in the late nineteenth century, which led to the view in Tasmania that developing the state's natural resources was the way to economic prosperity and an end to out-migration.

The development of the state's hydroelectric potential came to be bound up with the solution to depopulation, and electricity planning came to be a process whereby hydroelectricity could be developed as an end in itself – what we have earlier called reverse adaptation.

Electricity generation in Tasmania had its origins as a government rescue of a failed private enterprise in order to ensure development of the state's mineral wealth.[17] By the turn of the century the considerable hydroelectric potential of the state had been recognised. Great Lake in the Central Highlands offered the best prospects for development, largely because it had a very high head, and therefore a large amount of energy was available. The problem was that there was insufficient demand for the electricity until a proposal for an electrolytic zinc refining plant was made in 1908. This set the tone for the industry as one of a potential means in search of suitable ends. The zinc refinery developer, the Complex Ores Company, wanted the government to undertake development of the hydroelectricity, but the Cabinet rejected government ownership and legislated in 1909 to enable Complex Ores to develop the potential and supply surplus power to the public. The company was required by this law to consume a certain amount itself or forfeit its rights.

Provision was made, at the insistence of the ALP, for public ownership after twenty years at cost. It was argued that the legislation would increase employment and promote industry – the first support by Labor for a policy that was to become known as hydroindustrialisation. However, the Hydro Electric Power and Metallurgical Company created to develop the scheme ran into financial problems when its estimates for the cost of constructing the scheme proved optimistic. Then the closure of the London financial markets because of the outbreak of war in 1914 finished the company off. The ALP opposed financial assistance for the company in favour of public ownership, and the Tasmanian Hydro Electric Department was formed as a full ministerial department and assumed responsibility for power development. The engineer-in-chief of the former company became the head of the new department.

The state therefore saved both the zinc smelting operation and the electricity industry. The smelter opened in 1917, followed by a carbide works the following year. Eventually, further sales to industry were made – to the cement industry in 1930 and the developing pulp and paper industry from the 1930s onwards. In the case of the latter, considerable government assistance was provided in order to bring about industrial development based on the state's natural resources. It was during this period that the Cosgrove ALP Government perfected hydroindustrialisation, which was to serve as the basis for a long run of electoral success that lasted until 1982, save for a brief period of Liberal Party government between 1969 and 1972.

The establishment in 1927 of the Australian Loans Council, an inter-governmental body to coordinate loan-raising, ensured Tasmania access to a share of loan funds at cheap rates, and it used them to build hydro-electric schemes. Since the interest rates attached to Loans Council borrowings were low, the cost of electricity from these capital-intensive schemes was also low, and it could be sold at rates that were particularly attractive to 'footloose' industries with large energy demands and which could be supplied in bulk. By the time of the Gordon Below Franklin controversy, these bulk industrial consumers accounted for about two-thirds of sales. One industry alone, the Comalco aluminium smelter, accounted for almost a third of all consumption. The state benefited not just from the establishment of the industries themselves but also from the employment created in building the hydro schemes to supply them.

Hydroindustrialisation came to be embedded in the electricity planning institutions of Tasmania – in the policies of successive governments, in the enabling statute and organisational structure of the utility, in the strength of the beneficiary interest groups and (perhaps most importantly) in the attitudes of the citizens of the state. Much as did the Tennessee Valley Authority in the United States, the Hydro Electric Commission of Tasmania brought the trappings of modern society to many remote areas of the state with each successive hydro scheme, so it became synonymous with progress in Tasmanian political culture.

This cultural support reinforced structural features, which were to make reverse adaptation difficult to throw off. The first of these was a general constitutional feature that took on special significance in the Gordon Below Franklin case: the power, independence and insulation from the popular will of the upper house of the Tasmanian parliament, the Legislative Council. This body had been created quite deliberately so as to be immune from any popular enthusiasms. Its nineteen members were returned from electorates that gave little equality to the value of the vote, which gave the council a distinctively non-urban composition. Members were elected for six-year overlapping terms. Elections for three seats were held annually, and four members were elected in one year in each cycle. The Legislative Council could never as a whole be forced to an election and, since it enjoyed power over money bills, it could force the government to the people while itself being protected from such a discipline. The Legislative Council had a key role to play in electricity planning because all new utility investments required the approval of empowering legislation by both houses of the legislature.

The other important structural feature in Tasmania was the way the utility itself was formally constituted under the *Hydro Electric Commission Act 1944* (Tas.). This statute changed the utility from ministerial department to an independent commission with considerable power. The minister was still answerable to parliament for the actions of the commission, but he could not issue instructions to the commission. The Chief Commissioner chaired the commission as well as being chief executive officer and enjoyed considerable power, since there were only three other members of the commission. Since he possessed both a deliberative vote and a casting vote, the Chief Commissioner could prevail with the support of only one member; he could both force a tied vote and then resolve it in his favour, although – such was the support for the commission's policies – it is doubtful that he would ever need to do so. The office of Chief Commissioner was given particular prominence by the force of personality of Sir Alan Knight, who had been Chief Engineer of the Public Works Department from 1937 and served as Chief Commissioner of the HEC from 1946 until 1976. The membership of the commission at the time of the Gordon Below Franklin controversy consisted of three engineers plus the president of the Tasmanian Trades Hall Council, who was also the long-standing secretary of the Building Workers Industrial Union, whose members were beneficiaries of dam construction.

The large degree of independence, together with the high general support for the commission's activities and the highly technical nature of the details of those activities, prepared the ground for the reverse adaptation of the HEC, which became a highly proficient dam-building agency. It employed its own construction workforce and was dominated internally by its Power Division (where most of its senior executives came from), which was particularly favoured by expansion. It had little or no expertise in thermal electricity generation and required a continuous program of hydroelectric construction simply to stand still as an organisation. It occasionally undertook consulting overseas to keep its civil engineers occupied and built a reputation for excellence in this area.

The planning process itself encouraged reverse adaptation. Parliamentary approval was required for each new power scheme, but demand forecasts were published only when the HEC was seeking approval for a new scheme. This process diminished still further any external accountability of the utility since the forecasts traditionally contained little detail that could have been challenged – should anyone have wished to challenge it. Indeed, there was little questioning of the HEC's activities, save for a few landholders who were displaced by schemes such as those on the Derwent River. The demand forecast always provided the 'problem' of capacity shortfall, which the scheme recommended by the HEC would solve. Alternative 'solutions' were rarely discussed in any detail in these reports, which tended to seek rapid endorsement from the legislature lest delays cause shortages. A compliant legislature – both houses – invariably obliged. Detailed consideration of the demand forecast and of alternatives to the preferred scheme were kept largely within the commission.

These weaknesses were masked as long as the expansion of the hydro system accorded with the preferences of the government and society as a whole, which it did until at least the 1970s. The success of hydro-industrialisation was forged on the anvil of strong political support for the strategy. While long-serving Premier Robert Cosgrove might have developed hydroindustrialisation in the 1930s, it was Eric Reece (known as 'Electric Eric') who perfected the approach and used it as the basis for a long period of stable government. As long as the cost of electricity from each new scheme was less than the last, the interest costs of the schemes were subsidised by Australian taxpayers as a whole, and industries could be enticed to establish in Tasmania, it was a formula for political success. But hydroindustrialisation was a process of planning for a particular kind of future, and any idea that the demand forecasts had any basis outside that planning process was a convenient fiction.

In the two decades after World War II demand growth was vigorous and the disruptions of war had caused delays in construction, as was the case in most other systems. Nevertheless, the HEC was active in finding consumers, so much so that in 1951 a select committee of the House of Assembly had been established to inquire into the HEC entering into contractual commitments with Electrolytic Zinc, Australian Newsprint Mills, Associated Pulp and Paper Manufacturers and Tasmanian Board Mills for 82.8 MW of demand, more than it might have been able to supply at a time when wartime interruptions and a difficulty in labour recruitment had delayed the HEC's construction program.[18] One important accounting change at this time helped to keep prices down by reducing the reliance on internal financing for power station construction: the HEC started capitalising interest during construction (adding interest charges to capital cost until the scheme was commissioned) in 1951.[19]

In the 1960s, however, demand began to level out and the HEC caught up with the construction backlog; there was even the prospect of surplus capacity. It was during this period that the establishment or expansion of the significant footloose electricity-intensive industries occurred. Most of the earlier bulk consumers were engaged in processing the ores from Tasmanian mines or the wood from Tasmanian forests. The new industries, the Comalco aluminium smelter and Temco's ferromanganese plant (both at Bell Bay), were there primarily for the cheap electricity, although there was some evidence that Temco (a subsidiary of steel giant BHP) was relocating from Newcastle in New South Wales at least partly because of the laxity of Tasmania's pollution laws. The relationship between the HEC and the bulk consumers was the key to the utility becoming totally reverse-adapted, and Comalco was the most significant bulk consumer, so the relationship between it and the HEC bears closer examination.

Comalco and the HEC

Aluminium smelting began at Bell Bay in 1955. It was undertaken by the Commonwealth Aluminium Production Commission, which had been established during the war to produce the strategically important metal for aircraft construction. Initially, the smelter produced only 12 000 tons of aluminium a year and consumed only 38 MWav of electricity, and it was under public ownership, with the Commonwealth Government holding a two-thirds share and the Tasmanian Government a third. When there were rumours that the smelter at Bell Bay would reduce production with the decline in demand, Reece gained Commonwealth Government approval in 1959 for an expansion of capacity from 12 000 tons to 16 000 tons a year to be funded by the Tasmanian Government.[20]

Reece had a particular enthusiasm for power development and pushed hard for development of the lower Derwent River, introducing authorising legislation in 1961. The Liberal Opposition was critical of this scheme – one of the few to cause much disruption to landholders. Opponents raised concerns over the HEC's drain on loan funds, and the prospect that major industrial load consumers were being advantaged, with tariff increases for other consumers rising by 7.5 per cent in 1960 and 10 per cent in 1961, despite the relative absence of inflation and low prevailing interest rates.[21]

The aluminium industry changed from a strategic to a commercial concern with the discovery of bauxite at Weipa, in far north Queensland, and a private company, Comalco (a subsidiary of Conzinc-Riotinto of Australia) acquired the Commonwealth share on favourable terms in 1960 and assumed management of the smelter. The Tasmanian Government retained its share, which was reduced to 17.5 per cent when the capital of the company was expanded. With further expansions to process the output from Weipa, the power demand at the smelter was increased to a little over 150 MWav by the late 1960s. Another 84 MWav was added in the early 1970s.

This expansion of footloose energy-intensive industries marked the apotheosis of reverse adaptation in Tasmania. The expansion of demand by industries processing Tasmania's resources was minimal from 1960 onward. The Electrolytic Zinc Company, for example, increased its demand by only 12 MW between 1962 and 1979; the demand of Australian Pulp and Paper Mills increased by 27 MW and Australian Newsprint Mills by 36 MW in the same period. These were moderate increases but not enough to soak up the output of the Poatina, Lower Derwent, Mersey-Forth and Upper Gordon hydroelectric power schemes and the 2×120 MW Bell Bay thermal station commissioned over this period. This additional demand came from Comalco (199 MW) and Temco (61 MW), in addition to growth in general load demand.[22]

The HEC by now enjoyed a symbiotic relationship with its bulk industrial consumers and strong political support by both capital and labour. And rather than just providing for forecast demand, it began making provision for capacity that would enable it to provide additional electricity at the convenience of these industries. Its forecasting and planning at this time can be appreciated by examining the report in which the commission recommended construction of the Pieman power scheme and the second generating set at Bell Bay in 1970.[23]

The general load (that not supplied to bulk industrial consumers) was forecast by simple statistical projection techniques, with the HEC maintaining there was 'no reason to doubt that the increase in the General Load ... will continue to follow a pattern similar to that established in the past'.[24] But the general load constituted only a third of total demand, and the major industrial load was more significant. Here, the HEC stated that its policy was 'to make provision to meet all firm contractual commitments and to make some allowance for prospective and unforeseen demands'.[25] The HEC was thus providing slack in its forecasts to encourage further hydroindustrialisation. It justified approval for the second generator at Bell Bay on the basis of the anticipated requirements of industry, which would lead to a shortfall in capacity between 1974 and the commissioning of the Gordon Stage 1 scheme in 1976.[26] In addition to this temporary shortfall, however, the HEC argued that the additional capacity at Bell Bay 'would provide a margin of capacity at a low capital cost which would be very valuable in the event of a large block of power being requested by a new industry ...'.[27]

What is particularly interesting is that the HEC then entered into contracts for the sale of electricity equal to the output from this additional capacity at Bell Bay immediately after parliamentary approval had been given, even though these contracts were to be supplied from hydroelectric schemes such as the newly commissioned Mersey-Forth project rather than the oil-fired Bell Bay station, which became prohibitively expensive to operate after the 1973 oil price rises. The **capacity factor** for oil-fired plant is usually 80 per cent, so that the new capacity provided an additional energy contribution of 96 MWav. It might be coincidental, but this was almost exactly the amount of the new bulk industrial sales entered into with Comalco, Temco, Mount Lyell Mining and Railway Co. Ltd, Renison Ltd and Electrolytic Zinc – 95.5 MW.[28] Most of this additional contracted load went to Comalco (40 MW) and Temco (40 MW). In the event, the HEC could meet this demand from the Gordon Stage 1 scheme because a post-1973 slump in metals prices depressed demand by bulk users until after the new hydroelectric capacity had been commissioned.

This supply of new industrial load from the Gordon saved costly oil, but it did mean that the HEC was now subsidising Comalco. In 1974 it had agreed to a price of 0.52 c/kWh for this new block of 40 MW (referred to as Block F),[29] compared with the estimated cost for electricity from the second set at Bell Bay of 0.42 c/kWh in 1970.[30] The cost of electricity from the Gordon Stage 1 project came in at about twice the price set for Block F – about 1 c/kWh.[31]

The emerging problems for the HEC and its hydroindustrialisation policy were foreshadowed by this rising cost of new capacity. Cost escalation drove the estimated cost of electricity from the Pieman project to 3 c/kWh by 1980 – above the prices at which electricity based on coal-fired generation was being offered in the states of New South Wales and Victoria. Much of the blowout in Pieman costs was due to the need to delay construction as a result of the mid 1970s slump in major industrial demand and the HEC's practice of capitalising interest during construction. One analysis calculated that the HEC overestimated demand growth in the period 1971–81 by 300 MWav or about 30 per cent.[32] The Pieman scheme had been estimated to cost $114m in 1971. By 1980 the estimated cost was $531m (including $148m interest during construction) and in 1984 $681m (including $185m interest during construction).[33] The HEC appears to have underestimated direct costs by about 20 per cent and overhead costs by about 70 per cent.

The dangers attaching to the policy of hydroindustrialisation with rising real costs and the long lead times associated with hydroelectric schemes were considerable. The HEC by the mid 1970s was not struggling to build capacity to meet burgeoning demand but rather struggling to ensure that new capacity being commissioned would generate income to pay its interest bills. This concern was evident in the HEC offering a 4 per cent discount to Comalco for the Block F contract until the end of 1978, which the commission explained in a letter to Comalco as being aimed at encouraging 'incidence of the new block of load at a time when it suits the Commission's operations'.[34] The pending commissioning of the Gordon Stage 1 project was about to increase the HEC's interest bill, and it was thus keen to sell its output. This offer was made with the support of the politicians, with both the Premier and the Minister for Industrial Development involved in the negotiations.

Justifying Gordon Below Franklin

The increasing difficulties in finding bulk industrial consumers for the output of new power schemes, and the related rising cost of electricity from those schemes, should have resulted in caution over a demand forecast produced in 1979, which provided the justification for the Gordon Below Franklin dam. In addition to Tasmania's price advantage slipping, the scale of modern energy-intensive footloose industries was passing the state by. The entire output of the new proposed power scheme was barely enough to meet the needs of one **potline** of the new generation of aluminium smelters such as that planned by Alcoa in Victoria and by Comalco itself at Gladstone in Queensland. The latter project, together with expansion of Comalco's smelter in New Zealand (see chapter 3), were inauspicious portents for Tasmania.

The HEC could not, however, look to its 180 000 general load consumers for load growth that would justify a capacity increment of the size of the Gordon Below Franklin – about 20 per cent of the then total demand or about half the then General Load – and it had to find industrial markets. While the HEC therefore used its traditional statistical projection techniques to derive a general load forecast, it had to produce a convincing major industrial load forecast. The controversy over Lake Pedder and the Gordon Stage 1 project had focused attention on its activities as never before, and Premier Lowe had warned that its recommendations would not be accepted uncritically.

To derive its MIL forecast, therefore, the HEC surveyed its existing bulk consumers, asking them what their future power requirements were likely to be 'assuming the availability of power at commercially acceptable prices'.[35] This was, of course, a fiddle since the commission dodged the question of what the future price of power *would* be and thus removed the effect of any price elasticity of demand from the equation. But then the HEC was still in expansionary mood, considering it was 'reasonable for established industries to expect that relatively small increments of energy will be made available without undue delay'.[36] This survey indicated foreshadowed increases in MIL demand of 281 MW by 1990, with a further 225 MW between 1990 and 2000 – a total of 506 MW over twenty years. Nearly half this total, 228 MW, was foreshadowed by Temco, with 60 MW from Comalco. None of this increased demand eventuated, and in 1982 Comalco and Temco both told the Senate Select Committee on South West Tasmania that their electricity consumption would not be increasing.

Tighe has pointed out just how suspicious this survey was since, the year before it was conducted (1978), an inquiry into Tasmanian industry had surveyed the same companies and found that they did not envisage any significant growth in existing activities or new areas of development.[37] Helpful as the bulk industries were to the HEC's cause, their optimism provided the commission with an embarrassment of riches because neither the Gordon Below Franklin nor any other hydroelectric project in the state could meet this projected demand, and none could meet that which would supposedly emerge by 1990. The HEC response to this difficulty demonstrates as clear an example of reverse adaptation as one is likely to find because it had to adjust the demand forecast to match its preferred means: construction of the Gordon Below Franklin as the first stage of the Integrated Development.

The HEC weighted the foreshadowed increments signalled by each consumer according to what it saw as the probability of each eventuating. This produced a total figure about half that generated by the raw survey data – an increment of about 10 MWav a year. When combined with the general load projection, this produced a load forecast that fitted like a glove with the commissioning of the Gordon Below Franklin in 1990 according to the commission's preferred construction schedule. The forecast growth was not so fast that demand could not be met by the Gordon Below Franklin – thus justifying a thermal station – nor so slow that it could be satisfied by construction of the Gordon Above Olga dam in the 'Separate Development', which had both a lower output and a longer construction period (by two years).

The neatly constructed forecast of demand thus determined not only the timing of the addition to generating capacity but also the very nature of that additional capacity. This fact was not lost on the Directorate of Energy established within the Premier's Department to assist in responding to the HEC's report. The directorate noted:

> The commission's forecast has been strongly influenced by the available supply of hydroelectricity, if not governed by this factor. Indeed, one is left with the impression that the arbitrary allocation to major industry serves only the tactical objective of allowing the total load projection to dovetail neatly with the developmental lead time for the Integrated Development.[38]

The Directorate of Energy attempted to play the HEC at its own game, arguing that the HEC was being too pessimistic about the economic prospects of the state and thus acting as a brake on development in order to justify its preferred hydroelectric scheme. It argued that demand was likely to increase so rapidly that the Gordon Below Franklin could not be built soon enough to meet it. Instead it argued that demand could be met only by building coal-fired thermal capacity (with its shorter lead time) and that the Gordon Above Olga plus some conservation would both meet the load thereafter and preserve the Franklin River. It was an innovative piece of lateral thinking to try to outdo the HEC at reverse adaptation, but it was ultimately to prove unsuccessful.

The hearings conducted by the Senate Select Committee on South West Tasmania in 1982 provided some additional insights into the planning process in Tasmania, particularly the close relationship between the major industrial load and the commission's development plans. Some of the exchanges between members of the committee and Chief Commissioner Ashton are particularly instructive. For example, despite the massive forecasting errors over the course of the Pieman project, Ashton denied that the uncertainty in load forecasting had risen to new levels.[39] Rather, he thought that hydro schemes should be built regardless of forecasts since their output would undoubtedly be sold:

> SENATOR CHIPP – If you follow that statement to its logical conclusion, even if you did not have palpable evidence of increased demand, you would advocate building a new hydroelectric station anyway.
> MR ASHTON – It may be difficult to convince the Parliament on that, but I think it would be a wise thing for the state to do … This is the way it has worked in the past, that never at any time in the past have we had customers lined up to take the major lump of these energy sources that we have developed.
> SENATOR CHIPP – Do you think all this trying to project demand and doing lots of figures and stuff really is irrelevant?
> MR ASHTON – In many ways I think it is. I would say about the general load again, for instance, that maybe we are out in our estimates of general load; maybe we can achieve better results with conservation than we assume and that will drop down the general load a bit. But all that does is give us a little bit more for industry, and it is a mighty valuable thing to have. I do not see any problems about it.[40]

The difficulty here was that the HEC was seeking to continue hydro-industrialisation as a strategy of industrial development when the government of the day had rejected that approach. The commission was using its considerable independence, expertise and control over the information that constituted the discourse of the issue to seek to continue its construction business as usual. The construction of a demand forecast that justified that outcome was a crucial device in ensuring that the ends of Tasmanian society were adapted to its preferred means.

The HEC consistently saw its forecasts as vital to the future economic well-being of the state, and any consideration of possible slower demand growth as a result of poor economic performance as unacceptable, as is witnessed by the following two statements:

> This pessimistic outlook is not in accordance with past behaviour or Government policy and is one which cannot be assumed for planning purposes. To do so would be to assume reduced community expectations, and result in load limitations and inherent self-fulfilment.[41]

And:

> Above all, the Commission does not accept that expansion of the Tasmanian electricity supply system should be based on the proposition that over the next 20 years Tasmanians become progressively poorer compared with people in the rest of Australia.[42]

The way the HEC used its control over information to structure options available to politicians is exemplified by another case. The HEC managed to have the conversion of its only thermal station at Bell Bay considered at the same time as, but as a separate issue from, the issue of the next new power development program. This measure had been recommended by the HEC in an interim report produced in June 1980 just before the Cabinet deliberations on power development options.

This was a considerable coup by the HEC in defining the alternatives for the politicians, who at no time were presented with information about an important option: the construction of a new thermal station both as a replacement for oil-fired generation at Bell Bay and as a means of meeting the next increment of load growth. The economics of this option compared favourably with hydro, and the option had the added advantage of providing flexibility to meet low or high load growth more cheaply because it involved a higher proportion of variable costs.[43]

In the event, Bell Bay was not converted to coal but continued to provide 'firming' capacity, which increased the load the system could meet. By 1986, with the completion of the Pieman scheme and other minor planned works, the assessed system average capacity of the Tasmanian system (including **thermal firming**) was 1215 MWav. The average output from the hydro stations alone was 1087 MWav, to which the King and Henty-Anthony schemes were to add 112 MWav (some 70 fewer than the Gordon Below Franklin would have provided). This capacity would have barely coped with the demand of 1216 MWav in 1990, which had been forecast in the 1979 report recommending the Gordon Below Franklin, but demand exhibited only minimal growth during the 1980s, and by 1990 had not exhausted even the capacity of the Pieman project. The forecast load compared with the actual load that resulted is shown in table 2.1.

Subsequent developments

The realities of the slackening in demand growth took some time to sink in with an organisation that was still growing. HEC staffing levels had increased steadily from 4168 in 1975 to 5166 in 1984, with salaried staff increasing slowly and wages staff (including construction workers) making up most of the increase.[44] By 1985 the commission had 5247 employees.[45]

As late as 1984 the HEC maintained its faith in the demand forecast it produced in 1979 to justify the Gordon Below Franklin dam, stating: 'No evidence was found to indicate that any substantial change to the forecast was necessary'.[46] A year later it reported that a review of the long-term load forecast was underway and, although incomplete, it was expected that loads in the 1990s would be two or three years later than had been anticipated in 1983.[47] A new load forecast published in 1988 showed a downward revision of load forecasts to 1160 MWav in 1995 and 1227 MWav in 2000.[48] This reflected internal changes in the HEC.

Long-time Chief Commissioner Russell Ashton retired in February 1987,[49] which provided the Gray Liberal Government with the opportunity to restructure the commission. In late 1987 the government separated

Table 2.1   HEC load forecast and actual growth 1980–90

Year	System load (MWav) Forecast	Actual
1980	923	891
1985	1065	935
1990	1216	948

Source: Hydro Electric Commission, *Report on the Gordon River Power Development Stage 2; Appendix 2: The Forecast of Demand,* Hobart 1979, and Annual Reports.

the role of Chairman from that of Chief Executive Officer and appointed prominent businessman Sir Geoffrey Foot as Chairman and (from February 1988) Don Williams as General Manager.[50] Williams had a background in mining, engineering and manufacturing. Foot had once been government leader in the Legislative Council and Chairman of the Tasmanian Permanent Building Society and the Gas Corporation of Tasmania. The organisation was also downsizing, shedding 604 staff in 1987–88, to make for a reduction of about a thousand (or 20 per cent) in two years. A flatter organisational structure was put into place with the aim of reducing lines of communication and providing greater flexibility.

The reform of the HEC was disrupted by the accidental death of Williams in September 1989. He was later replaced as General Manager by G. J. Longbottom, whose previous appointments were with General Motors-Holden, IBM and Mitsubishi Australia. Foot was succeeded as Chairman by Brian Gibson, formerly manager of Australian Newsprint Mills. All these changes indicated a reorientation of the HEC away from an engineering orientation to more of a marketing orientation. Paralleling these organisational changes, the utility also began to show altered behaviour; an effort was made to reduce real net debt and to increase productivity. It began the preparation of a corporate plan, appointed its first marketing manager and began demand-side management. It was no longer deemed necessary to project an air of prescience in forecasting, noting instead of future load growth in its 1989 annual report that: 'In such difficult and uncertain times a load growth of between one and two per cent seems a reasonable forecast'.[51]

By 1990 the HEC was boasting that it had been quick to adopt demand-side management,[52] having begun an energy efficiency campaign in April 1990, and was proclaiming that: 'It is now generally believed in Tasmania that the so-called "era of large dams" is over'.[53] In line with this transition, and with construction work winding down, the number of commission employees fell to 3729, with a further thousand jobs expected to be shed over the next four to five years.[54] By 1992 staff numbers were 2929.[55]

In 1992 the HEC could point not just to the opening of the King River Power Development but also to the launch of its environmental policy and the Tasmanian Integrated Energy Management Centre.[56] It was also investigating a Bass Strait cable to join the South-east Australia Electricity Grid and welcomed the government's establishment of an Energy Council, supported by an Office of Energy Planning and Conservation. The HEC was also undergoing 'commercialisation', being organised into six business units, and shedding a further 20 per cent of its workforce as a result of both commercialisation and an end to construction activities.

This end to reverse adaptation came not through the anticipative response of the HEC and other institutions that had supported hydro-industrialisation. Rather, it came when the economic (and considerable environmental) damage was done. Reform of the HEC was a belated and inevitable reaction to the magnitude of the errors, which was reduced only by the Commonwealth subsidy for the construction of the King and Henty-Anthony schemes. The appreciation of the dangers of the HEC's course was reached too late to save it from overcapacity, and the costs of this error were exacerbated when Comalco – still the consumer of a quarter of all electricity in Tasmania – in 1993 announced its intention to close its Bell Bay smelter at the turn of the century.

In December 1985 Comalco had announced it was to reduce its workforce at Bell Bay by a hundred (from 950), having already reduced its administrative staff by fifty.[57] Then in July 1993 Comalco abandoned plans for a new smelter at Bell Bay after failing to come to terms with the government over a new power contract for 287 MW.[58] The existing contract for 237 MW was due to expire in 2001, and the company wished to conclude a new power contract and build a new smelter. It had attempted to buy power stations from the government, but those negotiations had also broken down over price. Comalco was prepared to offer about $800m for three stations in the Lower Pieman, Mersey-Forth and Derwent schemes, but the government's lowest price was $1 billion. It was reported that Comalco was paying about 1.7 c/kWh under its existing contract and was prepared to pay up to 2.5 c/kWh, but the government and the HEC would not go below 3.5 c/kWh.

Comalco therefore intended to close its smelter at the expiration of the current contract and possibly earlier. Comalco had just paid $200m to raise its equity in the Boyne Island smelter near Gladstone in Queensland from 30 per cent to 50 per cent. The Boyne Island partners were also planning to commit $1.65b by the end of 1993 to buy the Gladstone Power Station ($750m) and expand the capacity of the smelter by 200 000 tpa by the addition of a third potline ($900m).[59] In December 1993 Comalco announced a $300m upgrade to its Tiwai Point smelter in New Zealand after concluding new price agreements on its electricity contract with the government, which saw the price for two-thirds of its demand rise from 2 c/kWh to 3.5 c/kWh by 2010.[60] The upgrade would lift production by 32 000 tonnes to 290 000 tonnes, Comalco having previously sought to buy the 700 MW Manapouri power station.

Conclusion

In his 1976 analysis of the economics of electricity supply in Australia G.D. McColl found that 'the continuation of hydro-electricity developments in Tasmania appears to have been very doubtful in economic terms'.[61] The Poatina power station using Great Lake held up to McColl's scrutiny, but the Mersey-Forth scheme (completed in 1972) was of questionable economic merit, and the Gordon Stage 1 scheme (which flooded Lake Pedder) did not compare favourably with coal-fired generation. The rather poor state of project evaluation techniques in Tasmania go a long way to explain why the State Government approved of such schemes,[62] but (as this chapter has shown) the forecasting and planning processes in the state are of fundamental importance in understanding conflicts such as that over the Gordon Below Franklin.

The case studied in this chapter suggests some factors that might have contributed to the reverse adaptation of the Hydro Electric Commission of Tasmania. The effective monopoly on expertise that the HEC enjoyed was one factor since its demand forecasts could not effectively be challenged by any institution within the state. The HEC was responsible for generation, transmission and distribution of electricity, so there were no distribution utilities whose perspectives on load growth patterns might have countered those of the HEC. The fact that forecasting traditionally was undertaken only in conjunction with the justification of the construction of additional capacity would also appear to be a contributing factor. Of significance, too, would appear to be the fact that the HEC had its own construction workforce. This probably did not alter the organisational dynamics in favour of both growth and the selection of hydroelectric means, but it did provide an important constituency within the labour movement (and thus the Labor Party) that favoured the continued construction of dams. Federalism can also be seen to have played a part; hydroelectric construction was long seen as means of ensuring that Tasmania received a share of Loans Council funds for development. And, finally, both the statutory independence of the HEC and the power of the Tasmanian Legislative Council were important.

We might expect from this brief analysis of the factors conducive to reverse adaptation in Tasmania that the problem might be addressed by reforms to counter some of these factors and, indeed, some reforms along these lines have been suggested. Thus we might expect that the opening up of the forecasting and planning process to other agencies and to public scrutiny, the separation of generation and retail distribution, the decoupling of forecasting and planning, the absence of a construction workforce employed by the utility, and the assertion of ministerial authority over the utility might help to minimise the risk of reverse adaptation. Similarly, we might expect that such planning occurring in a unitary system of government and in the absence of a legislative upper house might be somewhat less afflicted by the problems we can point to in Tasmania.

We shall discuss such factors later in trying to reach some conclusions on the basis of four further case studies. But the exegesis of the cases themselves will throw some light on these matters, and none more so than the case examined in the next chapter on forecasting and planning in New Zealand. New Zealand has a unitary system of government without an upper house in its legislature. It has a similar political culture and economy to Tasmania, and its electrical utility at the time of the case study was a full ministerial department with only an electrical design and construction workforce and no civil construction workforce; it had no responsibility for retail distribution; forecasts were published annually as a result of a process that involved several agencies.

What we shall find in the next chapter, however, is that – despite these supposed institutional improvements – electricity planning in New Zealand became equally reverse adapted. What the two cases, taken together, underscore is the importance of politics – particularly the politics of development – in creating conditions conducive to reverse adaptation. We will then move on to look at cases in which reform of utilities occurred.

CHAPTER 3

New Zealand:
The triumph of distributive politics

Federalism in Australia is blamed for many things, including the poor management of resource development and environment issues. The experience of electricity planning in New Zealand in the 1970s, however, suggests that this blame is largely misplaced for the political attractions of development prevailed there even in the face of institutional arrangements different to those in Tasmania. Indeed, these differences in institutional arrangements were mostly of a kind that, on the basis of the Tasmanian case, might have led us to expect a less reverse-adapted pattern, yet this was not the case.

In the 1970s and early 1980s New Zealand possessed what we might have expected to have been a number of institutional advantages over Tasmania in the field of electricity planning. Yet these institutions proved to be just as adapted to expansion by the construction of the preferred hydroelectric means. Even after demand levelled off, the momentum of the development projects embedded in these institutions proved unstoppable, and the consequences were costly, especially since (unlike Tasmania) there was no Federal Government to pay the bill. An expensive dam was built much earlier than it should have been, and it should have been deferred in preference to thermal capacity. In this case demand-side management and least-cost planning techniques were ignored as means of responding to planning uncertainties, and the planning process continued as usual.

This chapter will examine these developments, focusing on the decisions to build two power stations and the forecasting and planning processes in general. First, however, we shall look at the institutional setting for electricity planning in New Zealand, which suggested in many ways the reforms suggested in Tasmania.

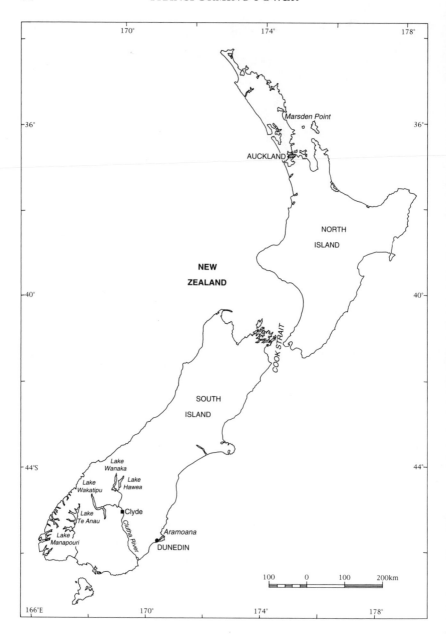

The institutional background

The dominant role for the state in the electricity industry in New Zealand began with the *Electric Lines Act 1896*, the result of a deliberate intention to create a public power system rather than a case of the state stepping in after the failure of private enterprise, as in Tasmania. Then the *Water Power Act 1903* reserved the rights to develop the country's hydroelectric resources to the Crown. The agency initially charged with developing the considerable hydraulic potential was the Department of Immigration and Public Works, created in 1870 by Sir Julius Vogel, who was responsible for the emergence of a strong role for the state in developing New Zealand.[1] Public works was separated from immigration in 1872 but, as the name of the original department suggested, Vogel saw public works as a way of combining immigration and development as a natural progression from the Wakefield system of immigration used to settle the country.[2] The Public Works Department was an unambiguously distributive agency.

The distribution function was separated from generation and transmission under the *Electric Power Boards Act 1918*, and retailing was thereafter undertaken by a number of electric supply authorities, either regional power boards or electricity departments operated by local governments. When the industry was restructured in 1987 there were ninety-four such authorities.

The administrative arrangements for electricity planning and generation were amended on 1 April 1946 by the *Electricity Act 1945*, which established a State Hydro-electric Department responsible for planning, design and operation of generation and transmission. Thereafter the Ministry of Works conducted civil construction of power schemes, and the Hydro-electric Department installed electrical plant. However, two years later the civil engineering section handling design and construction was transferred back to Works, which established a separate Power Division in 1959.

The next twenty years became known as 'the great hydroelectric era'.[3] By 1993 the New Zealand system had an installed capacity of 7400 MW and generated about 30 000 GWh pa. There was minimal thermal development, although the coal-fired Meremere station was commissioned in 1958. An undersea cable laid in the 1960s allowed interchange between the systems in the two islands, supposedly minimising the need for thermal firming because the high winter rainfalls in the North Island would balance the low winter inflows in the snow-fed South Island dams. The flow would in theory be in the opposite direction in summer, with the annual thaw flowing into lakes that provided little more than enough storage to regulate annual inflows.

Nevertheless, the growth of demand in the North Island and additional development in the South was to exceed the capacity of the Cook Strait cable. Eventually the relative lack of thermal capacity or long-term water storages caught up with the strongly hydro-oriented institutions that dominated forecasting and planning, and there was a supply crisis in the winter of 1992. With a dry, cold winter in 1992 there was a need for emergency conservation, and the Comalco aluminium smelter was closed (with compensation paid to its owners).[4]

Before 1967 power development relied on s306 of the *Public Works Act 1928*, which vested the power to use water in the Crown, subject to any right lawfully held. Similarly, s254 gave the Crown the power to take land by proclamation. In 1967 the Water and Soil Conservation Act imposed a regulatory approach to water resources development, including the use of water resources by the Crown for hydroelectricity and other purposes. All users of water were then required to make application to regional water boards for water rights, but with Crown applications decided by the National Water and Soil Conservation Authority, after considering the recommendations of the regional water board involved. This authority was close to the government, being chaired by the Minister of Works, but its decisions could be appealed to the Planning Tribunal and ultimately the courts. The Crown could avoid any such problems, however, by first declaring water to be 'of national importance'.[5]

World War II disrupted the development of the system. Capital and manpower were diverted to the war effort at a time when the electricity market was expanding rapidly. Shortages of both energy and power capacity were the norm in the postwar years, and outages were commonplace. These factors resulted in the emergence of strong popular support for hydro construction, a task that required considerable planning and coordination. To meet this need a dual committee system was developed in the mid 1950s, consisting of what were essentially interdepartmental committees. The first of these, the Committee to Review the Power Requirements (CRPR), dealt with demand forecasting, and brought together the Department of Statistics and the Treasury with the representatives of the electricity industry – both the New Zealand Electricity Department (NZED – two representatives) and the local retail suppliers' group, the Electric Supply Authorities Association (ESAA – two representatives).

The Committee to Review the Power Requirements used as the starting point for its forecasts the quinquennial projections generated by the Planning and Finance Utilisation Committee (PFUC), comprised of one NZED representative and six ESAA representatives. It then produced a fifteen-year forecast of demand, which was updated annually. In addition to the perspectives of the industry itself, demand forecasting was thus informed by the Department of Statistics' population projections and the Treasury's forecasts of economic activity. From 1973 representation was also given to the newly established Commission for Energy Resources. These forecasts were produced annually and tabled in parliament, but rarely excited much interest before the 1970s.

A Planning Committee on Electric Power Development (PCEPD) then produced annual reports setting out the preferred development plan to meet the forecast demand. This committee coordinated construction schedules with both the demand forecast and capital and labour availability. Its report adjusted the timing of the development plan on this annual basis to ensure that the median load forecast would be met. The committee consisted of representatives of the NZED (three), ESAA (three), Ministry of Works (two) and Treasury. Electricity development projects were then coordinated with other public works projects by the Cabinet Works Committee.

The institutional arrangements for forecasting and planning in New Zealand were thus in a form that has been advocated as a reform in other situations. Forecasts were produced annually, instead of only when a new power station was proposed so the risk of reverse adaptation should have been lessened. These forecasts were also produced by a process that was not monopolised by the utility itself and which had nominal accountability to parliament built in. The fact that this process (as we shall see below) went awry in the 1970s might, therefore, be disheartening to advocates of utility reform, although in fairness it must be stated that the accountability mechanisms were rather weak. The reports might have been published, but the processes by which they were produced were still shrouded in secrecy. So too was the extent to which utility dominance was checked by the presence of others illusory rather than real. The expertise of the electrical industry was not matched by any other agency with an interest or a brief to regard either demand forecasts or expansion plans critically. And the whole political climate in which the process occurred favoured expansion of the system.

With seemingly ever-increasing demand through the 1950s and 1960s a strong alliance developed between the NZED and the Power Division of the Ministry of Works (later the Ministry of Works and Development), which usually undertook construction of the schemes on behalf of NZED.[6] Both political parties supported the rapid development of the nation's hydroelectric resources. This was no more evident than with the deal struck to attract the Australian aluminium company Comalco[7] to build a smelter at Tiwai Point near Bluff at the south of the South Island, using electricity generated from the resources available at Lake Manapouri. The need to raise the levels of this scenic lake to extract more electricity politicised the electricity planning and construction process significantly for the first time. The government sold electricity to Comalco at a very cheap rate (claimed by critics to be as low as 0.17 c/kWh before being increased in 1977)[8] under a ninety-nine-year contract in a deal that enjoyed bipartisan support.[9] Price increases were limited to 1 per cent a year under the original contract, but a fourfold increase was extracted by the government in 1977 under the threat of legislation to impose an increase.

While governments of both persuasions were drawn to the use of electricity as a lure to attract footloose industrial investment, however, the controversy surrounding both the Comalco contract and the associated proposed raising of Manapouri set the scene for controversy over electricity planning in the 1970s. This controversy revolved around specific power station proposals, such as the Upper Clutha hydroelectric development or Auckland Thermal No. 1 Station proposal, rather than the demand forecasting and planning process itself. That process was to become highly politicised by the end of the 1970s, but it was when the process was not yet so highly charged in the early 1970s that it provides a case study of just how wrong electricity planning can go under conditions of uncertainty when utilities are adapted to growth.

The case study shows that the poor planning resulted not from a simple case of technocratic rule by the engineers of the electrical utility but from deeply embedded institutional factors that included an element of diminished accountability because of technical complexity, but which resulted more crucially from political support for growth. When combined with a positivist approach that took forecasts as objective reality, this provided a recipe for error.

The Marsden B debacle

The Marsden B power station had its origins in the planning process described above but a process influenced by the demands of the Comalco smelter.[10] The decision to preserve Lake Manapouri within its natural limits carried the cost of diminished output from that scheme as a result of the lower generating head available.[11] Further, Comalco was planning to increase its electricity demand by expanding its smelter from 112 000 tpa to 150 000 tpa, and this gave rise to an anticipated shortfall in generating capacity from the winter of 1978 until the commissioning in 1981 of plant already approved (a thermal station at Huntly on the Waikato River). Marsden B was originally conceived as an oil-fired thermal station with a 500 MW (2×250 MW) capacity to be built alongside the Marsden A station. Like that station, it would burn residual fuel oil, a by-product from the nearby Marsden Point Oil Refinery.

The capacity shortfall identified in August 1973 posed a particular problem for a predominantly hydro utility. There was no possibility of building and commissioning a hydro station with the available lead time of only five years. Even with thermal plant (other than combustion turbines) the lead time was normally six or seven years. Therefore even thermal options were limited to those on sites where geological surveys of foundations had been conducted and cooling towers would not be necessary on environmental grounds. There was only one station in the power plan that fitted these requirements: Marsden B. The decision to build it was to prove a difficult one, which made all the more crucial the acceptance as objective reality of the demand forecast and the looming supply crisis.

There was never any consideration of anything other than a supply-side response to the demand forecast indicating the shortfall in 1978. One demand-side option would have been to negotiate a deferral of the commissioning of the new capacity at the aluminium smelter. Another possibility was to embark on conservation in order to avoid the shortfall until the commissioning of new plant in 1981. Ironically, the conservation path *was* followed at the very time the policymakers were deliberating over Marsden B, but it was never seen as anything other than a temporary expedient. The oil crisis following the Yom Kippur war in October 1973 pushed oil prices from around $US2 per barrel in August 1973 to about $US10 per barrel a year later. This caused fuel costs at Marsden A to rise sharply and necessitated the introduction of stringent demand management measures from February 1974. These included such strictures as a ban on display and advertising lighting, which might not have saved much electricity but underscored the urgency of the situation by plunging cities into gloom. Some of these measures were temporary, but this crisis also resulted in the modification of building codes to ensure adequate standards of insulation and, for many years, a scheme providing interest-free loans for insulation that could be repaid as part of electricity bills. While these measures succeeded in slowing demand growth, the forecasters argued that these results 'must not be allowed to obtrude into longer-term forecasting'.[12]

Marsden B was unveiled in August 1973 as the response to the anticipated 1978 shortfall, but it was quickly overtaken by events. It was to be a 1×250 MW oil-fired station to be built at a cost of $48m. The rapid escalation in oil prices gave rise to concern among the cabinet, and the Prime Minister, Norman Kirk, reportedly told the NZED in April 1974 that he wanted the station to be coal-fired rather than burn oil, which was not only expensive but also imported and added to the nation's rapidly deteriorating balance of payments. The difficulty with this proposal was

that the only coal deposits in the vicinity of the site had not been established to have enough reserves to fuel such a station. The closest producing coalfield was 250 km to the south, and it was not clear that the
State Coal Mines would be able to increase production there by the
necessary 800 tonnes per day. An additional problem was that a coal-fired
station would be a more complex plant, with coal-handling and ash disposal equipment required, and it might not have been possible to meet
the seemingly immovable 1978 commissioning date with a coal-fired
station.

Despite these difficulties, the NZED acceded partially to the Prime
Minister's wishes and published an environmental impact report in May
1974 describing a dual-fired station, which would run on oil for the first
year, while coal-handling facilities were built, and coal thereafter
(although it would, of course, be capable of burning either fuel).[13] The
coal would have to be transported 250 km and the capital cost was
estimated at $85.9m, or 79 per cent more than the oil-only station. It was
this higher capital cost (particularly the cost of imported items) that
finally counted against the dual-fired station when the Minister of
Electricity, Tom McGuigan, announced the decision to proceed with the
oil-only option in August 1974. (The dual-fired option was rejected on
these grounds in an unfavourable Treasury report.)

Ironically, balance of payments problems resulting in large part from
the escalation in the price of oil led to a decision to place greater future
reliance on imported oil. That eventuality was averted if only because the
demand shortfall that had made the construction of Marsden B so
urgent never eventuated, despite the fact that the station was not completed until 1980. The anticipated deficit had by then become an overcapacity, and Marsden B was put into mothballs without being
commissioned. The final cost of this white elephant was $120m. In
February 1981 it was announced that the conversion of the station to coal
was being investigated.

The Marsden B debacle underscores the costs of risk and uncertainty
in electricity planning. Electricity generating capacity constitutes a costly
investment, and overcapacity is one way the costs of uncertainty become
apparent. In this case we can see the undesirable impact of incremental
decision-making. A series of decisions was made at the margin, each
rational within a limited frame of analysis, but each leading inexorably
to a fundamentally irrational decision. The reason for this macro-
irrationality was the failure to reconsider the fundamental assumptions
on which the decision process proceeded. Given the absence of a satis-
factory option, there was a need for the decisionmakers to re-examine
the basic causes of the situation confronting them. Failure to do so

resulted from their acceptance of the forecast of demand as a parameter, rather than as a variable over which they had some control. This point was made by a key bureaucratic actor, the Ministry of Works and Development, which warned in 1974 that a 'better explanation of why the April 1978 deadline [was] so urgent' was needed.[14] The Ministry of Works and Development can be seen as relatively neutral in this process, or even as being potentially hostile to the selection of a thermal station, since its Power Division usually built hydro schemes. It preferred hydraulic means and was quite willing to debate the ends that justified thermal means. The electricity interests, as we have seen, had argued in 1974 that the success of conservation efforts should not detract from a supply-side approach of adding new capacity. That approach continued in 1975 even after the demand forecast for the winter of 1974 (when the Marsden B decision was still under consideration) overestimated actual demand.

The warning signs were there for the politicians, but the expansionist approach prevailed and the failure of reality to match forecasts was rationalised away by the Planning Finance Utilisation Committee with such tortured logic as 'the *potential* for consumption continued to increase, and the *apparent* low growth of the last two years should not be allowed to distort forecasts and planning to the point where future, unrestricted supply may be jeopardised'.[15] This treatment of reality as illusory because it failed to accord with forecasts is reminiscent of the observation that forecasts often seem to tell us more of the future than we know of the past or the present.[16]

Planning under uncertainty

The Marsden B fiasco was not, unfortunately, an isolated mistake but a portent of a deeper malaise in the electricity forecasting and planning process in New Zealand. As forecasting became less predictable in the wake of the 1973 oil crisis, institutional arrangements developed in the era of market expansion and seemingly limitless growth found it difficult to adjust to a situation in which not only was the rate of future growth uncertain but also whether there would be *any* growth in the foreseeable future was problematic. The response of the planners to the emergence of uncertainty was to err on the side of overcapacity, an error that was to prove costly for New Zealand, particularly since institutional bias resulted in an undue reliance on hydro capacity. As we shall see, however, this error was not solely the fault of empire-building technocrats in a reverse-adapted utility but resulted at least in part from the maintenance by political actors of an environment conducive to such hubris. We now turn to this larger forecasting and planning process.[17]

By the early 1970s the Committee to Review the Power Requirements was making provision for major industrial load growth on the basis of estimates provided by industries such as Comalco and New Zealand Steel. In making its 1973 forecast, however, CRPR argued that such forecasts failed to make adequate provision for 'unforeseen electricity intensive industrial loads'. It therefore made provision for 600 GWh (about 70 MWav) in the load forecast. In this way, CRPR hoped to avoid the problems created by the differential lead times for power stations (at least six years) and industry (two to three years). Thus the state was effectively to assume the uncertainty costs associated with such industry and pool them across all consumers of electricity, who would have to pay for the capacity to meet this margin on a continuing basis.

This margin was used initially as a justification for building Marsden B but was replaced as a justification in the PCEPD 1974 Report by the lump of additional demand in 1978–79 'due mainly to changes in Comalco's requirements'.[18] The 600 GWh was retained, but could now be covered only from 1980–81 onwards. Now that the extra 600 GWh for industry was no longer needed to justify the urgent construction of Marsden B, the planners were happy to reveal that it had been incorporated into the demand forecast at the government's request rather than because of an expectation that it would be needed. Forecasting was in reality becoming planning.

The winter of 1974 saw a marked slowdown in demand growth as a result of the conservation efforts of consumers, and this trend continued in 1975 after the introduction of formal conservation measures, including (as we have seen) zero interest loans for domestic insulation. As we saw above, however, the planners were inventive in explaining away these results, which did not accord with the organisational goal of expansion. While the 'potential for consumption' might well have continued to increase, actual consumption did so at a much diminished rate and did so in a manner that did (eventually) 'obtrude into longer-term forecasting'. What was interesting was that doubts about overestimation of demand had been raised in 1975, at a time when Marsden B could have been stopped at little cost, but had not reached the politicians. The minutes of the Cabinet Economic Committee meeting on 7 June 1978 recorded:

> Three years ago concern had been expressed by some members of the Power Requirements Committee that the demand forecasts were too high and that not enough consideration was being given to a levelling off in demand and a slower rate of economic growth. This view had however been over-ruled by the majority of the committee.[19]

It was not until 1978 that the forecasters were found out and then only after more divisions in 1977 between representatives of the electricity industry on the one side and the Commission for Energy Resources, Treasury and Department of Statistics on the other. The emerging over-capacity caused some problems for the government, which responded (as we shall see) with a costly orgy of development, but it also cancelled several power projects and ended the independent existence of the NZED by incorporating it in a new Ministry of Energy.[20]

While the CRPR report was not published until September 1978, Cabinet was informed in June that there were serious errors in the forecasts resulting in a surplus that would last well into the 1980s. These revelations put an end to a debate over the ultimate need for nuclear development in New Zealand and resulted in the cancellation of two thermal stations and three hydro stations then on the development plan for the North Island. In the South Island, completion of the Clyde Dam was postponed four years and the Luggate Dam (next scheme in the Upper Clutha development) was cancelled. There was some irony in the Clyde Dam deferral because one of the reasons given for choosing it over an alternative scheme in December 1976 was that it could have been completed four years earlier. The capacity of projects shelved in 1978 totalled 3200 MW.

The slackening in demand growth had been obscured by the extra demand resulting from the Comalco expansion in 1976. Ironically, the needs of the smelter had never been specified separately in public precisely because of the long-running sensitivity of the pricing of electricity for the smelter and the controversy over the related Manapouri power scheme. The surplus was to benefit Comalco, which was able to soak up 1350 GWh from 1982 with a third potline at its smelter because the government chose to continue with all power schemes under construction and, in the view of Prime Minister Robert Muldoon recorded in the minutes of the Cabinet Economic Committee, 'If there was a surplus, consideration could then be given to introducing a new energy intensive industry to utilise this power'.[21]

This surplus capacity led to some rather confused policymaking with simultaneous steps being taken in several directions. First, the 1973 energy crisis had signalled the need for a coordinated approach to energy policy so the government incorporated the NZED into the newly established Ministry of Energy. The new ministry undertook a strategic planning process, which it opened to public participation, and the resulting *Energy Strategy '79* marked a move away from what had been essentially a trend towards a planning process that included the explicit identification of particular goals and the selection of the means appropriate for achieving them. This innovative approach by this new agency was undermined, however, by decisions taken by the politicians.

The severe reversal in New Zealand's terms of trade after the election of the Labour Government in 1972 led to its defeat in 1975 in a landslide by the National Party led by Robert Muldoon. That government had been returned narrowly in 1978, although it attracted fewer votes overall than the Labour Party. The economic miracle it had promised in 1975 had failed to materialise, and it very nearly paid the ultimate price at the 1978 election. It needed a plausible 'miracle' for the 1981 election if it was to avoid defeat and came up with a strategy of energy-led industrial development, which became known by the title 'Think Big'.[22]

This strategy involved not only the electricity surplus but also the use of natural gas from the offshore Maui field for use in motor vehicles (as compressed natural gas), a methanol plant, an ammonia–urea plant and a highly risky synthetic petroleum plant. These ventures were, however, related to the electricity surplus because the government had signed take-or-pay contracts with the Maui developers in 1973 to get that project under way and had intended that the gas would be used in thermal electricity stations, the construction of which could no longer be justified. The hubris of the electricity forecasters, therefore, had ramifications beyond the electricity sector.

Thinking big

In February 1980, as part of the program of developing energy-intensive industry, the government released an international marketing document called *Growth Opportunities in New Zealand*. The document invited proposals for electricity-intensive industries to take up a surplus generating capacity estimated at 5000 GWh. A concessional rate for new industry locating in the South Island (a 25 per cent discount) had been announced after the 1979 plan had confirmed a surplus. Among those proposals that emerged were the third potline at Comalco's Tiwai Point smelter and a proposed new aluminium smelter at Aramoana (near Dunedin).

The problem was that much of the surplus generating capacity was oil-fired thermal plant, or combustion turbine plant, and oil fuels escalated rapidly in price after the 1979 Iranian revolution. Much of the surplus capacity was therefore in plant that carried high avoidable costs and low capital costs, precisely the kind of plant that could be used for covering risk by providing 'firming' for the hydro system, rather than base-load capacity suitable for supplying aluminium smelters. Critics of the government made this point and argued that only 2000 GWh were available, which had been committed to the second potline at Tiwai Point and an expansion program at New Zealand Steel.[23] (The Minister of Energy was later to admit that there was not a big enough surplus for both the new smelter and the third Comalco potline.[24]) Few smelting companies would have been likely to be in the market for electricity at the marginal (largely fuel) costs of this thermal capacity. Unlike Australia, New Zealand did not have abundant supplies of cheap steaming coal. Smelting capacity worldwide was being relocated from areas reliant on high-cost oil and gas generation to areas with cheaper coal-based or hydraulic-based electricity generation. The relocation of smelting capacity from reliance on oil-fired base-load generation in Japan to reliance on oil-fired base-load generation in New Zealand was not likely to occur.

The Aramoana smelter in particular became inextricably linked with the hydroelectric development of the Upper Clutha River, especially the Clyde Dam, construction of which was already under way. The relationship between the two was to cause problems, as we shall see, as construction of the Clyde Dam was again advanced to provide electricity for the smelter. There was widespread opposition to both these projects. The Clyde Dam would flood the scenic Cromwell Gorge and had for some time been the focus of heated political conflict.[25] Aramoana was a site of some ecological sensitivity and had been proposed as the site of a smelter in 1972. Opposition to the proposal then was reactivated when the smelter reappeared as part of the 'Think Big' strategy with the announcement on 27 July 1980 of government approval of a second smelter.

In September the government signed a memorandum of intent with a consortium involving New Zealand's Fletcher Challenge, Alusuisse and Australia's Gove Alumina for a smelter, which would consume 3140 GWh of electricity. In April that year New South Wales had found it had offered power to too many smelters, and the Australian–Swiss consortium of Alusuisse and Nabalco was told it would have to miss out.[26]

Unfortunately for the government's ambitions, electricity from the Clyde Dam was going to cost considerably more than any smelter could afford to pay, and it soon became apparent that a subsidy would be necessary to lure the smelter to New Zealand. Criticism of both the dam and the smelter escalated as a result.

Electricity for a smelter was offered at a subsidised rate, but even that was not enough to attract investment from two successive consortia, the first involving Alusuisse and the second the French company, Pechiney Ugine Kuhlman. Estimates of the cost of electricity varied from 4–5 c/kWh at a 10 per cent discount rate (from critics of the smelter project) to 2.3 c/kWh at a 5 per cent discount rate (from the Minister of Energy, Bill Birch). The government had already announced that it was prepared to offer a 25 per cent discount for new industry in the South

Island, ostensibly to foster regional development, but also because the Cook Strait transmission cable was already at capacity and, therefore, any further electricity would have to be used in the South Island or water would simply spill to waste from South Island dams. The price on offer was therefore about 1.74 c/kWh – an annual subsidy of about $20m at a 5 per cent discount rate, but closer to $100m at 10 per cent.[27]

The withdrawal of Alusuisse from the consortium on 1 October 1981, just before the November election, caused problems for the government, which had used the smelter to justify the controversial Clyde Dam. The participation of Pechiney was therefore particularly helpful, but since it reached an electricity deal for a smelter with Hydro Quebec in April 1982, its interest in Aramoana might have been nothing more than a bargaining chip in negotiations in Canada.

The questions of whether there really would be a smelter and (regardless) whether there was a surplus did not sway the government from its decision to proceed with the Clyde Dam, which had seen some tortuous decision-making. Successive reviews had recommended a development program known as Scheme H.[28] The National Party in opposition had promised to review the height of the first dam in this option, which would have flooded parts of the town of Cromwell. Once in government, National announced on 20 December 1976 that it had decided on another option, Scheme F, involving a high dam at Clyde that would flood the Cromwell Gorge. This power station would have a capacity of 432 MW and would have an annual output of 1939 GWh for a cost of $565m (1983 dollars). The decision was reached on the basis of strong support for the Clyde Dam from both Treasury and the Ministry of Works and Development. One of the reasons advanced by the latter was the 'better foundation conditions for a "high" dam at the Clyde site'.[29] This was somewhat ironic since unstable rock conditions were to cause extensive delays and cost escalations while the dam was being built.[30]

The Minister of Electricity applied for a water right in July 1977. The Otago Catchment Board (as regional water board) received 209 submissions on the water right application; 206 opposed it. The board therefore recommended a low dam of 30 m, rather than the 64 m high dam, at its meeting on 25 October 1977. The National Water and Soil Conservation Authority (chaired by the Minister of Works) rejected that recommendation on 6 December 1977 when it decided to grant the water rights needed to build a high dam.

A group of fifteen landowners, joined by the Royal Society of New Zealand and the Environmental Defence Society, then appealed the granting of water rights. (The Royal Society and EDS appeals were rejected as the groups lacked standing to sue.) By a four to two decision on 16 December 1980 the tribunal dismissed the appeal. The two judicial members on the tribunal dissented, finding that the difference between the high and low dams did not justify the loss of agricultural, horticultural and scenic land. The landholders lodged an appeal against the decision in the High Court on 22 December 1980, arguing that the tribunal erred in law in disallowing evidence on the end use of power from the dam. Justice Casey delivered his judgment in the High Court on 13 May 1982, finding for the appellants and referring the matter back to the tribunal.[31]

Within two weeks the National Party had decided to use special empowering legislation to get the water right. Three backbench members of parliament indicated that they would oppose the legislation, however, and the decision created a constitutional uproar. Two dissenters reluctantly gave in on the grounds that they were faced with a *fait accompli*. However, one backbencher, Mike Minogue, said he would not vote for the legislation. As the government had a working majority of only one seat (after supplying the Speaker), Minogue voting against the bill would have meant a 45–46 defeat; if Minogue abstained, parliamentary convention would have required the Speaker to vote to preserve the *status quo* – again meaning defeat for the bill.

Work had begun on the project in 1977 (initially on associated roads), and the time was fast approaching when the river would have to be diverted, but the Auditor-General would hold any expenditure without a water right to be illegal. Without a water right, work would have to stop, jeopardising the employment of a thousand workers. The opposition Labour Party offered to support legislation allowing a low dam, which would not have infringed the rights of the appellants as they did not oppose a low dam, but the government rejected this offer on the grounds that it would cause delays while redesign work was conducted and would produce more expensive electricity.

Less than a week after the government rejected the Labour offer, the minor Social Credit Party offered to support the legislation if the government first allowed the tribunal to hear the appeal again. This was a *volte face* since two months earlier the party leader, Bruce Beetham, had stated that Social Credit opposed the legislation and favoured a low dam. In exchange it wanted five concessions, including guarantees that Lake Wanaka would not be raised (its level was already guaranteed by the *Lake Wanaka Preservation Act 1973*) and that electricity would not be sold to the Aramoana smelter at less than the current average price for South Island generation (which was below the price the government was offering). One condition in particular explained why Social Credit had changed its mind: it wanted a feasibility study of ways to keep open a freezing works at Patea in Beetham's electorate.[32]

The tribunal was reconvened in August and upheld the appeal, overturning the grant of the water right on the grounds that there was insufficient evidence to suggest that a second aluminium smelter would be built to consume the output from the power station. The government then introduced the empowering bill, which was referred to an all-party select committee (another Social Credit condition), and then passed in October 1992. The rebel backbencher, Mike Minogue, abstained.

The dam case thus saw the expediency of distributive politics triumph over the rule of law, a point made by the Law Society in its submission on the bill to the select committee and by two retired High Court judges, who warned of 'fascism' and 'dictatorship' respectively. And, typical of distributive politics, party discipline was severely tested both by those concerned about the propriety of the empowering legislation and by those with allegiance to those who benefited from the dam on regional or employment grounds. The Labour Party's ties to the unions whose members were employed on the dam caused it some difficulties, and one member from the region flirted openly with the idea of voting for the bill against party discipline. The opportunities to engage in logrolling for political advantage in one of its electorates was attractive enough to override Social Credit's principles. And voicing public doubts over the 'Think Big' program led to the resignation of the Minister of Works and Development, Derek Quigley, in the midst of all this on 14 June 1982.[33]

The vanishing surplus

Once the Aramoana smelter proposal fell through, the planners were forced to find another justification for the Clyde Dam. They did so in future demand growth in the North Island, but one complication was that there was no spare transmission capacity in the high-voltage under-sea DC cable that linked the hydro-rich South Island to the more populous North Island. Relying on the Clyde Dam to meet North Island demand required the reinforcement of the Cook Strait cable, and the demand could have been met more cheaply with thermal capacity in the North Island than with Clyde plus cable reinforcement.[34]

The political linking of the Clyde Dam with the Aramoana smelter led to the more costly option being selected, because the government needed to have a hydro source of electricity to offer the smelter proponents, and thus it became committed to Clyde regardless of other, more strategic considerations. The hydro option had been supported most strongly by the Power Division of the Ministry of Works and Development, the organisation that ordinarily constructed dams for the Ministry of Energy and the NZED before it. But this was not a case of pure technocracy, however, because the quest for ends to justify the means the MWD had available was actively aided and abetted by the National Party government, seeking to boost development in order to secure re-election. In an ironic twist the government then gave the majority of the construction work on the dam to private contractors, probably the first time it had done so at a time when the MWD had spare capacity to undertake such a project.[35] Fascinating as the twists and turns in the Clyde Dam and Aramoana smelter cases might be, they are interesting to us primarily as providing context and background for the electricity planning process. More important is the crucial question of what had happened to the surplus of generating capacity, which had encouraged the politicians to seek to lure electricity-intensive industry to New Zealand in the first place. After all, if there was a surplus, which it was better to sell cheaply rather than waste, why did the Clyde Dam plus reinforcement of the Cook Strait cable become necessary to meet load growth in the North Island? It is to this question we shall now turn.

The answer to the riddle of the vanishing surplus lies in the fact that much of the surplus capacity lay in oil- or gas-fuelled combustion turbine and conventional steam turbine generating plant, but the disappearance also owes much to some adept conjuring. A number of adjustments, which justified a continuation of capacity expansion by stressing technical rather than economic approaches to risk and uncertainty, were made to planning parameters. The surplus disappeared in a number of assumptions made in the 1980 electricity sector report of the newly introduced Energy Plan. This comprehensive plan marked an advance over the previous electricity-only planning process from the viewpoint of national energy policy, and most of the assumptions appeared reasonable enough in their own terms. However, the net result was extremely dubious in economic terms.

We saw above that, as the result of a Cabinet decision, provision had been made for about 70 MWav to cater for unforeseen industrial expansion, given the problem of differential lead times between power station construction and industry construction. The 1980 plan now added an additional 'planning margin' of 7 per cent to the forecast, intended to cover breakdowns, commissioning delays and 'higher demands than forecast'.[36] This margin amounted to approximately a further 170 MWav. On the face of it, this seemed a prudent move, although it came in addition to the existing 70 MWav margin and did not replace it.

Another innovation in the 1980 plan was the conduct of planning on a 'dry year' basis whereby it was assumed that water yields from the catchments of hydro stations were 15 per cent below the long-term average. This event was assigned a probability of occurrence of about one in twenty. The need for it stemmed from a lack of water storage or firming thermal capacity in the South Island and the absence of capacity on the Cook Strait cable. These factors limited the energy that could be generated in the South. As the Ministry of Energy put it, 'Because of the lack of long-term storage in the South Island the utilisation of inflows there for electricity generation is about 86 per cent'.[37] This loss of potential was about 3000 GWh a year – about one and a half times the output of the Clyde project. Regulation in the North Island was 97 per cent, thanks to the storage available in Lake Taupo. This higher wastage in the South Island reflected both the refusal of the government to allow Lakes Wanaka and Manapouri to be raised to provide storage and the continuing aversion to building thermal capacity, or even using the thermal capacity that did exist. The Electricity Division maintained that only the dry-year capacity of the hydro system could be relied on because 'oil is too expensive for power station use, gas is restricted in supply, and coal difficult to mine and expensive to supply...'.[38]

Again, this view seemed to make prudent sense, and it and the new planning measures discussed above marked a more sophisticated approach to electricity planning than had prevailed in the past. These new planning parameters introduced some provision for uncertainty, but it was introduced as a technical consideration, rather than as an economic concept, and carried some costs with it. Moreover, and probably because of this strictly technical approach, it dealt with only one side of the risk equation: the risk of failure to meet demand. The approach gave no consideration to the risks of overestimating demand and thus the costs of overcapacity. This was a notable omission, given that the experience of the recent past had been one of overcapacity. The electricity planning institutions were thus failing to learn from their recent experience and were instead erring on the side of overcapacity, which accorded with goals of bureaucratic expansion. Both the planning margin and the dry-year planning basis eroded the surplus, but what eradicated it was one further assumption – one that, on the surface, again seemed reasonable.

In 1980 the planners had written down the capacity of thermal plant and then written down hydro yields to 85 per cent as well as planning for a 7 per cent margin on top of this. The Ministry of Energy was essentially relying on high fixed-cost hydro capacity to provide system reliability. It admitted this point in its report to the select committee considering the Clyde Dam empowering bill when it wrote that the 'Clyde power station [was] required to maintain target energy margins even if the second smelter does not proceed'.[39] Conventional power planning wisdom would have said that system security would be provided more cheaply by thermal means and that there would be definite advantages in operating a genuinely mixed hydro-thermal system. Instead, reverse adaptation prevailed, with the planners arguing that: 'Construction of the Clyde power station, and the retention of a skilled workforce, is essential in providing the power system with the ability to respond flexibly to a wide range of future possibilities...'.[40] Flexibility was precisely what further hydro development did not provide (as the 1992 crisis showed), but that was not the real goal here.

There was more than ample political support for 'retaining a skilled labour force', which is perhaps why the planners no longer thought it necessary for them to establish too firmly a need for the scheme's electricity. They argued: 'The need to prove an end-use for the power before a power station is approved is seen to be impossible and would lead to continuous energy restrictions.'[41]

Thus, in establishing the year-by-year generating plan to meet the margin for industrial expansion and the planning margin in the dry-year scenario, the supply of natural gas to gas-fired generating plant was constrained by restricting gas availability as the range of 'Think Big' projects using Maui gas were commissioned. While these projects were of dubious economic value, and were susceptible to falls in the price of oil (since they were mostly aimed at substituting for oil), the use of gas for these purposes at least made better sense thermodynamically than burning it for electricity generation. There was, however, no indication that the opportunity cost of committing gas to these uses had been analysed, and what made much less sense was the restriction of genera-tion at oil-fired stations, both steam turbine and combustion turbine.

The planners justified this measure by pointing out that the cost of fuel at oil-fired stations (Marsden A and the newly completed Marsden B) was 6 c/kWh. The cost of distillate at combustion turbines was twice that figure. The energy plan therefore restricted the contribution of oil-fired steam plant to 15 per cent **capacity factor** and that of distillate-fired combustion turbine plant to 5 per cent capacity factor. This had the effect of writing down the capacity of the system by about 400 MWav as a base assumption in the plan. This amount was approximately the output of the entire Upper Clutha scheme – which then became necessary to fill the gap.

The net effect of these new planning assumptions – industrial margin, planning margin and restriction on thermal capacity – was to make a difference to the demand-supply equation greater than the capacity of the Clyde Dam. The dry-year assumption added further justification for new capacity. The additional capacity was only needed, however, if the planning margin were needed to cover faster-than-anticipated general load growth (the planning margin) and unforeseen industrial load without delay in a dry year (one year in twenty). The planners used these low-probability assumptions to justify the construction of capital-intensive hydro capacity. They advocated a continuation of construction of a scheme with a final capital cost of about $1300m, or an annual cost of

$130m at a 10 per cent interest cost. (The final cost of the Clyde Dam in 1991 dollars was $1573m.[42]) With oil costs at 6 c/kWh, the planning margin (170 MWav) and the industry margin (70 MWav) could be met for fuel costs of $126m a year. This sum would not be required every year; the average annual cost if it was needed only every twenty years would have been only $6.3m. While there would be restricted output of less than 15 per cent with greater frequency than one year in twenty, this is probably not an unreasonable estimate of the cost since the costs would have to be borne only when such a low-output year coincided with a spurt of load growth and the establishment of a new industry.

It would have been preferable to have approached the uncertainty question by finding the least-cost means of covering the various risks. Almost certainly, this would have entailed running thermal plant if and when required rather than building new high fixed-cost hydro plant. That is usually the result when the least-cost utility planning approach is used for future expansion programs; in this case the thermal capacity already existed and, if sunk costs were ignored (as economists require), the security of having the capacity available would have had no capital cost.

Counting the cost and achieving reform

This examination of the electricity planning process in New Zealand has shown the way the relevant institutions failed to adapt to the new, uncertain circumstances that prevailed after the oil crisis of 1973. The power shortages of the 1950s had stimulated the evolution of strong institutional support for expansion, and these institutions did not adapt well. It took a long time for the realisation to dawn that the future would not resemble the past.

John Culy has explored the size of the forecasting error since the mid 1950s. While the size of the error in the CRPR forecasts over a ten-year period was less than 10 per cent in the period 1956–70, the forecasts of the early 1970s went wildly astray. The forecasts of 1969–77 all over-estimated demand ten years in the future by more than 30 per cent. The forecasts for 1973, 1974 and 1975 proved – a decade later – to have been overestimated by 50 per cent.[43]

These errors were extremely costly. A Treasury analysis in 1985 estimated the costs of the overestimate in the early 1970s at about $1 billion. A further half billion dollars might have been saved if the cheapest equivalent scheme had been selected in preference to the Clyde Dam.[44] In 1991 dollars, the cost of energy from the Clyde Dam – finally commissioned in 1992 – was 11.3 c/kWh, compared with around

5c for combined cycle gas stations. The costs resulting from the old institutional arrangements went beyond excess capacity, however, and extended to pricing and investment policies.

In 1984 Treasury estimated that the difference between the then current price of electricity and the costs of supply, using a 10 per cent real rate of return and long-run marginal cost principles, implied an effective annual subsidy to electricity consumers of $800m.[45] During the second smelter debate the Minister of Energy questioned whether a 10 per cent discount rate should be applied to electricity projects. His motivation here was the fact that the lower rate approximately halved the apparent cost of electricity from the Clyde Dam and brought it within the ballpark of a figure that might, with the 25 per cent concession, have been attractive to a smelter company. That was after the government finally appeared to understand the implications of marginal cost pricing when they realised they were bargaining over new capacity rather than a surplus with an opportunity cost near zero. But whether the discount rate used is 5 per cent or 10 per cent affects not only the timing of pricing and investment decisions, it also affects the nature of investments made. The Treasury's insistence on a 10 per cent rate imposed a discipline on what had previously been a much more arbitrary decision process in an economic sense, with technical judgments prevailing. This was particularly because those technical judgments tended to favour hydro schemes over thermal.

The old NZED was adapted not just to expansion but also to hydro expansion, assisted by the influence of the Power Division of the Ministry of Works and Development. Decisionmaking was not influenced by notions of marginal cost and market rates of interest, which reinforced expansion and pro-hydro tendencies. The extent to which hydro was the norm is indicated by the fact that until 1967 the NZED recovered bulk supply costs from the distributors by means of a peak demand charge only. Energy (as opposed to power) was treated as a free good. (By 1983 it was using a 40 per cent peak charge and a 60 per cent energy charge.[46])

This institutional aversion to thermal generation was responsible for the fact that it was possible to have both surplus capacity and energy restrictions. It is in this context that the shortages of the winter of 1992 must be understood. Not only were the planners reluctant to build thermal capacity, they were also reluctant to use what they had, or even assume that they would use it in dry years, on very dubious economic grounds. Rather than follow least-cost utility planning techniques, attention to uncertainty focused solely on the possible costs of shortfalls. Thermal capacity was held down to low plant factors even then, and there was a preference for high fixed-cost hydro plant. This meant lower system reliability and greater spilled energy than could have been achieved with a fully integrated hydro-thermal system.

While the electricity planners in New Zealand managed to prevail largely unaffected until the demise of the National Party Government in 1984, the Electricity Division of the Ministry of Energy was to pay a high bureaucratic price under the new Labour Government. The Treasury had been a consistent critic of the electricity technocrats since the mid 1970s and presented the incoming government with some radical (and debt-reducing) options for reforming what they termed 'state-owned enterprises'.

The organisation of electricity supply in New Zealand was to undergo radical reform as a result. The former Electricity Division of the Ministry of Energy was corporatised in 1987 under a State Owned Enterprises Act to form Electricorp, which was divided into business units responsible for generation, transmission, engineering services and marketing. A new bulk supply tariff with a short-run marginal cost pricing option was introduced. The former regional electric power boards were corporatised into distribution entities, and franchise areas were abolished. Ownership of the grid company, Trans Power, was transferred to a company with equal shareholdings for the generation and distribution sides of the supply industry, plus other participants. And to counter the problems that commercial secrecy causes for the flow of information to the public domain, information disclosure requirements were introduced.[47] Within a year of its establishment Electricorp had reduced overall staff numbers by more than 20 per cent.[48]

Conclusion

The New Zealand case study shows a picture of a set of electricity institutions adapted to the means of system expansion, and hydroelectric means at that. The costs incurred by New Zealand as a result of this reverse adaptation were considerable. What was surprising is that this result came about despite the fact that many features of the institutional arrangements for electricity planning in New Zealand differed from those in Tasmania in ways that we might have expected would have prevented reverse adaptation.

First, forecasting proceeded on a regular, annual basis, so we might have expected that it was less likely to degenerate into justifications of preferred specific projects. But this is to ignore the point that a number of preferred projects existed and had been investigated for many years before the forecast was made. The annual forecasts under these circumstances merely became annual justifications of not just one but a whole raft of projects. And while the reports were published, the process by which they were generated was closed to outsiders, and the represent-atives of the electricity industry were able to dominate. There were no alternative loci of expertise or policy advice on electricity matters. It was finally up to the Treasury to bring the situation to attention solely on economic grounds.

Further, there was less vertical integration in New Zealand. The distribution agencies and the construction agency were separated from the planning and generation agency. But, again, the planning institu-tions allowed these interests to come together and dominate the fore-casting and planning committees respectively, so the separation was more illusory than real. Neither was there the problem of diminished account-ability and an obstructionist upper house since the NZED was a depart-ment of state subject to ministerial direction in a unicameral political system.

The fundamental institutional factor leading to reverse adaptation appears to have been the distributive politics that supported both expansion generally and the hydro means in particular. The political attractions of development and the related reliance on a distributive, means-oriented engineering agency proved enough to overwhelm – at least temporarily – the regulatory regime introduced by the Water and Soil Conservation Act in 1967. The politics surrounding the Clyde Dam empowering bill displayed the classic distributive attributes of dimin-ished party cohesion and logrolling, usually masked by the need for constant tight party discipline in a parliamentary system of government, in which they are usually confined to the secrecy of the party room.

Finally, this triumph of distributive politics cannot be attributed to federalism. New Zealand has a unitary political system, so the result cannot be blamed on interstate competition. But colonial socialism is not just a pattern found in federal Australia. The same problems of capital formation that beset the Australian colonies also resulted in an activist state and considerable reliance on the politics of development in New Zealand. We shall bear these points in mind when we examine the response of other governments to the planning challenges of uncertainty in following chapters.

CHAPTER 4

British Columbia:
Winning reform after losing the Peace

The experience of successful reform of the electric utility in the Canadian province of British Columbia undermines still further the view that federalism is necessarily a key factor in leading to reverse adaptation. The process of reform allows us to explore some of the elements that had to be overcome to bring about change in a utility very much adapted to expansion.

In 1981 the Chairman of the British Columbia Hydro and Power Authority reported that the utility was expecting to invest $22.6 billion over the next decade in new generating capacity and other assets in order to meet an ever-increasing demand for electricity.[1] After the Revelstoke hydroelectric project, which was nearing completion, would come a dam on the Peace River by 1987, then a thermal station at Hat Creek and massive hydro developments in the north of the province. BC Hydro was looking forward to a decade of unprecedented activity building power stations.

Yet a decade later construction of the Peace River dam had not even begun, and plans for the other schemes had been shelved indefinitely. Rather than building dams Hydro was actively promoting conservation, and a thousand staff had been cut from its design section. By 1993 BC Hydro was exporting its Power Smart conservation brand name to US utilities,[2] and its incentive programs had made high-efficiency electric motors the norm rather than the exception.[3] This chapter examines these dramatic changes.

BC Hydro is the third largest electrical utility in Canada (after Hydro Quebec and Ontario Hydro). In 1990 it had a total installed generating capacity (predominantly hydro) of 10 466 MW, with annual sales of almost 43 000 GWh. BC Hydro was formed in 1963 from a merger of the Public Power Commission and the British Columbia Electrical Company

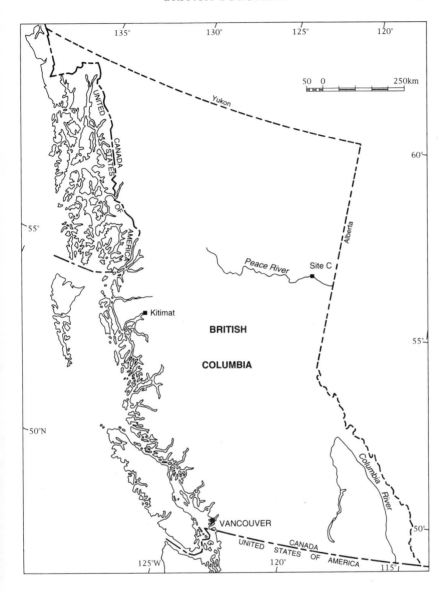

with the purpose of developing the province's hydroelectric resources. The resources most at issue then were those of the Peace River because negotiations with the United States over the Columbia River Treaty, which later allowed development of that river, were stalled.[4] It is ironic, therefore, that the Peace River featured in the process that brought about a change in BC Hydro's approach to planning in the 1980s.

BC Hydro was formed when the Premier, W.A.C. Bennett, had the government take over the BC Power Corporation, the parent company of British Columbia Electric Company. BCE was not keen on either the Peace River or the Columbia, as it had a huge coal deposit at Hat Creek east of Lillooet, and it could readily transmit energy from a power station there through its existing Lillooet–Vancouver transmission lines. For BCE, this was preferable to developing the Peace, remote from any existing transmission lines. Bennett, on the other hand, was keen on 'northern development' and created BC Hydro to ensure that it occurred.[5] (BC Hydro operations also included gas and rail operations, which were sold in 1989.)

BC Hydro set about developing the potential of the Columbia and the Peace Rivers but, like Ontario Hydro, it ran into financial difficulties in the mid to late 1970s. It recorded losses in 1976 and 1977, and a mounting debt burden made it particularly vulnerable to a downturn in either supply or demand caused by weather, conservation or economic circumstances.[6] It nevertheless intended to continue development of the Peace River in the 1980s with a dam at a location designated rather prosaically as Site C – a location downstream of the W.A.C. Bennett and Peace Canyon Dams, about 5 km from Fort St John. Whereas previously hydro-electric development required a water licence to be issued by the Comptroller of Water Rights of the Ministry of the Environment, the Peace Site C proposal also came up against the new approval procedures administered by the recently established BC Utilities Commission. In the face of a slackening of demand growth, BC Hydro was denied permission to build Site C by the British Columbia Utilities Commission, and this precipitated far-reaching change for the utility.

Planning for Site C

Load forecasting at BC Hydro was conducted on a regular basis, but the forecasts became public only when approval was being sought for a new project. Forecasts would be based on market trends, economic data and indications from potential large consumers. The demand forecast was clearly part of an implicit planning process, however, because in the late 1970s it was forecasting over only eleven years whereas (as it noted) the lead time for planning, designing, licensing and constructing major new projects was ten to fifteen years.[7] Because projects would thus have to be identified and planned beyond the forecasting period, there was a danger of reverse adaptation.

The planning process was to be changed considerably, however, by an institutional innovation introduced in 1980. The Utilities Commission Act establishing the BC Utilities Commission was proclaimed on 11

September 1980. It required all rate changes to be approved by the commission and required all new power developments – including transmission lines of 500 kV or higher voltage – to be granted Energy Project Certificates before proceeding. The Utilities Commission Act provided for public participation in matters of energy management and brought BC Hydro's operations under regulatory control. BC Hydro made application for an Energy Project Certificate for the $1.3b 900 MW Peace River Site C project immediately after the act was proclaimed in September 1980, with a view to completing the project in the autumn of 1987.[8] The project would provide an average annual energy output of 4770 GWh.

In 1980 BC Hydro was also planning to build a 2000 MW thermal station using the coal deposits at Hat Creek, scheduled for completion in 1988 to serve expected increases in demand. The need for both these projects was identified in a planning document called *Energy Blueprint 1980*.[9] Demand growth in excess of 6 per cent a year was forecast for the 1980s, and both Site C and the Hat Creek thermal station were seen as being necessary to meet this demand. Indeed, Hat Creek had initially been planned for commissioning in late 1989, and this was advanced to August 1988 in the 1981 plans.[10] That neither project was built and that by the early 1990s neither was needed underscores just how far astray these forecasts were.

The Utilities Commission began public hearings on the application for Site C in November 1981. The inquiry was conducted through both formal and informal hearings. Eighty individuals and groups appeared during the 116 days of formal presentations, and funding was provided for the expenses of some witnesses. The major questions before the commission centred on the benefit-cost of the project, at what time the energy would be needed and whether Site C was the appropriate means of meeting the demand. While the inquiry was also concerned with social and environmental issues, it really hinged on the matter of the demand forecast. Indeed, while there was opposition to the scheme on environmental grounds from groups such as the Society Promoting Environmental Conservation, the environmental issues figured less prominently than the economic consequences of any demand forecast errors.[11]

Annual demand growth had been as high as 14 per cent in the 1960s when hydroelectric development formed (together with forestry) the cornerstone of economic development in the province.[12] The initial 7 per cent growth forecast justifying the Site C project thus appeared reasonable, but it begged a whole range of questions. The forecast was reduced to 6.1 per cent in 1980 and then to 5.7 per cent in September 1981.[13] The commission observed that the Hydro's forecasts during the

1970s had run consistently above actual load growth, and those prepared in 1981 were well above those prepared by the Ministry of Energy, Mines and Petroleum Resources. The commission was therefore sceptical, and asked BC Hydro in March 1982 for an updated demand forecast with an explanation of any deviations from the forecast it had submitted in September 1981. The reason for this request was that a severe recession had brought about a sharp decline in electricity consumption, which had already resulted in the deferral of the Hat Creek thermal project.[14]

BC Hydro's forecast, it should be noted, was driven almost entirely by the industrial component.[15] The utility reported inquiries from present and potential industrial consumers in the two years before 1981 requiring a total of 8800 MW – in excess of the then system capacity of 7491 MW, to which was about to be added the capacity of the 1843 MW Revelstoke project. The Chairman, R.W. Bonner, stated: 'Hydro recognises that only a portion of the potential requirements for electricity represented by such inquiries is likely to materialise and has allowed 920 megawatts as a conservative estimate.'[16] Conveniently, this estimate was enough to justify the 900 MW Site C project – seen as but a part of a construction program costing $22.6b to meet rapidly increasing demand over the next decade. There are parallels here with the Tasmanian case, with the production of a forecast that dovetailed nicely with the available means of the technically preferred hydro scheme.

In a significant step, BC Hydro was required by the Utilities Commission to consider the new least-cost planning techniques. BC Hydro developed a resource planning model (RPM) that took into explicit account the costs of uncertainty by examining a range of five forecasts and a number of resource options including cogeneration, conservation, combustion turbines and energy purchases. Most significantly, the model included an explicit economic value for load *not* served so that it did not accept the assumption (usually made by utilities without any explicit justification) that all demands on the system must be met. It accepted the possibility that under some scenarios it might be worth purchasing conservation; that is, paying customers not to consume electricity.[17] It had been assisted with the development of this model by external consultants.[18]

These new approaches to planning were to undermine considerably the old deterministic planning approach of BC Hydro. The general thrust of considering uncertainty costs was reinforced by an 8.5 per cent decline in sales for the 1982–83 year. BC Hydro's System Planning Division later refined its probabilistic model from April 1984 onwards and first used it as the basis for developing the system plan in December 1984, initially in parallel with traditional deterministic planning methodology.[19] In December 1985 the RPM was adopted as the basis for selecting the ten-year resource plan, and in late 1986 it was used to develop a twenty-year Resource Plan spanning the period 1987–2007. The requirements of the Utilities Commission in hearing the Site C case were thus important in stimulating a change in planning approach.

As a result of the uncertainties over demand, the Utilities Commission found, in its decision handed down on 29 September 1983, that the project was not needed immediately to meet future demand and that BC Hydro had not demonstrated that Site C would be the most economic project to expand supply, if and when expansion was required.[20] Should demand growth be slower than that forecast by the utility, the commission found that other means of meeting the load might be cheaper. Possibilities included changing the role of the existing Burrard thermal station from peaking to **base-loading**, importing electricity from Alberta or buying surplus electricity from the aluminium smelting company Alcan, which had its own generation capacity.

On the basis of the Utilities Commission finding, the government therefore declined the application for an Energy Project Certificate in November 1983.[21] This outcome had been facilitated by the experience of the staff engaged by the Utilities Commission to assist with the Site C hearing. The least-cost utility planning approach had been adopted wholeheartedly by the Northwest Planning Council, involving four states just across the US border, and key players in the Site C hearing were aware of this approach and other probabilistic approaches to planning for uncertainty. The contagion of ideas did not respect political boundaries, and the spectre of the cost of planning failures in neighbouring Washington state was raised in British Columbia.[22]

After Site C

The British Columbia Government was under no obligation to accept the decision of the Utilities Commission. It could have rejected the BCUC decision and authorised construction of Site C regardless. Why it did accept the decision had much to do with the overall macroeconomic thrust of the government at the time, which, like many 'New Right' Western governments in the early 1980s, was intent on winding back the role of the state. In British Columbia this policy was known as 'Restraint', and it made it much more likely that the Site C project would have been rejected than if the government had been of an expansionary complexion.[23] Thanks to the recession, there was surplus generating capacity available, and the conservative Social Credit Government was favourably disposed towards deferring investment in Site C.

But Site C was deferred, rather than cancelled, and still offered an attractive opportunity to stimulate development in the north of the province should a market for its output be found. The initial response of the utility was a reverse-adapted one, and it was supported in this by the government. In the absence of demand growth, they searched for export markets to justify construction: the means were available; they just needed to find the ends to justify them. Previously, export sales had been restricted to non-firm energy on a short-term basis when water yields provided a surplus that might otherwise have gone to waste over spill-ways. In November 1983 the government adopted a new policy permitting export sales of firm electricity for periods in excess of six months.

Markets were found in California. In January 1984 an agreement was concluded with the Los Angeles Department of Water and Power and three adjacent cities for the supply of up to $200m worth of surplus firm electricity over a three-year period.[24] However, this would have required the conclusion of an agreement with the intervening Bonneville Power Administration to 'wheel' the electricity through its transmission network for consumption in California. There was considerable doubt (given transmission losses and other costs) whether the electricity could be delivered to California at an attractive rate. That question was rendered moot by the decision of BPA in September 1984 to limit access by extra-regional utilities to its portion of the Pacific Northwest–Southwest transmission intertie. This severely limited Hydro's ability to export both its existing surplus and any future output from the Site C project.

The recession and the industrial strife stemming from the Restraint program had serious consequences for BC Hydro at a time when the Revelstoke project was about to be commissioned, the major factor in a $2.2b (25 per cent) increase in the utility's assets in the 1985 fiscal year. Additionally, it lost about $25m in revenue in 1983–84 due to a ten-week dispute in the pulp and paper industry, and was itself hit by an eleven-week strike. The recession meant more than just lower than expected sales, although that was serious enough, with sales down 1.1 per cent in 1983–84 after an 8.5 per cent decline the previous year. The cost of the forced cancellation of future projects as a result of overestimation of demand also contributed to costs. Usual accounting practice was to charge development costs (and interest accruing to them) to individual projects, capitalising them and beginning recovery only after commissioning. Once the projects were cancelled these development costs had to be paid, and they amounted to $243m between 1982–83 and 1984–85. The main items were associated with Hat Creek, the 2800 MW Iskut-Stikine river basin project in the north-west, the Meager Creek geothermal explorations and evaluation of a possible 4400 MW project on the Liard River near the BC–Yukon border.[25]

Hydro also attempted to sell its surplus electricity by offering discounts to industry, beginning in 1983 with a one-year discount of 30 per cent for purchases above normal consumption. It sold about 190 million kWh for an additional $4m revenue.[26] This program was continued, with $8m in revenues generated in 1984–85, until it was replaced by concessions under the *Industrial Electricity Rate Discount Act 1985*.[27] In February 1985 a discount scheme for off-loading oil-fired turbogenerators was added, and from July 1985 the Critical Industries Act provided for discounts to bulk industrial consumers (the 'transmission' customers).

What finally put an end to the reverse-adapted situation of BC Hydro was the combined effect of the BPA decision and one other factor: the regulation of its rates by the Utilities Commission. BC Hydro was faced with rising interest charges and falling demand – and, therefore, falling sales. Rather than simply increase charges to cover costs, BC Hydro now had to apply to the Utilities Commission for rate increases. As we have seen, in 1983 it had suffered a decline in electricity sales for the first time in its history, with a smaller decrease in the following year. Despite being granted rate increases of 11.5 per cent in 1982 and 6 per cent in 1983, its capital plant consisted of predominantly high fixed-cost hydro plant and, with the Revelstoke project being commissioned and therefore coming on to its books, BC Hydro was being squeezed financially. It was also squeezed organisationally since it had been dominated by construction-oriented staff, initially from the Public Power Commission, throughout its history,[28] and with Site C deferred indefinitely it had no new projects on the horizon to occupy design staff.

These factors contributed to losses on the domestic electricity side of BC Hydro's operations, the size of which were masked in overall results only by export revenue and profits from the gas and rail undertakings.[29] Operating losses on the domestic electricity side of the operation were as shown in table 4.1.

The BPA decision in September 1984 to limit access to its transmission system denied BC Hydro the opportunity of generating significant additional revenue through export sales of its surplus capacity, and it was forced to seek rate increases to increase revenue. It had instigated an interim increase of 6.5 per cent in April 1984, and on 9 November 1984 it lodged an application with the Utilities Commission seeking approval of that increase, plus a further increase of 6.5 per cent from 1 April 1985. However, the Utilities Commission questioned the cost structure of the utility, particularly staffing levels in sections of BC Hydro concerned with design and construction when no construction on Site C was now planned and other projects had been cancelled.

Hydro responded by reducing its workforce by almost a thousand in 1984–85. Of those whose employment was terminated 914 were from the permanent workforce – 14 per cent of all such employees. This came on top of reductions of 788 employees over the two previous years, and it was

Table 4.1   BC Hydro operating losses

Year ending	Operating loss ($m)
1982	4
1983	3
1984	38
1985	170
1986	201
1987	112
1988	36
Total	564

Source: BC Hydro Annual Reports.

It should be noted that the domestic electricity operation has since been returned to profitability, as shown below:

Year ending	Operating surplus ($m)
1989	10
1990	55
1991	166
1992	313

to be followed by a further reduction of 550 in 1985–86.[30] Almost half these cuts came from the Engineering Division, which was reduced from 1300 staff members in 1980 to 350 in 1987.[31]

Even with these savage cuts BC Hydro was not fully successful in its rate application. First it sought to amend the application to a 3.75 per cent interim increase for 1985 in an application lodged on 13 May 1985. The Utilities Commission gave interim approval to this and the earlier 6.5 per cent increase, but it was later (on 9 May 1986) to grant a final increase of only 1.875 per cent for 1985 and (retrospectively) a further 1.875 per cent from 1 April 1986.

Demand-side management and LCUP

BC Hydro was required by the Utilities Commission in this 1986 decision to justify its planning approach because the commission was concerned that Hydro was not making adequate provision for future demand by placing considerable reliance on non-traditional sources. This was somewhat ironic since Hydro had adopted LCUP techniques at the commission's behest. The Resource Plan relied on demand-side management and purchases to such a degree that the projected load exceeded firm hydro capacity by 1991 and non-traditional sources accounted for 9.3 per cent of the total forecast domestic load by year 19 (2005).[32] This enthusiasm for demand-side measures amounted to a remarkable turnaround for a utility that had once been seen as essentially a dam-building company. Here was BC Hydro having to justify to a regulatory commission its preference not to construct additional power stations, whereas only five years previously it had been determined to press ahead with Site C, Hat Creek and other hydro schemes to follow. To help it persuade the commission that its allowance for non-traditional energy was prudent, BC Hydro engaged Stone and Webster Canada Ltd as consultants to audit its planning process and report to manage-ment on the adequacy of the procedures followed. Stone and Webster concluded:

> We believe that this probabilistic approach is state-of-the art and a tremendous improvement over the old approach of developing a least-cost plan for only the probable load forecast without considering the uncertainties in the planning assumptions.[33]

The Utilities Commission also required BC Hydro to report to it on purchased conservation, which the commission had noted on 9 May 1986 (in its decision on a rate application) was costed at about half the cost of new hydro capacity. The Utilities Commission had directed BC Hydro to begin the demand-side management program immediately and report on progress by 31 March 1987. BC Hydro responded with a report that identified demand-side management load reductions totalling 1420 GWh a year after twenty years, with a reduction of about $500m present value in revenue requirements (5 per cent discount rate). The projects put into place included an Energy Efficient Motor Program (748 GWh p.a. at 0.75 c/kWh), an Energy Saver Lamp Program (202 GWh p.a. at 0.28 c/kWh) and a Hydro Home Program with new building standards (279 GWh p.a. at 3.5 c/kWh). These measures were not only cheaper than new energy generation projects, they also allowed the whole development program to be delayed by a year.[34]

Strategic planning in BC Hydro evolved rapidly after the mid 1980s. In April 1989 a Twenty-year Resource Plan for the Period 1989–2008 was produced, and a special effort was made in the presentation of the report to ensure that the general public would understand the issues involved. This plan treated conservation as a resource rather than something that could be achieved on the demand side of the demand-supply equation, and it included a number of contingency options that could be used to meet any risk from a demand-supply gap emerging. These included site banking, projects to improve output from existing plant (the 'Resource Smart' program), purchases and coordination, independent power producers (IPP) and cogeneration, accelerated construction schedules and a review of rate structures that would focus on both efficiency and economic development objectives.

The 1989 Twenty-year Plan recommended a resource plan that relied on some generation from existing thermal plant (Burrard) to meet expected load growth. No new capacity would be commissioned before the turn of the century. Growth until then – expected to be about 10 000 GWh or almost 25 per cent of existing load – was to be met by non-conventional sources. These included conservation initiatives, which were given the program name 'Power Smart', and 'Resource Smart' programs, which consisted of using improvements to the existing system and better management to make the most of the output from the system.

Power Smart (conservation) programs were now seen as providing 2400 GWh of this 'capacity' at an estimated cost of 1.8 c/kWh for residential programs (500 GWh), 1.9c for commercial (800 GWh) and 1.6c for industrial (1100 GWh). These amounts were in addition to the 'natural' conservation brought about by the voluntary actions of customers, the results of which had already been taken into account in preparing load forecasts. Costs estimates were based on total unit cost for both consumers and BC Hydro over a twenty-year period at a 6 per cent discount rate. The report noted that it was now possible to save twice as much electricity as could have been saved five years previously and at half the cost. BC Hydro stated an intention to invest in cost-effective programs as they became available since the technical potential could be as high as 8000 GWh/year.[35]

In 1990 an Electricity Plan was introduced to replace the Twenty-year Resource Plan as part of the planning process, which was still undergoing considerable evolution. The process at that stage involved preparation of demand forecasts and the definition of the range of uncertainty associated with this forecast. Then the planning process involved the consideration of a variety of demand-side and supply-side options with a consistent treatment of their contributions and costs. The meaning of 'costs' was expanded to include environmental and social costs. This process involved public consultation to reconcile the values of a variety of stakeholders in order to overcome the difficulty of quantifying many of these costs. A plan was then developed in terms of a Development Strategy and a Risk Management Strategy.

One significant change from the 1989 plan in the techniques used in developing the 1990 plan was the adoption (in consultation with the provincial government) of an 8 per cent discount rate (previously 6 per cent) in order to provide a more equitable assessment of proposals for generation or load displacement from the private sector. This was an important step because public utilities have often employed a discount rate as low as 5 per cent – a figure that largely reflects the long-term bond rate for public finance, and which favours hydro plant over thermal in electricity project assessments. It has been argued by economists such as Swann that a figure of 8 per cent is more appropriate since this is about the opportunity cost of capital in the private sector, and to use a lower rate would bias analyses in favour of public projects and skew societal investments.[36]

Ordinarily, that skewing is a matter of degree; it might mean more energy projects than private industrial investment (where the former are in the public sector), but in this case it can be seen that failure to apply the higher rate would alter the kind of electricity project pursued since the demand-side management techniques are in the private sector while the supply-side options are in the public sector. Choosing the lower discount rate would thus bias the analysis in favour of supply-side approaches to electricity planning at the expense of demand-side management. Further, if two different rates were used, there would be an interface problem as the benefit-cost of demand-side management would appear different to consumers than to the utility, and the utility would be more likely to err in its forecasts of future demand.

Using the approach outlined above, the 1990 plan ranked the resource options in the following order (from least cost to highest cost):

1 Power Smart
2 coordination and purchases
3 Resource Smart
4 private sector generation (independent power producers)
5 new hydro plant already identified
6 hydro projects in undeveloped basins and thermal generation projects.

This rank order indicates the extent to which the old BC Hydro, well adapted to designing and building dams, was maladapted to the economic circumstances of electricity planning in the 1980s. BC Hydro by now had embarked on a program to develop these non-conventional resources and began active marketing of non-use using a coordinated media campaign under the Power Smart brand name. The utility achieved 84 per cent product recognition for its energy conservation brand name by using advertising, the distribution of information material about the program and financial incentives to save energy. The financial incentives were aimed at reducing the payback period for consumers on their investment in conservation to less than two years. The campaign was so successful that the standard fluorescent tube in British Columbia became 34 W rather than 40 W, and appliance manufacturers began shipping only the more efficient refrigerators and other appliances to British Columbia, so poor were the sales of those that did not offer substantial savings on electricity consumption.

BC Hydro encountered some difficulty in persuading people that they were serious in their efforts to achieve conservation as the utility still had surplus generating capacity at the time the program began and the public perception of BC Hydro was one of an expansionist utility. The utility tackled this problem by making a concerted effort at public relations and by extensive advertising of its newly introduced Twenty-year Resource Plan, in addition to the campaign to establish the Power Smart brand name.

The direction of the utility has thus been turned around from that of the early 1980s when the organisation had built up considerable momentum as a 'hydro construction company'. From the 1988 resource plan onwards conservation has been added on the supply side as a resource to be developed rather than subtracting it from the load forecast. As has been noted, voluntary conservation – that which would occur without intervention on the part of the utility – was factored in this way, but purchased conservation was treated differently. Purchased conservation was fully integrated into the resource plan and was expected to provide at least 25 per cent of load growth in the 1990s, and perhaps as much as 50 per cent. Whereas once BC Hydro planning focused on new, large additions to capacity, the emphasis moved to conservation and alternative supply options, with the large supply projects kept very much 'in the back pocket'. Previously, the emphasis was on new projects such as the Site C dam, and the supply- and demand-side alternatives were (in the words of one Hydro planner) simply 'nice things to do'.

This change in corporate direction was helped by the opportunities for public participation provided for by the regulatory process administered by the BC Utilities Commission, together with those opportunities for participation added by the utility. BC Hydro now involves the public fully in the formulation of the annual electricity plan and in decisions on bids from industry for the purchase of blocks of power. The utility invited bids from independent power producers and received bids for 150 MW of proposals and up to 5 MW of small hydro capacity.

The role of institutions in utility reform

These changes in planning approach were accompanied by a number of institutional initiatives that should help to ensure that the reforms will persist and that BC Hydro will be better attuned to public views on resource options and environmental issues than it was previously. A series of about ninety public meetings was held when the annual electricity plan was released. In addition, an annual energy forum was held in conjunction with the Ministry of Energy, Mines and Petroleum and the

Ministry of Environment, and keynote speakers (such as US energy consultants Amory Lovins and Hazel Henderson) were invited. This practice began in 1988 with the first forum on the theme of 'IPP and Conservation'. In 1989 the theme of the forum was 'Electricity and the Environment'.

Part of this realignment to public preferences involved changes to the way the public relations function of the utility was performed. This function had been wound down considerably during the downturn that struck the utility in the early to mid 1980s. The fate of the utility is reflected dramatically in its documents. Organisational charts ceased to be prepared, and the utility's annual reports changed from glossy, full-colour documents (1983–84) to a single colour, unadorned booklet that reported the $170m loss on domestic electricity operations in 1984–85. The medium certainly was the message as the drab reports continued for a further two years before the gloss returned in the 1988 report. Whereas public affairs staff formerly had been assigned to specific development projects, now there were regional public affairs officers who were not tied to projects – indeed, there were few projects remaining to be tied to! These staff now worked on finding out the public's perceptions of BC Hydro, identifying issues of concern to the community, advising BC Hydro on the appropriate processes to follow, methods of community consultation, who the key community influentials were and so on for when projects might arise in future.

Much of the work on estimates and design was now handled by a project management group in the reformed utility, and there was less emphasis on 'selling' the project. There was more of an emphasis on fitting the project (mostly transmission route selections) in with programs such as Power Smart. There were now deliberate efforts to involve the public in study and project teams to provide meaningful participation. This was helped by having utility staff no longer talking about preferred projects and by constantly referring back to the conservation program. They maintained regular contact with interest groups, invited them to attend the two-day energy forum and gave them access to consultants' reports. The utility also established resource committees with community representation in each of the two major river basins within the province.

The question that these changes poses is this: What factors resulted in a reverse-adapted, dam-building company becoming a risk-adapted, conservation-oriented utility that prefers environmentally benign alternatives to new generation projects? We now turn to this question.

It should be apparent from the discussion so far that the role of the BC Utilities Commission in bringing about the reform of BC Hydro was quite important. What needs to be stressed, however, is that this was but one factor among several in bringing about change. There is a need for

caution in assigning all the credit for the successful reform to the Utilities
Commission or to any other single factor.

It needs to be stressed that both the recession of the early 1980s and
the response of the 'New Right' Social Credit Government to that
downturn – the 'Restraint' program – provided an environment conducive to reform. Restraint meant that the government was receptive to
policy measures that resulted in a reduction to the public sector rather
than continued expansion. Had a less conservative government faced
with different economic circumstances received the recommendations of
the Utilities Commission on Site C, it might well have ignored them. The
BCUC recommendation accorded with, rather than went against, the
general thrust of government policy. The recession itself and the
subsequent slackening in electricity demand growth effectively softened
up BC Hydro as an organisation, making it more responsive to the
reforms that were to follow. The Utilities Commission therefore could
not only require that LCUP methods be considered but subsequently it
could also draw attention to the high levels of design and construction
staffing in an organisation geared to expansion, and legitimately raise
questions of whether these excess staff should be allowed as an expense
in the utility's rate base.

The least-cost utility planning approach had been adopted wholeheartedly by the nearby Northwest Planning Council across the US
border, and BCUC staff involved in the Site C hearing were aware of this
approach to electricity planning under the uncertain conditions that
prevailed in the early 1980s. Also helpful in continuing the push for
reform were the appointment of a former BC Hydro vice-president to the
commission and the fact that the commission was provided with enough
resources (at Hydro's expense) to buy additional expertise. Bill Bell, as a
former BC Hydro engineer, was the most knowledgeable of the commissioners and the strongest advocate of demand-side management.
BCUC was therefore able to overcome one of the factors that often leads
to weak regulation or capture of the regulatory agency: the inequality of
expertise between regulator and regulated.[37]

Aside from the initial crucial decision to deny the utility an energy
project licence for Site C, the most significant factor from then on was
the point that the utility learned from its error. Construction of the Site
C project would have resulted in significant overcapacity since capacity
from the last project then under construction (Revelstoke) was still
available in the early 1990s when the utility was marketing conservation.
Site C will not be needed in the twentieth century.

BC Hydro found itself overstaffed with dam builders and with a
requirement (imposed by the Utilities Commission) to cut costs in the
face of rate decisions. The somewhat savage staff cuts that followed made

the task of reorienting the organisation much easier, but it was by no means a foregone conclusion that the utility would react to these challenges in a positive manner. After all, the initial government and utility response was to try to promote electricity consumption by offering discounts to industry and to export surplus electricity. The external limits placed on the export option by BPA again helped to determine the direction BC Hydro would take by limiting freedom of action, but the reforms in planning approaches would be unlikely to have been so fundamental without a series of changes to the utility that began as far back as June 1981.

BC Hydro was formerly governed by four directors, two of whom were government ministers (the Minister of Energy, Mines and Petroleum Resources and the Minister of Universities, Science and Communications). The utility was clearly an instrument of government policy. Changes in 1981 saw it restructured as a corporation with eleven new members – many with a background in business – appointed to the board.[38] BC Hydro was therefore governed by a board better placed to respond positively to the problems of uncertain load growth that left the utility with little financial resilience.

Leadership was also important in the reform process. The restructuring of the board in 1981 made the change from an engineering to an economic orientation possible, but the structure of the corporation itself had to be changed if the utility was to incorporate fully the new economic approaches to planning. This reform process was carried out by two successive chairmen and chief executive officers, each of whom was responsible for a quite distinct (but probably equally necessary) phase, each of which alone was insufficient to bring about the necessary changes. The major part of the 'purge' that resulted from the denial of the Site C licence and the 1984–86 rate increase case occurred under a CEO, Chester Johnson, who was incumbent for only a short time; he was appointed in June 1984 and served until the end of May 1987. Significantly, Johnson was appointed from outside the organisation. Therefore he was unencumbered by any loyalties or obligations to any part of the utility and was free to take the necessary hard decisions – without favour, if not necessarily without fear.

The Chairman and CEO who led the positive side of the reform process, Larry Bell, was appointed in April 1987 and took up his duties on 1 June. Bell was well connected politically, having once been Deputy Minister of the Treasury.[39] Bell was able to rebuild the organisation without having been associated with the destructive phase of the reform process. He essentially built a new utility from the ashes of the old one and did so in such a way as to incorporate demand-side management and risk sensitivity into its goals.

These changes were reflected both in the structure of the organisation and in its culture or ethos, both of which were addressed by Bell. The structure of the organisation had already undergone considerable evolution away from an engineering dominance after the utility was reorganised as a corporation. In the late 1970s there were two vice-presidents in the Engineering Division, one of whom was also the Chief Engineer. There was also an engineering Vice-President in charge of the Electrical Operations division (as well as vice-presidents responsible for the Gas and Transportation undertakings). Other vice-presidents were responsible for the Administration and Finance and Corporate Affairs divisions, plus one who (as General Counsel) reported to the Chairman.[40] If we ignore the gas and transportation divisions, we can see how the structure of the electric utility was changed from the six divisions at the end of the 1970s; the three most important of which were engineering-oriented.

The evolution occurred, understandably, by initially adding new vice-presidents and divisions. Amalgamations came later as divisions of declining importance were down-sized. By 1985 there were no fewer than ten officers with the title of vice-president (excluding the one for Gas Operations). Two of these were executive vice-presidents, of Finance and Administration and Business Operations – a new post to which the Vice-President of Electrical Operations reported, along with a new Vice-President for Business Development. The second position of executive vice-president had initially been an engineering one (in operations). The other two new vice-presidential posts were in the Corporate Planning and Public Affairs divisions, reflecting (respectively) the need to chart a new corporate future in less certain times and to function in the new regulatory environment brought about by the establishment of the Utilities Commission.

In 1986 the number of vice-presidents was reduced to seven, with two senior vice-presidents (System Development and Research and Finance) and five others (Administration, Electrical Operations, Engineering, Legal and Personnel). Significantly, both senior vice-presidential positions were non-engineering posts, and the Chief Engineer, who had been a senior vice-president in 1985, now ranked alongside four other ordinary vice-presidents, only one of which was an engineering position.[41] Any distinction among vice-presidents was removed in 1987 even though the two former senior vice-presidents continued in office. In order to complete the move from deterministic to economic planning the System Development Division became Marketing and System Planning from 1987, and Customer Service the following year, with System Development replacing Engineering as a division. By April 1988 only two divisions of six (System Development and Production) were engineering-oriented.

In the other significant changes a position of Vice-President Energy Innovation was established in 1990. The division under this position was called Power Smart from 1991, reflecting the incorporation of demand-side management in the organisational structure. The System Development Division became the Resource Management Division in 1991.

These changes reflect an expansion in both executive positions and organisational divisions responsible for the new functions being undertaken by the utility. The number of engineering positions initially was unchanged. Then, taking advantage of both the prevailing circumstances and the new loci of power within the organisation, the influence and scope of engineering activities (and the number of executive positions) was gradually wound back.

These changes began under the chairmanship of Chester Johnson but were seen through by Larry Bell, who was also responsible for embuing the reformed organisation with a new culture. We have seen earlier how there was ambivalence during the Johnson years as to whether the utility would respond to the challenges confronting it by seeking markets so as to continue expansion or by developing risk-sensitive planning and demand-side management. The Bell years saw the latter path quite definitely taken. This commitment was reflected both in structures (as we have seen) and in the new corporate ethos Bell built.

An important part of Bell's approach was to create a more positive outlook after the traumas of the mid 1980s. This included not just developing a corporate plan oriented to the new mission of energy service, conservation and public involvement but also creating a climate of expanding employment opportunity after the period of retrenchments. A further 10 per cent of staff were induced to take voluntary retirement in 1988, which allowed the utility to start hiring again. The size of the permanent staff shrank by a further 341 that year, but then rose by nearly 400 the following year. (The size of the temporary workforce had also began to grow significantly.) There was also considerable redeployment of design and construction staff into positions that were in demand, such as customer service – a theme that featured prominently in the 1988 annual report.

The new ethos was reinforced by an emphasis on human resources planning and development. Training programs that had suffered cuts were reinstated, with the aim of creating a more decentralised organisation with 'greater employee autonomy and empowerment'.[42] The 1990 annual report indicated that it had been prepared by 'an empowered work team from the Corporate Accounting Department'. The utility also made a commitment to providing job security to its employees by establishing base staff levels, using redeployments and relying on temporary contracts to cope with peak demands.[43] BC Hydro sought to develop by 1990 a workforce that provided greater opportunities for women, the disabled and minorities and which was 'dedicated to the protection of the natural environment'.[44]

Bell was so successful at redirecting BC Hydro that the utility could in some ways be said to have gone further than required by the Utilities Commission. Indeed, the commission's approach to price regulation impinged on the utility's approach to conservation since minimisation of rates effectively precludes use of price as an instrument for demand management. There was a view in BC Hydro that the commission was understaffed and that this had prevented it from being more proactive when it had some opportunities to do so. It did not appear to be captive of BC Hydro; rather BC Hydro was being restrained from some innovative approaches to strategic planning (such as economic pricing) by regulation that focused on the allowed recovery of past costs.

Conclusion

This case shows that considerable reform is possible but that it depends on several causes for its success. This was neither a simple case of top-down or bottom-up reform, nor of simply reform through regulation. The board and the politicians played their parts, but they were not the only determining factors. The commission played its part but, again, it was one actor among many and probably not even first among equals. The public also played its role, both through the commission and alone, but its participation was not a direct factor in the changes within the organisation. The provision for public participation in the electricity planning process that developed will provide a supportive constituency for factions within the organisation favouring what is now the *status quo*, but provision for participation came about largely as a result of the changes and did not of itself assist the process of organisational reform.

The 1981 changes that established BC Hydro on a corporate footing were important, although at the time they were not intended to bring the development activities of the utility to an end, because (as we have seen) the utility was anticipating unprecedented expansion. The corporatisation did, however, facilitate the move away from distribution to a regulatory regime, of which the establishment of the Utilities Commission with power to regulate both development and rates was such a key component. These changes did not predestine the way the utility responded to the slackening in demand and the postponement of the Site C project, but they helped to make it possible. Even then, however, the distributive forces were strong as both the utility and the government sought markets for the power that would have allowed 'business as usual' – the construction of Site C and subsequent development projects. The effective denial of access by the Bonneville Power Administration to Californian markets was the final nail in the coffin for a distributive approach because with the contracts went not only Site C but also the subsequent projects. The capitalised development costs were brought on to Hydro's books at a time when its finances were already in trouble.

With the prospect of continuing a distributive, expansionary approach gone there was little option but to yield to the regulatory pressures and restructure the utility into something like an energy service provider, diminishing its construction-related engineering divisions and building up divisions attuned to the new realities. And in the absence of the professional norms of engineering as an integrating force, a new organisational culture, conducive to the pursuit of the goals of efficiency and environmental conservation alongside economic development of the province had to be created.

The case illustrates the relationship between structure and process suggested by Lowi's arenas of power approach to policy and administration. Yet the picture that emerges here is of a more dynamic *inter*-relationship, with policies requiring changes in structure (as Lowi suggests), but with prior changes in structure facilitating this policy change, which in turn give rise to further structural change. Electricity planning certainly moved from an expansionary phase we can recognise as distributive to something closer to a regulatory phase. However, we must see the reform of bureaucratic agencies as contributing to this process of change rather than just reflecting it. We shall see this pattern repeated in our next case, Ontario Hydro – a utility long thought to be immune to reform.

CHAPTER 5

Ontario:
The decline and fall of the electric empire

Ontario Hydro was included in the present study because it was widely
seen by its critics as the epitome of the powerful electric utility beyond
the control of the government of its province. It is significant, therefore,
that it too has undergone remarkable change, and it provides us not with
simply a case study of a reverse-adapted utility, but also another case of
successful utility reform.

Ontario Hydro is the largest electric utility in Canada and one of the
largest in North America. Since the 1960s its plans for future expansion
have placed great reliance on nuclear generation, which has resulted in
considerable controversy over its planning activities. At the beginning of
the 1980s it appeared that a further eight nuclear stations after the one
then under construction at Darlington were going to be needed by the
end of the twentieth century. The capital cost of this expansion program
would have been about $100b.[1] Yet by 1992 the utility was no longer
seeking approval for any new nuclear plant after Darlington and was
instead intending to invest $6b in demand management over the next
decade. Late in 1992, Maurice Strong (who had been Secretary-General
of the United Nations Earth Summit in Rio de Janeiro in June that year)
was appointed chairman of Ontario Hydro and, by early 1993, the utility
once described by its critics as the 'Electric Empire'[2] was considering ways
of implementing the concept of sustainable development.[3]

Ontario Hydro operates a system of about 30 000 MW capacity, and
sells about 135 000 GWh/year, about half of which comes from nuclear
capacity, with hydraulic and thermal plant contributing about a quarter
each. The utility can trace its history to the Hydro Electric Power
Commission of Ontario, formed as a result of provincial government
commissions of inquiry in 1903 and 1906. At that time Ontario
depended on coal from the United States for its energy, and the idea of
a public agency to exploit the potential of Niagara Falls and other

104

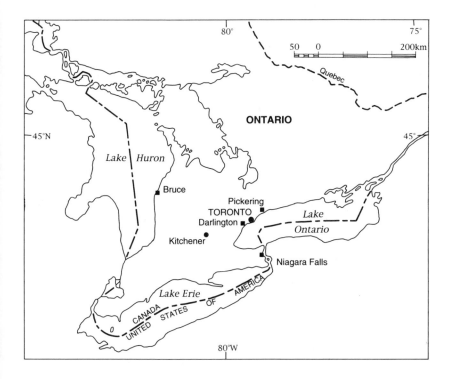

sources of hydroelectricity was first developed. The first commission of inquiry reported to an unsympathetic Liberal Government, but in 1904 the Conservatives won office, and after the 1906 inquiry a Conservative minister, Adam Beck, introduced legislation to establish the commission. Beck was to become the body's chairman for its first eighteen years.[4]

The commission was charged, under the Power Commission Act, with generation (initially from Niagara Falls), transmission and supply at cost to municipal utilities, which still exist today. It was self-consciously a *public* undertaking, with public service its avowed guiding principle, despite its origins in response to demands from business interests. When it supplied its first power to the city of Berlin (renamed Kitchener during World War I) in 1910 an illuminated sign above the street proclaimed it was 'For the People'.[5] That its first supply was to a provincial city rather than Toronto was also significant because its creation was also something of a response to fears that Toronto would control access to the immense resources at Niagara Falls. As one historian has put it:

> In Ontario there were many manufacturing towns of importance outside Toronto at the beginning of the electrical age. Indeed, the reluctance of those towns to see Toronto monopolise the electrical power of Niagara was an important force leading to the public ownership of electricity in Ontario.[6]

The commission was highly politicised for the first twenty-five years of its existence, with Beck campaigning vigorously against attacks on its public nature, especially those from United States interests.[7] The following passage gives an indication of the nature and vehemence of early criticisms:

> The Ontario Hydro-Electric System is customarily erroneously represented as an experiment in 'public ownership'. It is really an attempt on the part of a small number of politicians to establish an industrial monopoly and to manage this monopoly in such a way as to keep themselves in power.[8]

The Hydro Electric Power Commission saw such attacks as the work of US private utilities that feared an extension of public ownership, and was not averse to issuing pamphlets defending its single objective as being simply to provide low-cost electrical service.[9] The commission had been attacked in one US publication as 'a political Frankenstein ... recklessly expending the public funds in the promulgation of political propaganda ...'.[10] A Wisconsin publication even had the temerity to suggest that Hydro had made a bid for political support by bribing domestic consumers (and vastly increasing their numbers) by means of low rates. This, of course, was precisely Hydro's policy for achieving market penetration!

The Hydro also had to win the competition from other utilities within the province for the natural monopoly that existed over electrical supply and, seeing the Liberals as the tools of the private utilities, campaigned openly against that party. When the Liberals won office in the 1930s, having campaigned in part on the issue of the propriety of some of the contracts signed during the Conservative reign, they cleaned out the membership of the commission and many of its staff, but they did not change its policies. By then it had won both control of the province's market and the support of consumers with its low prices.

It also secured the support of the government, helped by the fact that its champions, the Conservatives, began a long run in office in 1943. The government had considerable formal power over the commission. It appointed the commissioners and had to approve any major construction project and all bond issues.[11] In reality, however, the government had little practical control over Hydro because it lacked any effective independent sources of policy advice. It could not have exerted much effective influence, especially given the strong support from grateful domestic and industrial consumers, had it so desired. It rarely exhibited any such desire, however, because Hydro came to be an important tool of provincial development. Close formal relationships developed between successive governments and the commission, with the Chairman liaising closely with the Premier of the day.[12] The relationship appeared a little too close in the early 1970s when there were allegations that the Chairman, George Gathercole, had used undue influence in the award of a contract for the construction of Hydro's new headquarters to a friend of the Premier.

The commission was eventually restructured into a corporation and named Ontario Hydro in response to an inquiry, Task Force Hydro, which ran from 1971 to 1973. It now reports to parliament through the Minister of Energy, a portfolio created at that time. Since corporatisation it has been the subject of almost constant scrutiny, most notably with the Royal Commission on Nuclear Power Planning (the Porter Commission, 1975–80),[13] as well as by inquiries by three legislative select committees, a Nuclear Cost Inquiry[14] and a Nuclear Safety Review.[15] As we shall see, Ontario Hydro has also been subject to review by a regulatory agency, the Ontario Energy Board. Its activities have become highly politicised, largely as a result of the massive nuclear expansion program embarked on in the 1960s.

Ontario's considerable hydraulic resources were eventually developed fully, except those in more remote locations, and it had to turn to other sources of energy. It turned first to thermal stations using imported fuel but soon enthusiastically embraced indigenous nuclear technology using Ontario uranium. It developed into a utility clearly adapted to nuclear means, building the Pickering, Bruce and then Darlington nuclear stations, and was widely criticised as being an unstoppable juggernaut – an 'electric empire'.[16] At the beginning of the 1980s it appeared that a further eight nuclear stations after Darlington were going to be needed by the end of the twentieth century. Yet by 1992 the utility was no longer seeking approval for any new nuclear plant as it did not see the need for one until at least beyond 2009. Instead, it was anticipating investing $6b in demand management over a decade to produce savings of almost 10 000 MW by 2014. It was also intending to build some further hydro-electric projects and buy electricity from Manitoba and from independent power producers. By 1993 it had cancelled the purchase contract with Manitoba and paid $100m in compensation for the privilege. Just how a utility that had come to be regarded as a nuclear construction company changed direction so dramatically is the subject of this chapter.

We shall look first at how Ontario Hydro became a reverse-adapted utility, looking for ends to suit its nuclear means, and then focus on both the policy changes and the accompanying organisational changes.

Hydro goes nuclear

Ontario Hydro's nuclear program has been almost synonymous with Canada's nuclear prowess. Beginning with a small reactor at Chalk River in 1945 – the first operating reactor outside the United States – the growth of Canada's nuclear industry has been linked inextricably with Ontario Hydro. It provided the platform for the distinctive CANDU (CANada Deuterium Uranium) reactor, beginning with a demonstration plant at Rolphton that began providing electricity in 1962, and leading via a small plant at Douglas Point (commissioned in 1967) to the large-scale developments at Pickering (commissioned in 1972), Bruce (commissioned in 1977) and Darlington (in the 1980s). Hydro Quebec also operates a CANDU plant (Gentilly) but, unlike Ontario, Quebec had massive hydraulic resources at James Bay and so did not have to place great reliance on nuclear energy. New Brunswick also has the Point Lepreau station, but Ontario, with 42 per cent of Canada's uranium reserves,[17] embraced the technology most enthusiastically and became a virtual showcase for it.

In the late 1960s forecasters at Ontario Hydro were predicting growth at an annual rate of 7 per cent, which would have required the installation of 80 000 MW of additional capacity by the year 2000.[18] The province's hydro resources would be inadequate to meet this demand so an institutional commitment to nuclear generation based on the CANDU technology was made. As a result, the internal organisation of Hydro developed to suit this anticipated nuclear expansion.

The evolution of Hydro into a reverse-adapted nuclear agency and its eventual transformation into a more responsive 'energy service company' is intimately connected with the place of engineers in the utility. From its establishment in 1906 the chief executive officer of Ontario Hydro was designated to be the Chief Engineer. From 1947 the position of General Manager existed, but the position was occupied by the Chief Engineer. It was not until 1955 that there was a position of Chief Engineer separate from the General Manager,[19] but (as we shall see) the real power in the organisation lay with the Chief Engineer.

The internal structure of Ontario Hydro became reverse-adapted to nuclear means from the 1960s. The decision to commit to CANDU technology was a high-risk one and related both to a desire for national technological achievement and to a desire to achieve energy self-sufficiency (rather than rely on imported oil or coal). The decision to build the first full-scale CANDU station at Pickering was taken in 1965 while the prototype at Douglas Point was still under construction. The decision to build the second, Bruce, was taken in 1968, with the prototype operating only sporadically and Pickering still under construction.[20] These decisions committed Hydro to a nuclear program based on unproven technology and dictated the kind of organisation it would become. Its willingness to take risks with CANDU, however, was in marked contrast to the conservatism it developed over its planning criteria.

The nuclear decisions were followed in the late 1960s by a shortage of generating capacity resulting from rapid load growth and ice limiting output from hydroelectric stations. The resulting near-failure of the system[21] led to the introduction of highly risk-averse reserve margin criteria at a time when larger unit size and the introduction of CANDU were themselves requiring increases in reserve margins. The planning criteria adopted even included a rule that no allowance would be made for imports from US utilities in an emergency.[22] Together with the legislative requirement under the Power Corporation Act to supply electricity at cost (meaning historic accounting cost, rather than marginal cost), the irreversible commitment to nuclear power and the introduction of conservative planning margins amounting to 30 per cent over peak demand[23] meant that Hydro became reverse-adapted to nuclear construction. This became reflected in the internal organisation of the utility.

This commitment to nuclear power was personified by the appointment as Chairman of Harold A. Smith, who had played a key role in the initial development of CANDU as Chief Engineer in 1957. Smith was strongly patriotic and was responsible for the strong push for CANDU in the face of a weak Hydro Commission. The General Manager at this time lacked a personal staff and was not well placed to counter the advice of the Chief Engineer.[24] Smith set up a structure that prevented the emergence of competing centres of expertise, to avoid what he called the 'five quarterback stuff'.[25] As Roberts and Bluhm observed, 'On technical matters, top management's ability to evaluate engineering recommendations [was] limited by the increasing concentration of engineering functions under the Chief Engineer's authority'.[26] Not only were the sources of alternative engineering advice severely restricted but also the financial (and other) evaluation of engineering recommendations was limited by a lack of strategic planning capacity on the part of the assistant general managers within the general manager's side of the organisation.

Smith merged the Design and Construction divisions under P. G. Campbell in 1965, and he and Campbell began a series of structural changes in 1966 to increase the integration of the functional groups within the Engineering Branch. One of the first was to move from a disciplinary basis for organisation within Design and Construction to groups based on facilities – generating plants, substations and transmission lines.[27] The Generation Projects Division was, understandably, nuclear in orientation. Its deputy was the chief designer of the Pickering plant. Then in 1969 a new advance planning group, the Generation Concept Department, was established within Generation Projects. Generation Concept took a project approach to new plants and, at Smith's insistence, the project teams, in addition to design and construction engineers, also included the operation engineers who would staff the plant when completed.

Design and Construction (later Design and Development) Division of Ontario Hydro became, with a staff of 1600 in 1980, the most powerful arm of the utility. And it was strongly oriented to nuclear design and construction. Despite the retention of the word *hydro* in the name of the utility, the Hydraulic Development Section had a staff of only twelve.[28]

'Nuclear men' were placed in charge in other groups. For example, when thermal operations were placed in a new centralised Operations Group within Engineering in 1970 the group was headed by Lorne McConnell, former head of nuclear operations.[29]

Not only did the forecasts of the 1960s produce the organisational structure of the 1980s, they also led to other substantial commitments to nuclear technology. To fuel the new reactors Ontario Hydro signed long-term contracts between 1974 and 1978 for the supply of uranium at a time when the world price was at a record high of $US40–50/lb. In 1981 the world price was about $US23.50/lb, while Ontario Hydro was paying as much as $US55/lb for uranium from Elliott Lake (Ontario) rather than (by way of example) $US35 for Saskatchewan uranium. The cost of this preference for Ontario yellowcake, with its advantages of political security of supply and jobs for Ontario, was about $40–50m a year.[30] Moreover, the Hydro erred on quantity as well as price. In contracts with Denison Mines Ltd (which were to run until 2012) and with Rio Algom Ltd (to run until 2027) it was committed to purchases in excess of requirements to the tune of 1000 megagrams a year (53 per cent above anticipated consumption of 1900 megagrams a year).[31] Given a fourteen-year lead time for new nuclear capacity, these arrangements might have appeared more prudent to the planners of the 1960s and early 1970s, but they amounted to an inflexible commitment once demand had become less predictable.

The cost of this commitment to nuclear generation was even greater when the hidden subsidies to various forms of energy use (especially for debt guarantee and R&D) are considered. A select committee of the Ontario parliament found that federal and provincial subsidies to the nuclear option amounted to $436m in 1984. The subsidisation of conservation measures at that time amounted to only $85m.[32] This last figure is particularly significant when it is realised that electricity consumption had been encouraged in Ontario by the adoption of pricing policies that deviated from marginal cost principles. (Marginal cost pricing reflects the cost of supplying electricity from the next increment to the generating system.) The implicit subsidy for Ontario amounted to $300–400m a year.[33] Soloman has even argued that, if true economic prices had been charged for electricity, there would have been no need for *any* nuclear generation in 1984.[34]

Things fall apart

The implications of the Ontario Hydro expansion program began to become apparent in the mid 1970s, especially as the projected capital cost of the capacity to meet the forecasts was around $70b (about $100b in 1990s terms). Simultaneously, load growth began to slacken to about

2 per cent a year,[35] raising the spectre of capital-intensive plant coming into operation in the absence of demand and, therefore, revenue to service the loans raised to build it. While work began on the 4×880 MW Darlington nuclear station in 1977, a fossil fuel station was scaled back from eight to one 200 MW unit and plans for another oil-fired station were abandoned.

The government established a Royal Commission on Electric Power Planning (the Porter Commission) in 1975, and when it reported in 1980 it found that only one four-unit nuclear station after Darlington would be needed by the year 2000, whereas eight had previously been thought necessary.[36] The government had already forced Hydro to slow down its expansion program as a result of its concern over the borrowing implications, which had led to a review of Ontario Hydro's credit rating. Net income was negative in both 1975 and 1976, and in 1976 it had to withdraw $35.1m from reserves to meet statutory debt retirement obligations. Rates jumped 25 per cent in 1976 and the fixed charge coverage ratio,[37] 1.37 in 1970, fell to 1.07.[38] In 1977 the government limited Hydro's capital expenditure to $1.5b a year for each of the next three years, using one of the few instruments of control it had over the Hydro: authorisation of borrowing.[39]

Soloman has argued that the way Hydro responded to these capital limits demonstrated just how great was its commitment to the nuclear option. Soloman pointed out that the board had decided in 1977 to build seventeen hydraulic stations, which had cost advantages over nuclear, yet they were cancelled in order to preserve the nuclear construction program.[40]

The cost of nuclear electricity was more expensive to consumers than the predominantly hydraulic electricity they had once enjoyed, and nuclear was becoming more expensive all the time. For example, hydraulic energy in 1981 cost 0.566 c/kWh and nuclear 1.450 c/kWh; by 1985 the former had increased to only 0.818 c/kWh whereas nuclear had doubled to 2.925 c/kWh.[41] As the system became more reliant on nuclear generation, this cost difference fed its way through into consumer prices. After bottoming out in 1970 real electricity prices began to rise, with a particularly sharp rise in the period 1975–77.[42] The increase was exacerbated by the end to cheap energy imports from Quebec.[43] This trend contributed to the slowing in demand growth, as did the recession of 1982–83, and progress on construction of Darlington was kept under annual review by Ontario Hydro as a result.[44]

The board of Ontario Hydro responded to these uncertainties with some faltering attempts at a change of direction, adopting a new cor- porate strategy, which included as a central component 'a shift away from the supply of new generation toward a greater effort to work with cus- tomers to determine how Ontario's electricity resources can best be used to meet their energy needs'.[45] Steps were taken to reduce staff; 1300 left under early retirement scheme, and staff were redeployed 'from engineering and construction activities to service and marketing efforts'.[46] But little was done to alter the structure of the utility, and the old pattern reasserted itself – with a rise in staff numbers – once growth returned. Which it did in 1983.

The return of demand growth provided the ends once again to justify Hydro's nuclear means. While the downturn in demand had resulted in some changes, the reverse-adapted attitude to risk in demand forecasting still prevailed, as evidenced by the following statement by Ontario Hydro President Milan Nastich (to a Liberal Party energy symposium) in January 1984:

> It's been said before, but it is worth saying again: if there are going to be mistakes in forecasting, then we have a responsibility to ensure that those mistakes are on the side of safety. It is still better, when all is said, to have an oversupply than to have an electricity shortage. Period.[47]

In the period immediately after this recession, however, demand growth was above forecast for four years, averaging about 3.5 per cent a year and bringing new uncertainty into the planning picture. Together with concern over rising costs to the consumer, this trend prompted the establishment in July 1985 of a Legislative Assembly Select Committee on Energy to inquire into Hydro affairs. It should be noted that the first Liberal Government in thirty years was in power, and the Liberals in opposition had been highly critical of the Conservatives' energy policies.

The select committee reviewed the Darlington station under construction in order to see whether cancellation of the $10.9b project would allow any relief from price increases. It found that 65 per cent of total costs had been irrevocably committed and that Darlington therefore enjoyed considerable cost advantages over coal-fired stations. It recommended that Units 1 and 2 – with 80 per cent of costs committed – be completed, but recommended that no new significant contracts be let for Units 3 and 4 (less than 50 per cent committed) while the committee studied demand and supply options.[48]

The committee eventually recommended that Darlington be completed, but it also recommended changes to the way Ontario Hydro conducted its planning. In particular, it wanted Ontario Hydro to develop a comprehensive conservation strategy and to develop, as the basis of its planning exercise, a range of plausible scenarios based on end uses. Alternative resource mixes were to be evaluated over a range of scenarios rather than a single 'most probable' forecast.

At Ontario Hydro there had been mounting concern from 1984 that higher than forecast growth (as we have seen, at 3.5 per cent, or about 650 MW a year) meant that there would be a shortfall of generating capacity by the year 2000. With a fourteen-year lead time for nuclear plant (five years planning and approval, eight to nine years construction) a decision would be required by 1986. Ontario Hydro therefore began a Demand/Supply Planning Study to try to plan for future uncertainty. This study resulted in the production of a report in December 1987, which set out a draft strategy for public consultation.[49] While this report included a wide range of demand-side management techniques, provision for energy imports, site banking, load shifting and purchases from independent generators, it did not include the economist's solution to the problem: marginal cost pricing. Instead, it was proposed that rates be based on average costs, with incentives to encourage load shifting, but no consideration of purchased conservation or other more radical approaches.

Most significantly, the project stopped short of proposing a planning approach similar to that being followed in British Columbia, which incorporated a probabilistic rather than deterministic approach to planning. Ontario Hydro was using instead a model it 'bought' from the Electric Power Research Institute, which was able to generate system cost data for a range of over- and under-capacity mixes.[50] The 'answer' this model gave to the planners was that the cheapest thing to do was to start preconstruction activities (site banking) as if the aim was to meet load growth about 1.5 per cent above the most likely load growth scenario. The model was not fully interactive and required the load forecast, technology mix and reserve margin policy preselected to be fed into it. However, it was an obvious improvement over former practice and allowed the sensitivity of planning to higher or lower load growth to be examined.

But even getting Ontario Hydro to do this much was difficult because the nuclear additions to capacity had resulted in balance sheets worse than they might otherwise have been and there was a need to increase sales to service loans. As a result senior management required persuasion that anything at all was necessary on demand-side management. Forecasts were being taken to represent what was thought *would* occur rather than what *should* occur, and the utility was not (in 1987) using the methods of planning for uncertainty to make decisions. Instead, senior management were in something of a non-decisionmaking mood, hoping that the situation would resolve itself.

The political power of Ontario Hydro was still quite considerable, and it is important to bear in mind when comparing it with BC Hydro that it operates in a largely unregulated environment with few meaningful controls in the hands of the government. As Vining has described the situation, Ontario Hydro had been criticised for 'its expansionary policy, its rate structure, its tendency to ignore both the provincial government and the Ontario Energy Board and, in general, its secrecy'.[51] As Vining notes, the utility is regulated by the Ontario Energy Board, but this is little more than a symbolic gesture, as can be indicated by reference to the Hydro's statement of its policy on rate setting.

The Hydro is bound by the Power Corporation Act to charge for power at its cost of provision, including operating and maintenance, depreciation, interest and an amount for debt retirement. The Ontario Energy Board Act requires a public hearing to be held for any rate changes proposed by Ontario Hydro that would affect its municipal utilities, direct industrial customers or (at the direction of the minister) rural retail customers. The process then followed underscores the largely symbolic nature of this process:

> The Ontario Energy Board submits its recommendations to the Minister of Energy. After considering the recommendations of the Ontario Energy Board, the Board of Directors of Ontario Hydro, under the authority of the Power Corporation Act, establishes the electricity rates to be charged to customers.[52]

Dr Roger Higgin of the Ontario Energy Board has advanced the argument that the board had been effective in restraining rate increases since 1975 despite the fact that regulation was not formal in the sense that the board only made recommendations and the Hydro then selected its own rate.[53] He has argued that the 'political regulation' provided by the Ontario Energy Board and other government inquiries and reviews could thus be seen as effective despite the largely informal nature of the regulatory process. According to this view, the process of a public hearing, in which evidence is tendered and the issues are aired, could be seen as being important even if effective control is exercised through a policy department and the political process; in the case of Ontario, through the Ministry of Energy and the corresponding minister. The annual rate reviews thus might help to identify the policy handles and levers for the ministry. There might be some validity in this argument, but the point remains that the formal external constraints on Ontario Hydro were not as strong as those in British Columbia.

Providing the balance of power

The change in Ontario Hydro's planning approach began in 1984 and was partly attributable to 'political regulation', at least in the form of widespread concern over its nuclear expansion plans. The utility had been hit by slower than expected demand growth from the mid 1970s and had responded by cancelling some expansion plans and mothballing some existing plant.[54] Hydro noted a resurgence of demand growth, which would necessitate a substantial addition to generating capacity by the mid 1990s. Hydro was by now a nuclear company; the problem was that it had come under increasing scrutiny for its nuclear expansion plans, and it seemed to realise that it could no longer count on automatic approval for new nuclear capacity.

It therefore began a study called 'Meeting Future Energy Needs' or the 'Demand/Supply Options Study'. One notable feature of this study was that it explicitly considered demand management approaches as well as capacity additions. The study found that savings of between 1000 MW and 4000 MW were possible by the year 2000. The study also saw the deliberate involvement of the public in the planning process.

It should be noted that Ontario Hydro had been slowly evolving a range of mechanisms for public participation for almost twenty years. In the early 1970s it began to run into opposition to its proposed siting of transmission lines, and these delays had adverse potential consequences for system reliability. We have already seen that Hydro had developed a conservative approach to system reliability. Public involvement became an important part of avoiding delays, and it was extended slowly to the planning process surrounding new generating capacity, again largely to facilitate and protect Hydro's expansion plan. Initially meetings were conducted to provide information to the public rather than seek their input. However, in 1973 it did make a siting decision on the basis of public comment and in 1975 began an open-ended public participation process to select a site for a new generating station.[55] By the mid 1980s, therefore, Hydro had built up considerable expertise in public consultation.

Hydro devised a 'Provincial Organisations Consultation Program' to carry out consultation on the Demand/Supply Options Study and actively sought involvement, rather than simply being open to it. Under this program 125 organisations were invited to a series of five meetings in Toronto between November 1985 and February 1986; fifty-eight accepted.[56] The meetings were addressed by a senior executive and then thrown open to discussion. Written submissions were then invited, and thirty-six were received. This program was followed by a Regional Consultation Program, based on participation by 300 community leaders in thirteen meetings throughout the province between January and June 1986, and a Municipal Utility Consultation Program between February and June 1986. In addition, a market survey of Hydro's residential, commercial and industrial customers was conducted.

Hydro also consulted provincial and federal government agencies, but it was simultaneously coming under political scrutiny. The Legislative Assembly's Select Committee on Energy was appointed in July 1985 and conducted hearings in September and October, releasing its first report in December 1985.[57] As we saw earlier, this report addressed the need for the completion of the $10.9b Darlington Nuclear Generating Station then under construction on the shores of Lake Ontario. To consider cancelling a nuclear station under construction was a radical notion indeed; although with 65 per cent of project costs already committed, there was little chance of that happening as proceeding had clear cost advantages over the next best alternative: a coal-fired station. A dissenting minority report from the New Democratic Party members did recommend cancellation.

The committee, however, recommended only that Units 1 and 2, with 80 per cent of costs committed, could not be cancelled on economic grounds but found that serious questions remained about the viability of Units 3 and 4, which were less than 50 per cent completed. It therefore recommended a six-month freeze on further significant contracts related to Units 3 and 4 while the committee studied demand and supply options. The committee expressed concern that Hydro was giving too much attention to supply-side options and too little to demand-side management. It also raised concerns about Hydro's planning processes and the delineation of operating and policymaking responsibilities between Hydro and the government.

This, then, was the political context in which the Demand/Supply Options Study proceeded. The calls for reform of the planning process and for demand-side management were to be reinforced in the committee's final report.[58] While the final report ended the uncertainty for Hydro over completion of Darlington, it called for substantial reform of the energy planning process, opening it up for public scrutiny and requiring the utility to promote conservation. It recommended (among other things): that end-use analysis be required; that a range of forecasts be published and subjected to external review; that a comprehensive conservation strategy be adopted and the Power Corporation Act be amended to require Hydro to pursue conservation; that the Ontario Energy Board be given power to set rates for electricity sold and set rates for purchase of electricity from independent power producers; and that the Energy Board conduct a public review of the Demand/Supply Options Study and then conduct biannual reviews of Hydro's resource development plan.

While the recommendations of the Select Committee on Energy indicate the existence of considerable bipartisan support for changes in the basic direction of Ontario Hydro, it would be a mistake to conclude that the organisation itself was hostile to change. During the committee hearings it sought direction from the committee on five questions relating to the adoption of conservation techniques and the evaluation of supply options. Significantly, Hydro saw the recommendations for the expansion of the planning process to include industry and informed public groups, and the biannual public reviews of the resource plan, as measures that could lead to a reduction in approval times by dealing with possible objections in advance.[59]

The Demand/Supply Options Study proceeded concurrently with the select committee deliberations. A draft planning strategy was approved by the Ontario Hydro Board on 16 November 1987 as a reasonable basis for public review and discussion on the strategic directions Ontario Hydro should follow. This draft strategy was then subjected to further review by the Select Committee on Energy,[60] government ministries[61] and by a Technical Advisory Panel appointed by the Minister of Energy, Robert Wong, in March 1988.[62] Chaired by a former Vice-Chairman of the National Energy Board, Ralph Brooks, this panel included an economist and, significantly, James Litchfield, Director of Planning at the Northwest Planning Council in Oregon (which had led the way in adopting LCUP techniques in the United States).

The Ministry of Energy, the most important of the ministries reviewing the document, welcomed the strong emphasis given to demand management, but considered that demand growth would be slower than that estimated by Hydro. Importantly, the ministry argued that the reserve margin planned needed to be reviewed and the cost of maintaining it assessed against the value of system reliability. This point was reinforced by the technical panel. Reflecting the Northwest Planning Council approach, the panel recommended that Hydro develop state-of-the-art planning techniques that would allow greater emphasis on probability planning, risk mitigation and demand and supply options that offered shorter lead times and more flexibility in sizing. The panel also found that Hydro's forecasting techniques were inadequate and recommended that it urgently commit the financial and human resources necessary to develop a comprehensive end-use forecasting system incorporating econometric techniques.[63]

The panel was also highly critical of Hydro's approach to public participation, stating:

> Hydro's process of public consultation for system planning appears likely to have important shortcomings that will affect not only the credibility of the consultation but also the soundness of the plans eventually selected.[64]

It argued that the process lacked 'the appearance, and perhaps the substance, of independence and neutrality', that no provision was made for scrutiny of the power plan by independent technical experts and that there was 'no established procedure for Hydro to seek, receive, and incorporate into the plans outside information and opinions (as distinct from disseminating information about the plans)'.[65]

The panel's recommended approach to these shortcomings was the establishment of an independent agency with the expertise and other resources to conduct continuing reviews of Hydro's plans. It had in mind the role the British Columbia Utilities Commission played in considering applications for Energy Project Licences. It did not see periodic reviews (such as its own) to be adequate since there would be no cumulation of wisdom, and there would be too much opportunity for stalling by Hydro. It pointed to its own inability to extract specific cost information on nuclear generation from Hydro, a failing that led it to recommend the subsequent Nuclear Cost Inquiry.[66]

The government did not follow the panel's recommendation on public review when the Demand/Supply Plan, *Providing the Balance of Power*, was issued in December 1989, but the criticisms did result in a concerted effort on the part of Hydro to incorporate public input in a more meaningful way. Moreover, this occurred before the election of the New Democratic Party government in 1990, which indicates that the subsequent changes in Hydro began before the NDP came to power. What is problematic, however, is whether the change would have been as far-reaching without that political sea-change. The Liberal Government's approach to public review reveals that, without the change of government, change might have been more superficial because the government supported Hydro in making external review of the plan more tokenistic. We shall examine the public participation process followed for *Providing the Balance of Power* below, but first it is instructive to look at the struggle over the selection of decision path for the plan.

The Ministry of Energy made a Cabinet submission recommending that the plan be considered at a joint hearing by the Ontario Energy Board and the Environmental Assessment Board under the *Consolidated Hearings Act 1981*. It also made a separate submission that there should be a review of Hydro's level of avoided costs, which formed the basis for its approach to demand-side management. Both were considered together, and both were rejected. Instead a proposal was 'walked in' from the Cabinet Office for an assessment by the Environmental Assessment Board only, and the Minister of Energy was outflanked by what was widely believed to be a proposal from Hydro, introduced with the assistance of the Premier. The government then realised that the arrangement would look suspicious as the Environmental Assessment Board had no expertise on Hydro affairs. It hurriedly appointed a new vice-chairman of the Energy Board and appointed him to the Environmental Assessment Board as the OEB representative.

In its planning document Ontario Hydro identified around 2000 MW of demand-side management by the year 2000 at an avoided cost of 3.7 c/kWh, amounting to about 10 tWh. The total expectation of the gains from demand-side management by 2014 (the end of the twenty-five-year planning period) was 5570 MW – about 1000 MW of peak reduction from load shifting, 700 MW from capacity interruptible load and the remainder from induced electrical efficiency. About a quarter of future energy demand in the plan would be met from demand-reducing options, but (unlike BC Hydro) these were included as subtractions from future demand rather than as additions to available resources. In order to achieve this reduction by the year 2000 Ontario Hydro intended spending more than $1b financed from its normal budget, with $28m to be spent in 1990 and $124m in 1991. Expenditure on demand-side management over twenty-five years would exceed $3b.

Hydro did not wait for the outcome of the Environmental Assessment Board hearing to follow this path and immediately set about pursuing demand-side management. As part of this approach the utility introduced cash-back schemes on energy-efficient appliances. For example, in October 1990 a $5 rebate was offered on 17 W (60 W incandescent equivalent) fluorescent globes at a major supermarket chain. The scheme proved so successful that the chain sold out of globes.[67] There were numerous other schemes introduced in conjunction with other retail chains, including a coupon scheme with Canadian Tire and a previous scheme with the Home Hardware chain. The R2000 Home program (a pre-existing national program marketed under the EnerMark brand by the Canadian Electrical Association) offered a $2000 rebate to homebuilders who met required standards of energy efficiency (insulation, caulking and solar efficiency). There was also a $500 payment to the builder. Meeting the standard typically added about $7000 to the cost of a house, but the house was not eligible if there was gas to the street. This point highlights an institutional problem: who should pay the costs of conservation in heating and cooling energy use when gas and electricity are both available and both distributed by different public utilities? We shall take this point up in chapter 7.

Ontario Hydro also paid 50 per cent of the incremental cost of the project (apparently, the additional cost for the energy efficient option) up to a maximum of $300 000 in the commercial sector energy audits through the 'Savings by Design' program, which applied to both new and retrofitted demand-reducing projects. It also offered free energy audits to commercial and industrial consumers under the Power Savers Plan launched in July 1989. Its EnerMark loan program offered domestic consumers convenient, cheap finance to install energy-saving appliances.

It was also planned to rely on non-conventional sources on the supply side, with a 1000 MW purchase from Manitoba and 2120 MW from non-utility generation. Despite this total contribution from non-conventional sources of 8690 MW, forecast growth still pointed to the need for further major capacity. Hydro's preferred plan, therefore, included 2008 MW of hydro capacity, 4368 MW of thermal capacity and two nuclear stations of 7048 MW capacity. Importantly, since the last unit of Darlington was to be commissioned in 1993, approval for CANDU Nuclear A was sought by 1991 so that it could be commissioned in 2003. (CANDU Nuclear B was to be commissioned in 2009.) This would have ensured that Ontario Hydro continued as a nuclear construction company over the twenty-five-year planning period – indeed, at about the same level of activity as over the previous twenty-five years.

Public participation in power planning

These initiatives were being pursued even while the planning document, *Providing the Balance of Power*, was before the Environmental Assessment Board hearing. But there was an assumption that this approach would be approved given the controversy over nuclear power and the need to achieve targets on greenhouse gas emission reductions. This change can be traced directly to the Demand/Supply Options Study begun in 1986. A cynical view of Ontario Hydro would suggest that it undertook the public participation exercise in order to assuage public concern over its nuclear expansion program, so that it would succeed in getting approval. This view would see the adoption of this limited amount of demand-side management as a necessary 'price' it would have to pay to be allowed to continue with nuclear construction. Such a view might be justified on the basis of Hydro's past nuclear ambition, and (as we shall see later) it does seem to have been held by its president. However, its motivation is not important here because this was in fact the beginning of fundamental reform of the utility, and the public participation process can be seen to have played an important part in bringing about that reform.

About 250 interest groups were invited to take part in the Demand/Supply Options Study during 1985–86. About half that number participated. Ontario Hydro also went into the local communities and attempted to find out what the public thought. The feedback was quite consistent: most people thought Ontario Hydro was a construction company that was not interested in conservation. The public preferred hydraulic supply options and was concerned about nuclear safety and waste disposal issues. Moreover, they wanted more attention devoted to renewable energy options.[68]

Within Ontario Hydro this information was incorporated with technical and economic considerations in the System Planning division to produce the strategy. The strategy was then considered by a government select committee, which provided further opportunities to groups to contribute. The strategy was then redrafted as the final strategy and released in December 1989 in the document *Providing the Balance of Power*, the result of four years of public consultation and government reviews (1986–89). Then there was a further (and major) consultation process on the *Providing the Balance of Power* report.

Care was taken in this process to 'factor the public in' in a meaningful way so as to avoid it becoming just a public relations exercise, although Ontario Hydro already had a preference for one plan. Factoring the public in extended to the design of the documentation. Special care was taken both in the way the material was written and in graphic design to clarify the issues for decision for ordinary citizens. Ontario Hydro public relations staff also recognised that they needed to work with its six regional offices and plug them into their planning – they needed to get close to the people.

The consultation process on *Balance of Power* involved visiting seventy locations for three to five days at a time, with five sets of movable displays. Even with the ability to target five areas simultaneously, this process took about three months to complete (from 8 January until 30 March 1990). A two-day training session was conducted for those who were going to take part in the consultation exercise at the information centres. This meant that they could take people all the way through the display and helped to develop in themselves a better appreciation of the whole problem and the concerns of other branches of the utility, rather than sending out planning engineers familiar with only their own areas of the plan.

The system planners were all sent out to the regions for two weeks each to try to find out what the community values were. This exercise was seen as being very beneficial for the planners. As one of them remarked in an interview, 'The system planners were the masterminds of the *Balance of Power* document, so we sent them out to see how their product was received. This helped the system planners factor in those views'. The teams sent out into the province consisted of five people: a systems planner; a member of the Energy Management Branch (by now dealing with conservation rather than just marketing electricity as formerly); a person with responsibility for environmental affairs; a public affairs officer (because they had a broad understanding of all the issues and an 'ability to dialog with the public and the media'); and a local person from the regional office of Ontario Hydro.

On the first day the team would have local Ontario Hydro employees in, on day 2 the local elected officials, on day 3 the interest groups (the likely interveners in subsequent hearings over specific projects) and on day 4, the general public. About 10 000 people saw the exhibit over the period; a questionnaire was distributed and 3365 were returned. (It had been intended to conduct a series of workshops but these did not occur.) If interest was shown in a specific aspect of the plan or a particular project, the inquirer was put in touch with the appropriate person at Ontario Hydro who handled that part of the plan. This started a process of continuing interaction, which subsequently became more related to specific site activities.

The participation process to this stage cost in excess of $5m. Hardware for the presentations alone cost $0.5m for the three months of tours, and the documentation alone cost about $1m to produce. The twenty-nine interveners in the Environment Assessment Board proceedings that were to follow sought $60m in costs but had to settle for about $23m. However, this amount did not seem excessive when it is considered that approval for a $61b capital expansion was being sought. (By way of context, total revenue for the utility was then a little over $6b a year.)

The employees of Ontario Hydro were an important target audience for the consultations as the planners recognised that they would play an important role in communicating with the wider public through their discussions with friends and families. This was the first time Hydro had sought to involve its employees to this extent. The planners had also targeted government agencies and sought their input early in the planning process rather than have them on the outside and thus more likely to criticise later.

This process marked a substantial change in approach. Never before had system planners gone out in the field to expose themselves to the views of the people, and never before had there been public involvement at such an early stage in the planning process and reaching such high levels in the organisation. There were signs that Hydro collectively saw the process as one of gathering legitimacy for continuing a nuclear expansion program. However, system engineers involved in the planning process – and exposed to the public for the first time – reported finding this experience educational.

The Environmental Assessment Board finally began hearing the application in April 1991. It had originally been hoped that the review process would take eighteen months (approval for the first of the new nuclear stations had been expected in 1991), yet the hearings were only just beginning after that time had elapsed. The passage of time ultimately made the plan redundant as recession was slowing demand growth.

Structural change and the New Democrat Government

There were, as we have seen, indications that the reform process was proceeding under the Liberal Government, with Ontario Hydro introducing a modest amount of demand-side management and some more flexible approaches to planning in its 1989 planning document, *Providing the Balance of Power*. These tentative steps in a new direction were given a boost by the election of the New Democratic Party (NDP) government in the September 1990 provincial election.

The period of Liberal rule from 1985 to 1990 was significant for Ontario Hydro. It came after more than three decades of Conservative government, during which time the nuclear commitment had been made and the close relationship between the utility and the Conservative Party forged. Many members of the board of Hydro and many of its senior executives during this period were reputedly Conservative sympathisers. The Liberal Party had come to power having promised to make Hydro more accountable but soon lapsed into what one bureaucrat described as a 'cosy relationship'. However, it was a period in which some important but gentle changes occurred.

First, the President and CEO of Hydro, Milan Nastich, retired. Nastich was very much a 'company man', having served with Hydro for thirty-seven years. On 3 February 1986 the Liberals appointed an outsider, Robert C. Franklin, who had been (among other things) Executive Vice-president of CN Railways, to replace Nastich. Franklin was subsequently also to become Chairman in 1988.

Franklin instituted a number of organisational changes both at the divisional level, a step below the (vice-presidential) branch level, and at branch level. The branch structure had already reflected the declining influence of engineering functions, moving from a seven engineering/ three administration branch structure in the late 1970s to a four/four structure in 1982. In 1988 Franklin established an Environment Division and a Non-utility Generation Division. He also reshaped the Marketing Branch into an Energy Management Branch and the Power System Program Branch into a Corporate Planning Branch, 'expanded to plan all long-term power supply, advocate environmental policy initiatives, and encourage non-utility generation'.[69] These changes can be seen as reflecting a mild shift from a distributive to a regulatory regime.

It is difficult to gauge with any certainty whether these changes were enough to overcome the forces that might have snapped Ontario Hydro back into its old ways once the opportunities for further development presented themselves. There were some indications that Hydro still cherished its goals of nuclear expansion, and (as we shall see) Franklin apparently favoured further nuclear construction.

While there was a political climate of concern over the size of Hydro's expansion program and its nuclear nature, there was not the same kind of formal regulation that had been so influential in bringing about change in British Columbia. Nevertheless, it could be said that the politics had shifted from distribution to regulation even if there were few signs that the regime had followed suit. At first glance there also appeared to be only minor structural adjustment to the organisation of

Ontario Hydro. After all, there had been no decimation of design staff (as there had been at BC Hydro); indeed, staff numbers continued to grow throughout the period when the utility was anticipating publicly that there would be a shift towards demand-side management. Overall staff levels, having been 31 000 in 1985, reached 35 000 by 1990 and declined only marginally in 1991. Numbers of 'regular' employees (essentially all employees other than those associated with construction projects) rose from 23 001 in 1985 to more than 28 000 in 1991.[70]

These figures do not readily suggest a picture of a utility down-sizing in anticipation of a change of direction from nuclear construction to energy service and conservation, although they do mask some internal changes that were not reflected in aggregate staff levels. From 1985 there was considerable redeployment taking place, with a shift in staff from design and construction to production and distribution. The corporation managed initially to achieve 100 per cent redeployment of redundant staff within Ontario Hydro.[71] That rate declined to 90 per cent by 1989 when a Career Centre was opened to assist with the process of redeployment; 547 employees used the centre's services in that year.[72]

This was rather mild change in a climate of overall employment growth and reflected the fact that Hydro still intended at this time to be involved (eventually) in further design and construction. But it reflected also a much more moderate imposition of regulatory politics than was the case with BC Hydro. Not only was the Ontario Energy Board a veritable paper tiger compared to the BC Utilities Commission but also the extent to which Ontario Hydro was still regarded as an instrument of provincial development was reflected in the low levels of revenue collected from it by the government. For example, it paid only $95m in water rental for its hydroelectric generation in 1989 or 0.287 c/kWh; BC Hydro was levied twice that amount – $196m or 0.49 c/kWh.[73] This situation was changing slowly, with the introduction from May 1989 of an annual debt guarantee fee to be paid to the provincial government. However, it was set at only 0.5 per cent of Hydro's outstanding debt and raised only $82m in that year.[74]

As we have seen, the internal reorganisation of the utility also suggested slow evolution, with a gradual and marginal waning in influence of engineering-oriented branches and the gradual development of branches and divisions, which reflected a change to a regulatory regime. This suggests that a modest policy shift had been wrought by the Liberals, but there was much more left to be done. For this reason the election of an NDP government was significant in this case in a way it was not in British Columbia, where it occurred in late 1991, long after the effective reform of BC Hydro. This was especially so in Ontario because the NDP had been one of the leading critics of Hydro's nuclear expansion program, and certainly the most critical political party.

A good example of the continuing strength of the old Ontario Hydro and the NDP Government's determination to reform it was the appointment of a new Chairman and CEO, Marc Eliesen, in 1991. The government wanted to appoint Eliesen to the chairmanship and to renew Franklin's five-year contract as President and CEO. However, it was reported that Franklin felt he could not work with the new government. Its November 1990 policy speech from the throne had indicated a new direction, including greater emphasis on energy efficiency and controlling demand growth ($240m was to be redirected from engineering to energy conservation) and a moratorium on all further nuclear development. Franklin reportedly considered that further nuclear capacity was urgently needed; a view that indicates that the *Providing the Balance of Power* exercise might have been intended (at least by Franklin) as a means of generating support for further nuclear capacity.[75] Franklin therefore indicated that he would not accept a renewal of his contract, and Eliesen was appointed CEO.

The board of directors Eliesen inherited consisted of an 'old guard' of eight who had been appointed by the previous Liberal Premier, David Peterson, and five who had been appointed by the New Democrat Party Premier, Bob Rae. In May 1991 the 'old guard' directors of the corporation sent a memorandum to the Premier in which they stated bluntly that Eliesen was not qualified to be a CEO.[76] Moreover, they announced the appointment of their candidate, Alan Holt, a Hydro executive, as President and CEO. This move conformed to the letter of the Power Corporation Act but ignored the government's traditional role in choosing the CEO. The Premier responded with retroactive legislation tying the CEO's job to the chairmanship. The bill had not been passed by the legislature when Eliesen began work, so that Holt was still technically CEO, but Eliesen reportedly asserted himself quietly and got on with the job of implementing the NDP agenda.[77] Eliesen was a political appointee but one whose expertise had received bipartisan recognition. He had long been an NDP supporter and had been Chairman of Manitoba Hydro until the NDP defeat there in 1988. In April 1990 he had been appointed Deputy Minister of Energy in Ontario by the Liberal Government.[78]

The new government also named four new board members to fill vacancies at this time. They too had a new look, signalling greater social and environmental sensitivity: an environmental consultant and head of the Canadian Coalition on acid rain for ten years (Adele Hurley); Chairwoman of the University of Toronto Department of Preventative Medicine (Mary Jane Ashley); a native affairs consultant (Anne Noonan); and (more traditionally) the Chairman of Sudbury Hydro (Elmer McVey). McVey, however, was an NDP supporter who could be expected to support the government's policies.

Among other changes to the Power Corporation Act Premier Rae instigated in May 1991 (along with tying the CEO position to the chairmanship) was the establishment of the government's right to issue policy directives to the board and a legislated mandate to promote a switch to energy-efficient fuels. He also expanded the board to twenty-two members, appointing a former provincial NDP leader, the Deputy Minister of Energy, and two people with strong environmental credentials: Barbara Heidenrich (Executive Director of the Canadian Institute for Environmental Law and Policy) and David Brooks (Associate Director for Environmental Policy at the International Development Research Centre).

The changes at board level reinforced the changes in direction already begun within the organisation. Holt had been regarded as competent but pronuclear. While Eliesen had been criticised initially by environmentalists over seemingly pronuclear and prodevelopment remarks in the past, he was quick to point out that the remarks in question had been made during expansionary times and were not appropriate in the recessionary climate then prevailing.

Eliesen's actions after assuming office also pointed to substantial change both in the structure of the organisation and in its policies. He established a senior vice-presidency in aboriginal and northern affairs (and moved the Senior Vice-president Human Resources into it) and changed the Corporate Planning Branch to Environment and Corporate Planning. He also elevated the vice-president responsible for the Energy Management and Corporate Relations branch to senior vice-president and restructured the utility so that all the vice-presidents and senior vice-presidents with regulatory or 'policy' roles reported to him as Chairman.

All three 'engineering' vice-presidencies plus the Senior Vice-President Operations reported to Holt, who was effectively Chief Operating Officer – 'effectively' because the 1991 annual report listed Eliesen and Holt as 'Chairman' and 'President' respectively. All reference to the contentious CEO designation was avoided. Each side of the organisation now had seven vice-presidential executives, but, significantly, four of the five senior vice-presidencies were on Eliesen's 'non-engineering' side.

Hydro also cancelled uranium contracts with the two Elliott Lake mines (Rio Algom and Denison Mines). The government used its power to issue directives to ensure that the social impact of this decision was softened, with Hydro required to subsidise the shutdown of the mines. The cost of cancelling these overcommitments – $717m – is to be amortised over a decade and paid for by consumers.[79] There could be no clearer indication that Hydro was no longer wedded to nuclear expansion than the cancellation of contracts for the supply of this excess uranium since it had only made some sense to continue the contracts if it was anticipated that their output would one day be needed.

By January 1992 the reforms to Ontario Hydro's approach to planning appeared comprehensive and conclusive. In January 1992 Hydro issued a revision to its *Providing the Balance of Power* report showing even greater reliance on demand-side management and non-conventional sources, to such an extent that the need for *any* major new thermal or nuclear capacity additions had been deferred until the end of the twenty-five-year planning period (2009–11).[80] It was no longer necessary to seek planning approval for any such plant from the Environmental Assessment Board, then hearing the application based on the 1989 plan.

The success in delaying new thermal or nuclear capacity resulted partly from the effects of recession on short-term demand growth but mostly from greater anticipated yields from demand management and non-conventional supply. The expectation in 1989 had been a saving of 5570 MW through demand management by 2014; in the 1992 *Update* this had been increased to 9860 MW. Most of this increase was to come from fuel substitution, particularly gas for electricity in domestic space heating, as a result of an anticipated amendment to the Power Corporation Act, which would allow Hydro to promote fuel switching where it was in the mutual interest of the utility and the consumer.

The contribution from non-utility generation had been increased from 2120 MW to 4200 MW. A further 4300 MW was to come by extending the life of existing thermal capacity beyond the end of the planning period. Purchases (from Manitoba) were unchanged at 1000 MW. These gains were offset slightly by a reduction in new hydraulic capacity from 2850 to 1800 MW before 2014 as a result of the new government's recognition of the rights of aboriginal peoples in the development area. Hydro officially suspended planning for six new stations and two extensions to existing stations pending approval by affected aboriginal groups of a process for co-planning studies.[81]

Strong leadership and sustainable development

As if the Eliesen reforms, coming on the heels of the more moderate Franklin reforms, were not enough, worse was to come for those in Hydro who might still have cherished being able to build a nuclear plant – or any new plant – one day. Later in 1992 Marc Eliesen resigned to take the equivalent job at BC Hydro. To take his place, in October 1992 the government appointed Maurice Strong, a former Chairman of Petro-Canada and more recently Secretary-General of the UNEP Earth Summit at Rio de Janeiro in June 1992.

Strong soon had Hydro considering ways of operationalising the concept of sustainable development, essentially taking the new demand-side management and non-utility generation initiatives for granted – or at least as settled and beyond debate.[82] But Strong went further. He cancelled the 1000 MW Manitoba purchase (paying more than $100m in compensation) and associated transmission line construction as part of a multibillion dollar cut in investment. As if to emphasise the demise of Ontario Hydro as a nuclear construction company, Strong began a purge of similar dimensions to that at BC Hydro in the wake of the Site C decision.

Strong set Hydro the new goal of becoming a world-class company in energy efficiency and competitiveness to further sustainable development. Clearly the old structure – even as reformed by Eliesen – could not serve this goal. Strong had the board meeting on 13 April 1993 approve a new structure that saw the establishment of three business groups within the corporation: Ontario Hydro Enterprises Group (which would operate consulting and research companies), Ontario Hydro Electricity Group (essentially a generation and transmission company) and Ontario Hydro Energy Services and Environment Group (to incorporate energy management and liaison with independent power producers). Each business group was to operate as a distinct entity within the larger corporation and would be required to provide a rate of return on its assets. It would also be required to meet policy, program and performance requirements to be set out in contracts with the Ontario Hydro Corporation. The Chairman and CEO and President and Chief Operating Officer (there was no longer any doubt) and the managing directors of the business groups were to be supported by a number of divisions: Corporate and Public Affairs, Corporate Finance, Legal Corporate, Human Resources, and Audit. The first four were to be headed by senior vice-presidents.[83]

There are two significant features of this structure. First, it builds in a degree of competition between traditional sources of supply and both conservation and IPP, and will allow the corporation to select the most economical source of new supply. There is little chance that signals about technical feasibility or price will be distorted by the organisational bias of reverse adaptation. Second, the design and construction branch is gone. Design expertise is now a commodity marketed by the Ontario Hydro Enterprises Group to Ontario Hydro, along with other customers.

The move to new structure would result in a flatter structure. Half of Hydro's 700 executive-ranked staff will go, and a total of 4500 staff will be lost by the end of 1993 by means of a Special Retirement Program and a Voluntary Separation Program. All staff would have to apply for positions in the new structure, and no position is guaranteed. The first casualties were at the vice-presidential level, with only six of fourteen vice-presidents or senior vice-presidents finding a place in the new structure.[84] Of the eight to retire, six were engineers of long standing with the utility, averaging thirty-two years of service. Of the six to find a slot in the new structure, only two came from engineering branches. The Electric Empire was in serious decline.

Conclusion

It took twenty years of public criticism to turn Ontario Hydro around. The Porter Commission and investment restrictions in the 1970s were not enough to divert it from its course. Faltering attempts to chart a more conservation-minded course in the early 1980s were swamped by resurgent demand growth.

Ontario Hydro is the largest utility in Canada and the largest corporation in Ontario. Like an ocean liner, its sheer size would have made it slow to change its course. It was not sheer inertia that made reform difficult, but the strength of the distributive regime that surrounded it. Its nuclear expansion program not only provided construction jobs, it also meant stimulation for the uranium industry in northern Ontario. Government imposts such as water rents were kept low as part of a general effort to keep prices down – again as part of a general policy of economic stimulation. Combined with the technical complexity of nuclear power and the desire of engineers to engage in construction, this policy amounted to powerful support by means of distributive politics for a reverse-adapted utility. To continue the maritime analogy, it was not a matter of the ship not answering the helm but of a strong hand holding the ship on the old course. The critics of Hydro provided nothing more than a cross-current until they could change the captain's mind – or change the captain. It took two changes of captain and seven years to replace the distributive regime with a regulatory one and for this change to be reflected in the plans of Hydro and its structure.

If there were those in Hydro who were not serious about the non-conventional elements in the demand-supply plan, who saw them simply as necessary to gain legitimacy for continuing nuclear construction, there was considerable irony in the recession-induced slackening in demand growth and the election of an anti-nuclear NDP government. The lower forecast and the non-conventional elements in the development plan before any new nuclear capacity gave the NDP the justification they needed to end nuclear expansion and curb the Electric Empire.

CHAPTER 6

Victoria:
Uncertain reform

'Electricity obeys its own laws, and not those of the
economist.'
George Bates, chief general manager,
State Electricity Commission, Victoria, 1991[1]

Chapter 5 has shown that extensive reform of electric utilities is possible
if the political forces favouring change are powerful enough and
persistent enough to overcome the factors producing reverse adaptation.
We now turn to a case that supports this conclusion if only by showing
that limited political support for reform will result in the pursuit of
divergent goals by governments, which is likely to limit the scope and
effectiveness of reform.

The State Electricity Commission of Victoria in 1993 operated a system
with an installed generating capacity of 6700 MW and annual sales of
about 32 000 GWh. It had only limited hydroelectric capacity (468.5
MW), but was entitled to a one-third share of the output of the Snowy
Mountains hydroelectric scheme. The SEC was established in 1919 for
the express purpose of developing the brown coal resources in the state's
Latrobe Valley in order to avoid reliance on imported coal from New
South Wales.[2] It was established as an independent statutory commission,
not just because of the need to ensure that technical rather than political
rationality infused the organisation but also because Victoria had pion-
eered this form of institutional arrangement after a series of scandals in
the nineteenth century involving political decisions over routing rail
lines to the advantage of particular land developers.

The SECV was thus established with a very clear mission to give
preference to resources within the state and with an emphasis on leaving
the details of pursuing such a goal to the technical specialists – the

130

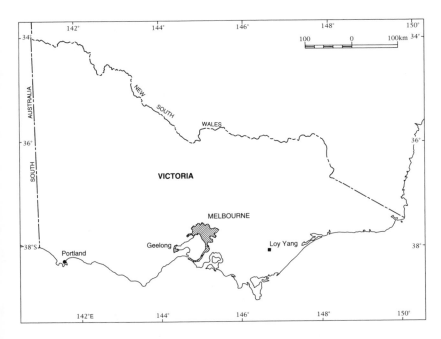

engineers. This free hand given to the technical specialists was probably just as well for the brown coal of the Latrobe Valley – while abundant – proved particularly difficult to burn, having a very high moisture content that made initial combustion difficult to achieve and flame regulation at low loads very troublesome. It proved to be a much more difficult fuel than that of Germany's Ruhr Valley, and the engineers of the SECV earned a deserved reputation for their skill in solving the numerous problems brown coal combustion presented for power generation. Almost certainly, these developments would not have occurred had matters been left to the market.

This political support for within-state fuel sources, the expertise of the SECV and the increasing reliance on electricity of the Victorian economy – long the industrial powerhouse of Australia – created the conditions for reverse adaptation, which was to prove difficult to overcome in the 1980s. It took some time for reverse adaptation to become established, but the lack of control over the SECV was seen as a problem as early as the 1930s. Yet the ever-increasing demand for electricity effectively overwhelmed such concerns. As was the case in most other places, the ability to meet a burgeoning demand was limited by the need to divert resources to the war effort in the 1940s, and there was post-war rationing of electricity in Victoria for seven years.[3]

The technical achievements of the SECV in meeting this growing demand from the state's brown coal resources, and the political support for this course of development in the towns of the Latrobe Valley that grew to depend on the SECV, did not necessarily mean that the SECV's decisions were in the state's best interests in economic terms. Latrobe Valley brown coal broke Victoria's dependency on New South Wales black coal, and ended Victoria's vulnerability to industrial disputes in New South Wales. However, a new vulnerability to disputes in the valley was substituted. And this result came at a price, because the economic basis for these investment decisions was very tenuous indeed.[4]

Brown coal did have one marked advantage over black coal, however: it had an effective opportunity cost close to zero. Thus, as the price of energy rose in real terms after 1973 (and again after 1979), the economics of brown coal appeared more attractive. Black coal could substitute for oil, and so it increased in value in line with export prices, but brown coal could never be traded competitively and so could be acquired for the costs of mining it. Electricity *could* be sold, even exported in energy-intensive exports, and did thus have an opportunity cost linked to world energy markets. The 1970s thus saw a widening gulf between the value of electricity and the cost of brown coal that could be used to generate it. Reinforced by efficiencies resulting from the trend towards larger boilers and turbogenerators, brown coal appeared to provide an attractive means of generating electricity. Furthermore, if the electricity could be exported either directly or in some electricity-intensive product, Victoria could share in Australia's resources boom which Prime Minister Malcolm Fraser saw as providing economic salvation in the late 1970s.

In this context a boom in electricity generation was seen as likely in Victoria. Plans emerged for a 4000 MW Loy Yang development to be built in two 4×500 MW stages, to be followed by a similarly sized project at Driffield to be commissioned progressively from 1993 onwards. Further substantial development was also planned. A report prepared by the Planning Department of the SECV in 1980 identified a possible twenty-one further power stations beyond Loy Yang. Planning on this scale was necessitated by acceptance of demand forecasts that predicted demand would treble in Victoria between 1980 and 2000 from 23tWh energy demand and 3800 MW peak demand in 1979–80 to 67 tWh of energy and 11 500 MW peak demand in 1999–2000.[5] Demand was expected to double again in the twenty years after that.

By 1993 – when the commissioning of Driffield had been planned – that project had been cancelled, the last 1000 MW of the Loy Yang project (Loy Yang B Units 3 and 4) had been deferred indefinitely, and the first unit of Loy Yang B only just commissioned after a majority share in the station had been sold to a private company, Mission Energy of the United States. The staff of the SECV had been halved, and it was being prepared for privatisation. The dimensions of the planning problems can be appreciated when the cost of one of these 4000 MW stations is made clear: about $5 billion. Turning around the SECV juggernaut took a decade and a half, and it is that process we shall examine in this chapter. As we shall see, the path of reform has been tortuous. The resources boom of the late 1970s (and an associated aluminium smelter project) and the industrial strength of the Latrobe Valley unions (and their influence in the Australian Labor Party) both complicated the issue. These factors combined at the beginning of the 1980s to contribute to a 'power crisis' that did much to mask the looming surplus in the medium-to-long term resulting from the SECV's expansion plans.

The power crisis in the early 1980s resulted largely from delays over the commissioning of the Yallourn W and Newport Power station. The delays were the result both of the arrogance of the SECV in trying to push throughout the Newport project on an inner-city site, with little regard for the growing concern for the environment, and of its poor record on industrial relations. The Final Report of the Newport Review Panel, which resolved the dispute over the project, noted a considerable reluctance on the part of the SECV to concede that any of its decisions – technical, commercial, financial or environmental – were open to challenge.[6]

On the matter of industrial relations, a costly dispute caused power interruptions for a month in 1977, and delays over the construction of Newport, Yallourn and Loy Yang A caused further interruptions in 1981. One observer has noted that: 'Prior to 1982, the SECV was in a state of constant war with its unions, which included some of the most militant in the public sector.'[7] Worker solidarity in the valley has traditionally been high because of the 'total' environment that exists, with workers interacting socially and as neighbours in a way not usual in industrial firms in large urban settings.

Ironically, the SECV had been attracted to the gas-fired Newport project because it would make it less vulnerable to industrial disputes in the valley, but the project worsened the overall industrial relations situation markedly. The union movement placed black bans on the Newport project, but in a building recession the (right of centre) Liberal Party government found enough labour prepared to ignore the bans and complete the station, although at the cost of industrial harmony and thus additional costs on the Loy Yang project. The Newport dispute was resolved ultimately by scaling down the size of that station from 2×500 MW to 1×500 MW and installing 466 MW of less efficient gas-turbine plant at Jeeralang.

This outcome was to affect electricity prices and the ability of the SECV to meet peak demand, but these were relatively short-term problems. In order to appreciate the longer-term issues we must examine the Loy Yang

A project and Alcoa's decision to construct an aluminium smelter on a site at Portland in the far west of the state. The problems surrounding the Alcoa smelter project and the Loy Yang project dominated electricity planning in the early and mid 1980s. Only once these related problems were resolved could the longer-term issues of planning and institutional reform be addressed. These issues provide considerable insight into the politics of the electricity planning process in Victoria as the government was torn between development and reform.

Before we examine that process, therefore, we must look at the Portland smelter project. It makes a fascinating case study in itself, but we shall confine ourselves here to the main features only and then only those aspects that bear most directly on electricity planning. That done, we shall then turn to examine the reform of electricity planning in Victoria.

The process was more drawn out than in our Canadian case studies and in many ways less profound. The political forces supporting the old institutions were perhaps a little stronger than in most of our other cases (with the possible exception of Tasmania) so the reverse adaptation took longer to overcome. Indeed, the faltering steps towards a less deterministic approach to planning, which found a role for demand management, coexisted with government policy (supported by the utility) to use cheap electricity to attract development in much the same fashion as Tasmania in its heyday.

Ultimately, the utility has undergone far-reaching reform in the face of pressures resulting from the breakdown of its monopoly supply position. This prolonged and indecisive struggle between development and conservation allows us to peel back the layers of institutional support for reverse adaptation and gain insights into both the support for the 'old' approaches to planning and the kind of institutional factors that must be addressed in moving towards new approaches.

The Portland smelter

Newport was a relatively minor hiccup in the expansion of the Victorian system as construction had begun on the giant Loy Yang A station in the Latrobe Valley in 1977. This station had been planned since 1974 and was the subject of a Parliamentary Public Works Committee Inquiry between 1974 and 1976. It was to be built in two stages (Loy Yang A and Loy Yang B), each of 4×500 MW capacity at an estimated cost (in 1977 dollars) of $1635m. Loy Yang was to be the largest electricity generating station in Australia, and it was to be followed by the 4000 MW Driffield station.

Before Newport the largest generator in the SECV system was 375 MW at Yallourn W. The new giant turbogenerators offered considerable economies of scale and were more efficient, but they did have an important disadvantage: they constituted large, lumpy increments of generating capacity. Although the four units of a station like Loy Yang A would ordinarily be commissioned progressively over about four years, the 'normal' growth in demand would take some time to use this capacity. At a time when electricity authorities had access to cheap capital and very cheap coal, it was an attractive proposition to work a high energy-consuming load such as an aluminium smelter into system expansion plans. Smelters have the additional advantage of taking an almost constant load regardless of the time of day or the time of year, ensuring that expensive capital plant was utilised more fully, and, because they can suffer short periods of disconnection, can reduce total investment requirements by serving as part of the reserve capacity of the system.

An aluminium smelter was thus attractive to the SECV because it would integrate well with its system expansion plans (although generation would have to come initially from more expensive gas-fired generation until Loy Yang was commissioned). A smelter was attractive to the Victorian Government because it would provide highly visible jobs and capital investment for which the government could (with some justification) take a large share of the credit. These benefits would, moreover, be provided in economically depressed regions where jobs were needed (in the case of the smelter) and in the Latrobe Valley (by ensuring that power station construction continued apace), thus furthering the government's desire to foster decentralisation.

The Portland deal was pushed through Cabinet in early 1979 by Digby Crozier, member for Western Province and Minister for State Development, Decentralisation and Tourism, despite opposition from the state Treasury. Crozier represented the Portland area and was later to become Minister for Minerals and Energy after the resignation of Jim Balfour on 15 December 1980. Balfour was member for the Latrobe Valley seat of Narracan, and the electoral constituencies of these two ministers with primary responsibility for the Portland project underscore nicely the political rationale behind the proposal. Development in the valley and in Portland added up to classic distributive (or 'pork barrel') politics, although at considerable cost.

In 1977 and 1978 Alumax and Nabalco approached both the New South Wales and Victorian Governments seeking electricity deals for aluminium smelter projects. The SECV was forced to tell the companies that it could not offer any special deals because it was required to disclose all its prices publicly and that if the published tariffs were too high they should discuss the matter with the government. This they did, but the Treasurer, Premier Rupert Hamer, refused to offer any subsidies beyond those available to all industries as part of general industrial development policy. Alumax then decided to seek a deal in New South Wales, but Nabalco indicated that it would prefer to set up in Victoria – at Portland – but that it could not afford the then lowest SECV tariff of 1.43 c/kWh.[8]

Crozier then presented a submission to Cabinet in January 1979 arguing that the government should pay the entire cost of the transmission line and offer a tariff of 1.15 c/kWh fixed for five years from the commissioning of the smelter in 1983. The cost of delivered power from Loy Yang was at that time estimated at 2.2 c/kWh, so the subsidy proposed was substantial. For this reason the Treasury was strongly opposed to the proposal and considered that Geelong or Westernport would be cheaper sites than Portland. The proposal for the government to meet the costs of the transmission line was crucial to Crozier's plan to get the smelter in his electorate since it guaranteed the same power price regardless of location and Portland is remote. By this time, Alcoa and Pechiney had also expressed broad interest in establishing a smelter.

Despite Treasury opposition, state Cabinet approved Crozier's submission and delegated the task of refining the details to a Cabinet subcommittee, which met on 28 February 1979. This subcommittee raised the electricity price marginally to 1.25 c/kWh. Even at this higher price, however, the deal was extremely attractive to aluminium smelters, and it was quickly snapped up – not by Nabalco, but by Alcoa, despite the fact that Crozier's letter to Hamer on the day of the Cabinet subcommittee decision referred to power for the establishment of a smelter at Portland by Nabalco. While the deal was to be available to any interested company, the speed with which the agreement was concluded with Alcoa was breathtaking.

Nabalco was a consortium of Sydney-based CSR and the transnational Alusuisse, while Alcoa was 48 per cent owned by Melbourne's Collins House group: Western Mining, Broken Hill South and North Broken Hill, with majority shareholding by the United States transnational parent. Alcoa's managing director, George Haymaker Jr was told of the package by Hamer on the telephone the day after the Cabinet subcommittee had agreed to it (1 March). Alcoa had only conceptual plans for a smelter at that stage, but Haymaker immediately called a board meeting, had it accept the package and sent a letter of acceptance to the Premier the same day. The director of the Department of State Development and Decentralisation was to have gone to Sydney that same day to put the offer to Nabalco. The government made no attempt to seek the best possible deal by involving the three companies in any competitive bidding.

Alcoa had expressed an interest in building a 120 000 tpa (220 MW demand) smelter at either Westernport or Portland as long as 'no significant economic penalty attached to either location'.[9] The deal concluded between Hamer and Haymaker did not specify where the smelter would be built; the government had agreed to sell power at the same cost regardless of site, and the Portland site would require trans- mission lines costing between $70m and $100m extra. Alcoa did not announce its decision to proceed at Portland until June 1979,[10] thus allowing the government to hold out the carrot of the smelter to all possible sites during the state election in May 1979. Enticing Alcoa to locate at Portland rather than Westernport Bay (much closer to the Latrobe Valley) reportedly cost taxpayers an extra $89m, and this cost was to escalate.[11]

This offer was so generous that an embarrassed Alcoa did not hold the government to it. The company agreed to allow the 1.25 c/kWh to rise to 1.35c in 1978 values in line with other electricity charges and later offered to pay for 21 per cent of the transmission line.

After the selection of the Portland site in June 1979 the government adopted a special piece of legislation, the *Alcoa (Portland Aluminium Smelter) Act 1980*. This act gave Alcoa rights to 880 MW of power in return for a commitment to build the first potline of the smelter (which would consume 220 MW). Allowing for transmission losses and plant availability, the generating capacity required at Loy Yang to service the load for the four-potline smelter was about 1350 MW. Thus a four-potline smelter would require the dedication of about three-quarters of the capacity of Loy Yang A. The smelter finally proceeded with was of two potlines at a slightly larger capacity per potline of 150 000 tonnes a year, with an electricity demand of 230 MW per potline. This required dedica- tion of about 700 MW of generating capacity at Loy Yang A.

 The government provided a number of additional sweeteners to cement the deal. The subsidies to the smelter included: an export market development grant; a rebate of turnover tax; a payroll tax rebate; a land tax rebate; a bulk LPG subsidy; an employment subsidy; an employee- removal subsidy; and a plant and equipment transport subsidy (in addition to electricity subsidies). It was estimated that with these sub- sidies the smelter would return 20.4 per cent on capital, while it would still earn 15.3 per cent without them – in excess of the 10–12 per cent return on capital usually considered sufficient to induce investment.[12] The value of the special subsidies other than for electricity included in the deal was estimated at $70m.[13]

The final agreement on conditions of electricity supply was not reached, however, until March 1981. Under this agreement Alcoa was to pay for electricity according to the published tariff for heavy industrial users, the so-called Tariff M, Option 5. Under this tariff Alcoa would have paid 1.95 c/kWh for electricity, less an interruptibility discount of 0.22 c/kWh – or about 1.73 c/kWh in 1981. Under this tariff the base price for electricity in August 1984 (at the time the Portland deal was renegotiated) would have been about 3.21 c/kWh. Significantly, a cost–benefit analysis of the smelter proposal was not undertaken by the Premier's Department until after the decision had been taken to proceed with the project.[14]

Unfortunately, SECV operating costs were escalating, and cost over-runs and industrial disputes were plaguing the Loy Yang project. Consequently, in August 1981 the SECV announced a general tariff increase of 25 per cent. The increase would also apply to the Portland smelter, which would have increased the basic tariff for Alcoa to 2.44 c/kWh at a time when aluminium prices were falling and the Australian dollar was appreciating.[15] Both meant lower returns to the smelter.

Alcoa immediately announced that it would have to reassess the economic viability of the Portland project. The government responded by establishing an inquiry, which confirmed the appropriateness of Tariff M but recommended that increases applying to the Portland smelter be less than or equal to increases in the consumer price index for the first ten years of operation. A subsequent review of the SECV tariff setting principles by the international consulting firm of Ernst & Whinney confirmed the approach taken. The final recommendation was for a base price (before interruptibility discount) of 2.256 c/kWh, with increases to be less than or equal to the rate of inflation (as reflected in movements in the CPI) for the first ten years of operation. This price was slightly below the 2.44 c/kWh price then prevailing under the published Tariff M.

The government accepted this recommendation in December 1981 but not before Alcoa had met with the Australian Labor Party opposition on 3 December. Alcoa had apparently told the government that it would strike a deal only if it was acceptable to the ALP because it feared that an ALP victory in the election due in 1982 would otherwise lead to the contract being renegotiated.[16] After this meeting, however, Opposition leader John Cain stated that under Labor there would be no electricity price subsidy,[17] but Alcoa then decided to proceed with the project. Part of the price of ensuring that Portland proceeded at this stage was a cut in the price of electricity for Alcoa's existing smelter at Point Henry near Geelong.[18]

Australian Prime Minister Malcolm Fraser had been active behind the scenes in trying to save the project, talking extensively with Victorian ministers, Liberal Party officials and Alcoa representatives. The site of the smelter was in the Prime Minister's electorate, and therefore he would no doubt have been keen to ensure that the project went ahead. Additionally, however, Fraser had won the 1980 federal election largely on the basis of promised benefits of the resources boom, and he was obviously keen to ensure that he was not embarrassed by having a major project in his own backyard come unstuck a little more than a year later. When Alcoa warned that it would withdraw unless it got an acceptable decision within three days in November 1981,[19] Fraser came to the aid of the party. He promised an investigation of the prospect of additional loan funds, which would keep prices down by decreasing the SECV's reliance on internal financing for its expansion program.[20]

One notable change in accounting practices had helped to feed demand growth by keeping costs down during the period of expansion from the late 1970s onwards: the capitalisation of interest during construction. Previously the SECV had entered all its interest charges as an item on its profit and loss account, and interest had to be covered by tariffs. Capitalising interest meant that the level of internal financing of capital works was halved over the 1970s, and the true (rising) costs of the massive expansion were not signalled to consumers, thus encouraging growth in consumption.[21] This change of practice was especially dangerous when it was coupled with special dispensations for Loans Council borrowings for infrastructure projects (including electricity generation) from 1978, as part of Prime Minister Fraser's attempt to stimulate the resources boom.[22] This change to Loans Council policy gave the utilities the means to finance this additional capacity.

The settlement on the price of 2.256 c/kWh less interruptibility discount allowed the SECV and Alcoa to sign a heads of agreement document in March 1982, just before the April state election. However, the smelter was not enough to save the government, and the ALP gained power. The renegotiated electricity price arrangement did not save the project from the effects of a further slide in metal prices and, with aluminium prices as low as $US1000/tonne and the Australian dollar above parity with the US dollar, work stopped on the smelter on 19 July 1982.

There followed two years of private negotiations between the new Labor Government and Alcoa. The government was keen to see the smelter proceed but refused to provide subsidies. Alcoa threatened at one stage in early 1983 to walk away from the project, but all the time its liability to the SECV under the 'take-or-pay' provisions of the contract was growing. With an improvement in metal prices to around $US1600/tonne by the March quarter of 1984 and a depreciation of the Australian dollar a new deal with the government was concluded. A new price was set for both the Portland and Point Henry smelters, the 'take-or-pay' debt owed to the SECV was picked up by the government, and the government took 25 per cent equity in the smelter. An agreement to proceed with a two-potline smelter was signed by Alcoa and the state of Victoria on 31 July 1984. The first potline of the smelter commenced operation in late 1986 and reached full production in mid 1987.

The Victorian Government had to go to considerable lengths to ensure that the Portland smelter proceeded in addition to taking equity in the project (and committing itself to marketing a share of the output). It also had to undertake to compensate the SECV for the delay in the smelter taking up its electrical load (estimated at between $130m and $160m in December 1983 prices), provide loan finance to Alcoa, sign a contract with Alcoa for supply of its 25 per cent of the alumina needed as feedstock for the smelter, and provide a flexible tariff structure that would insulate the smelter from external economic vicissitudes. Further, the new flexible tariff, with the price of electricity linked to the prevailing world price of aluminium, was extended to the contracts for all three potlines at the existing Point Henry smelter.

In order to ensure that the smelter proceeded the government had to expose itself to considerable risk by means of an electricity tariff structure that insulated the economics of the smelter from some of the vagaries of the world market. The electricity price was to vary according to a complex formula, so that it went up and down with the spot price of aluminium (specified in US dollars). A 'base tariff' was set initially at 2.669 c/kWh (in December 1984 values), with an allowance for interruptibility of 0.04 c/kWh. This allowance was 2.5 per cent higher than the tariff agreed to in December 1981, which would have been 2.564 c/kWh in December 1984 money values net of the interruptibility allowance. This base tariff was to increase in line with SECV construction costs until the smelter began operation and thereafter according to actual Loy Yang costs. The escalation was to be limited, however, to the rate of inflation initially and according to both the rate of inflation and wage costs thereafter.

The flexible tariff arrangements were designed not just to put a ceiling on escalation (as with the base tariff) but also to allow the cost of electricity to go up or down along with changes in the spot price of aluminium on the world market, taking a base price of $US1700 (in June 1982 values). The government could claim to have met its commitment not to subsidise the price of electricity to the smelter. It sought to achieve this objective by entering into an agreement with the SECV for the government to pay the short-term costs or receive the short-term benefits associated with deviations from the base tariff. The government also undertook to pay the minimum and holding charges owed to the SECV by Alcoa under the old agreement for the loss of revenue between the time of the original commissioning date (1983–84) and the new commissioning date (1986–87). The amount owing was estimated to be $162m (December 1983 values).

By ensuring that the output of Loy Yang A would find a market, the Alcoa deal saved the government and the SECV from immediate embarrassment, although with a potential for long-term costs, which was to be realised. The SECV described the decision to proceed with the smelter in the following terms:

> The decision is of major importance to the Commission and will ensure that the generation facilities at Loy Yang and the Moorabool to Portland transmission line constructed to meet the Portland smelter load are now utilised.[23]

However, caution should be exercised in attributing the smelter deal to the expansionary ambitions of the SECV. The commission had raised serious doubts about its ability to provide generating capacity in time for the first planned commissioning date in 1983. Furthermore, as we have seen, the deal would seem to be attributable more to the electoral appeal of distributive politics both at the national level, with Fraser's resources boom and at the local level, with Balfour and (particularly) Crozier pushing hard for a development project to benefit their constituencies – at very considerable public expense.

The rationale for the ALP's revised deal is less obvious since Alcoa's cancellation of the smelter left the company liable for compensation payments to the SECV that would have offset the costs of constructing the transmission line and building capacity at Loy Yang sooner than needed. The then Premier, John Cain, has described the 1984 smelter deal as follows:

> The solution of the complex problems around the smelter was a test of the resolve of a number of people. It involved a determination on our part to ensure that the SEC did not dictate to government: a determination to ensure that the SEC produced, without cross-subsidy, a tariff structure for a large user that maximised the prospects of our being able to restart the smelter and earn the considerable export income that was potentially there.[24]

The taking of government equity in the smelter project to get it started again was not a great obstacle to the ALP. Indeed, at a time when it had seen the smelter as being highly profitable thanks to the Liberals' subsidy, the ALP state conference had resolved that a Labor government would take equity in the project to ensure that taxpayers received a fair share of the economic rent.[25]

The successful renegotiation of the agreement in 1984 undoubtedly earned the Cain Government a reputation as being able to 'fix' the problems it inherited from its predecessors. However, it is debatable whether this boost to its reputation would have been a strong enough incentive to go as far as the government did to get the project rolling again, especially when one considers that the electricity price does not appear to have been the reason the project was halted. Alcoa reviewed the smelter project as a result of the 1981 electricity price increase, but it did not link its 1982 mothballing of the smelter project to that price rise nor with the price review initiated by the ALP when it came to government. Instead the company attributed its decision to depressed market conditions.[26] This information was public knowledge when the government attempted to get the project going again, and the renegotiation of the deal clearly reflected the government's unwillingness to wait for market conditions to improve.

This lack of patience appears to have been related to the need to guarantee continuity of construction-based employment in the Latrobe Valley as part of a package to deal with the perilous industrial situation the Labor Government had inherited. The smelter deal meant not just that the capacity of Loy Yang A would find a buyer, it also meant that work could begin on Loy Yang B, which was an important part of the relatively peaceful reform of the SECV and its industrial relations which was to follow.

Loy Yang and the need for reform

Legislation authorising construction of the 4×500 MW Loy Yang A power station was passed by parliament in late 1976.[27] Unfortunately, the SECV had seriously underestimated the cost of the project – by about $1000m in 1982 dollar values.[28] Poor labour relations problems also added to the cost.

The poor industrial relations that afflicted the Loy Yang project were partly a legacy of the Newport bans and the use of non-union labour to complete that project. A long-running dispute helped to bring about the resignation in December 1980 of Jim Balfour, who had been Liberal Minister of Minerals and Energy since 1967.[29] When the dispute began in April 1980 it had involved only a handful of concrete batchers. However, after 600 workers had been sacked it escalated into a major dispute, which was settled only late in November 1980.[30] The next year, three months of crippling work bans on the project by the Builders Labourers Federation were ended in December 1981 with a deal providing both higher wages and a shorter working week.[31]

Part of the price of the SECV's poor industrial record was a large degree of 'featherbedding' in work practices in the Latrobe Valley. A 1982 comparison with similar power stations in Germany's Rhur Valley (commissioned by the incoming Cain Government) revealed considerable overmanning in the valley in both the construction and operating phases of Loy Yang A.[32] Some of this difference was attributable to different maintenance practices due to differences in coal, but most was due to the costs of poor industrial relations.

These costs began impacting on demand. In October 1981, after a review of the load forecast in the light of tariff increases of 20 per cent in August and 14.6 per cent the previous November, it was announced that the construction of Loy Yang would be slowed. The second and third units were delayed six months and the fourth unit by one year.[33] The delay was also linked to Alcoa's reassessment of its plans after its tariff was increased by 25 per cent on 18 August. An immediate casualty was the planned Driffield station. Driffield, the subject of a Parliamentary Public Works Committee inquiry in 1981,[34] was originally thought to have been needed between 1993 (first unit) and 1999. However, its future was clouded by the likely effects on load growth of tariff increases associated with the effects of the agreement with Alcoa.[35]

On its election in 1982 the Cain Government, elected with a mandate to reform the energy sector, first had to deal with some of these problems it had inherited, in particular Loy Yang costs, security of supply and pricing. It tackled costs at Loy Yang swiftly by commissioning a series of reports into the situation.[36] Similar reports were compiled on the energy supply outlook (although it was becoming less of a problem with the commissioning of new plant),[37] energy pricing[38] and wider questions of policy and institutional structure.[39]

The Cain Government undertook a number of reforms after 1982. In particular, in 1983 it amended the *State Electricity Commission Act 1958*, restructuring the board both to place it on a more commercial footing and to achieve a degree of social accountability. Its department head at the Department of Minerals and Energy, Bill Russell, was appointed to the board, as was Ian Gibson, an economist from the Latrobe Valley. The commission began to hold 'annual meetings' to which the public (as 'shareholders') were invited. In 1983 a non-engineer general manager, Jim Smith, was appointed from outside the SECV. He became Chairman in 1990 following the retirement of Charles Trethowan, who had worked his way up from a clerical position within the organisation.

Several tentative steps towards conservation and improved energy planning were taken between 1982 and 1984, but the attractions of development rather than conservation became stronger with the need to provide employment continuity on Loy Yang B as part of the reduction in staffing levels on the Loy Yang A project. Thus the commitment to reforming energy institutions began to waver. In 1984 consultants to the Victorian Energy Planning Program recommended a number of structures be established to ensure adequate public consultation on energy planning issues, but these suggestions did not find favour with the government and were not implemented.[40]

The decision to proceed with Loy Yang B 1 and 2 was made in the wake of the conclusion of the Alcoa deal. In October 1984 it was announced that the construction of the first two units of Loy Yang B would be constructed according to a timetable that provided maximum flexibility.[41] The decision to proceed was an incremental one, with the Loy Yang B station treated as a stage subsidiary to the strategic decision to proceed with the entire project, rather than as a fundamental decision that required careful analysis. The reasons for this seem clear: Loy Yang B was the project that would provide continuity of employment in the valley, which was the sweetener in the deal with the valley unions to reduce costs on Loy Yang A by reducing overmanning. The authorising legislation in 1976 had provided for the whole 8×500 MW project, and the Alcoa deal allowed this prospect to be realised by avoiding considerable over-capacity in the SECV system and was thus a vital step in the process.

The decision to proceed with Loy Yang B was in reality a classic non-decision: it was decided not to deviate from the original intention to build the whole 4000 MW station, despite the opportunity to do so. Rather than reconsider this decision, the decision was to provide for flexibility. The contracts let for Loy Yang B from 1985 onwards included options to complete Unit 1 by 1992, 1993 or 1994, with Unit 2 to follow eighteen to twenty-four months later.[42]

The government had released an energy policy in 1984 that included some features of least-cost utility planning. Conservation, cogeneration, plant-life extensions, gas turbine plant and imports were all included as ways of providing planning flexibility at low cost. These measures were overshadowed subsequently, however, by the surplus in generating capacity resulting from the 'routine' decision to proceed with Loy Yang B, the inability to slow the construction of Loy Yang A and the decision to take advantage of the surplus by refurbishing the Hazelwood Power Station (which required units to be taken out of service). The dominance of these conventional supply-side options limited the attractiveness of demand-side management and other LCUP components because the prevailing short-run marginal cost against which such options had to compete was the relatively cheap brown coal of the Latrobe Valley, which has close to zero opportunity cost. On this point, a later inquiry noted that the

> SECV is committed contractually to the construction of Loy Yang B Units 1 and 2, and so has limited financial incentive to invest heavily in the short to medium term in conservation or other demand side measures which might reduce projected demand to the point where over-capacity would result from installation of these units.[43]

Additionally, as we shall see below, the SECV lacked the tools necessary to engage in LCUP.

The government's leaning towards development rather than conservation was signalled at the institutional level after the March 1985 state election, when it moved quickly to abolish the agency that had taken the lead in energy sector reform, the Department of Minerals and Energy. Its functions were absorbed within a Department of Industry, Technology and Resources. At the institutional level, therefore, the emphasis shifted towards industrial development.

However, limited steps continued to be taken towards both conservation and the use of non-traditional energy sources. The SECV had ceased marketing off-peak electricity for water heating in the mid 1970s, but this had resulted in a poor peak to off-peak ratio in its load curve, and it had recommenced marketing in 1985 and stepped up this effort in 1987.[44] Victoria launched an energy efficiency appliance labelling program in cooperation with the New South Wales Government in April 1987. The SECV also launched a Cogeneration and Renewable Energy Incentives Package in June 1987. By the end of 1989 it had identified more than 200 MW of potential capacity under this scheme, together with a further 350 MW outside the incentives package. (By 1991 the SECV had about 180 MW of cogeneration on line.) These measures were in addition to various information programs and energy auditing services.

NREC and aftermath

The tentative steps towards reform in the first five years of the Cain Government were to pale into insignificance compared with the changes to come in the 1990s. These flowed most directly from an inquiry conducted by a parliamentary committee, but they were helped along considerably by the emergence of real competition from private black coal and demand-side possibilities as the uncertainty costs of brown coal options became increasingly apparent. But all these factors were overshadowed by the emerging surplus of generating capacity as supply outstripped demand. (In its 1986–87 annual report the SECV noted that after the commissioning of the last unit of Loy Yang A in 1988 there would be a gap of four or five years before more capacity would be needed.)[45] In addition, the government continued to see cheap electricity as a means of fostering industrial development. Because of the key place this parliamentary inquiry played in shaping the reforms that followed, we shall now examine its proceedings and recommendations.

On 7 October 1986 the Natural Resources and Environment Committee of the Victorian parliament was directed

> To inquire into, consider and report to the Parliament by 1 October 1987 on the most appropriate sequencing of future power supply options to follow Loy Yang B Units 1 and 2 in order to meet the forecast range of load growth for the decade beyond the mid 1990s, as part of the development of long-term strategies for balancing electricity supply and demand.[46]

The NREC inquiry was the result of an SECV recommendation in a report forwarded to the government in August 1986.[47] The SECV knew how to play the game of distributive politics and moved to ensure that the concerns of community interests in the Latrobe Valley were communicated to the inquiry by establishing a consultancy to review the socioeconomic impacts of future power station development options with the Latrobe Regional Commission, the regional planning agency for the valley.[48]

The NREC inquiry was to be an important step in the reform of the SECV. It was able to bring to bear considerable consultant expertise and give detailed public consideration to the issues of demand forecasting and planning under the uncertain load conditions that the SECV faced in the 1980s.[49] While the extent of shared facilities between Units 3 and 4 and Units 1 and 2 of Loy Yang B (already under construction) gave that capacity a considerable advantage over any other supply projects, stiff competition was to come from both black coal and gas. Demand-side management, as we shall see, did receive some consideration, but it was very limited compared with the approaches followed in our Canadian cases, reflecting largely the relative lack of political support for such an approach.

The black coal in question was the Oaklands deposit in southern New South Wales, which the proponents (CRA Ltd) were keen to develop for electricity generation for both Victoria and New South Wales since the coal was not of export quality. CRA had undertaken considerable work in developing a power station proposal based on multiples of 700 MW units, with one possible site being at Yarrawonga in northern Victoria. Gas was being pushed by BHP Petroleum and Esso Australia, the partners in the Bass Strait oil and gas fields. The attractiveness of gas had been enhanced by the development of combined cycle technology, and the short construction lead time and low capital cost of gas-fired capacity were undermining a long-standing state policy that gas was not to be used for electricity generation.

Against these interests were pitted the SECV and numerous organisations representing interests in the Latrobe Valley. The latter included local governments (the Shires of Alberton and Morwell and the City of Traralgon), regional bodies (such as the Latrobe Regional Commission and Latrobe Valley Community Forum) and associations representing both labour (Victorian Trades Hall Council, Electrical Trades Union, Amalgamated Metal Workers Union, Federated Engine Drivers and Firemen's Association, Building Workers Industrial Union and the Federated Iron Workers Union) and capital (Victorian Employers Federation, Gippsland).

In contrast to this array of forces behind the various supply options, there were few organisations pushing for conservation of renewable energy sources. Those arguing for these approaches who made submissions to the inquiry were the Alternative Technology Association, Victorian Solar Energy Council, Australian and New Zealand Solar Energy Society, Wind Technology Pty Ltd, and the Fibreglass and Rockwool

Insulation Manufacturers' Association. What is significant about this list is that few of these groups were arguing for conservation as opposed to renewable energy sources. Furthermore, not one major environmental group thought the inquiry important enough to merit their making a submission to it. This is in marked contrast to the Tasmanian case and both of the Canadian cases, where groups were pushing the conservation cause vigorously.

The SECV recommendation to the NREC inquiry was to the effect that Loy Yang B 3 and 4 should be built, and that project definition be undertaken for both a 1000 MW brown coal station at Morwell or Yallourn and the Oaklands black coal project in southern New South Wales.[50] These recommendations were based on forecast load growth of 9.4 per cent over the year 1987–88 to 1988–89, 3.1 per cent a year growth in the period 1988–89 to 1991–92, and 2.4 per cent a year growth over the decade thereafter.[51]

The NREC inquiry found that the cost of electricity from Loy Yang B 3 and 4 was competitive with that from black coal from Oaklands at high load factors. However, prices for electricity from future brown coal stations were not competitive with black coal or gas. This finding raised the interesting question of whether the whole Loy Yang project had been competitive with imported electricity based on New South Wales black coal, since the equation was loaded heavily in favour of Loy Yang, and especially since the estimate on which approval had been based in 1976 had proved to be so optimistic. The site for the B station had been levelled, and the open-cut and coal-handling plant, the water and waste water services and most other operational infrastructure had been provided in common with Loy Yang A and were already being used there.[52] This tends to suggest that McColl's findings, that electricity based on imported black coal was cheaper than brown coal generation, still held in relation to Loy Yang.[53]

The NREC refused to recommend a preferred sequence of power supply options in its final report, which was released in April 1988. Instead, it recommended that no final commitment be made to construction of Loy Yang B 3 and 4 until the latest time consistent with maintaining a reliable electricity supply system – and after a review of all options, including demand-side options. The NREC also recommended that the Hazelwood and Yallourn W stations be refurbished to extend their life and enhance their performance, and that more attention be given to demand-side management. As a result a joint task force was established with the Department of Industry, Technology and Resources. It was necessary because the SECV had failed to present any evidence to show how the economics of each demand-side option compared with supply-side options, nor indeed with other demand-side options.

The NREC report made two principal recommendations. They were that:

1 The government and SECV should adopt an Electricity Development Strategy based on the Overall Objective, Strategic Principles and Key Elements described [in the report] together with the Specific Recommendations which [followed].

2 SECV should prepare and publish an annual Electricity Development Strategy and Implementation Review document for submission to the Parliament in accordance with the format suggested in Appendix 14 of [the] report.[54]

Later, in July 1989, a Powerline Review Panel, which had been established to resolve a controversy over a transmission line siting, recommended that development strategies be developed on a triennial basis and implementation reviews be conducted annually.[55] The NREC also recommended the development of an integrated least-cost planning methodology better able to cope with the uncertain future load outlook and the risks associated with making large capital commitments on projects with long lead times (recommendation 10). The committee recommended that it be given further terms of reference to explore this issue further to ensure that the SECV considered demand-side measures alongside supply-side approaches to planning.

The government did take steps to implement these recommendations. However, it found the electoral attractions of power station construction irresistible and, in its policy statement for the Latrobe Valley for the October 1988 state election, the ALP announced: 'The Government has decided that Loy Yang B3 and B4 will be the next base load stations [sic] in Victoria. Construction is expected to commence within 3 years to meet future demand'.[56] The government enjoyed a very slender majority of only six seats in parliament and harboured ambitions of winning the marginal Latrobe Valley seat of Narracan (held by the Opposition). It was also vulnerable in the nearby seat of Morwell, where a rebel 'labor' candidate, who had quit the party after failing to secure party preselection, was opposing the official ALP candidate. About half of all employment in the valley was provided by the State Government (principally the SECV). The Commonwealth electorate there (McMillan) had the highest level of public sector employment in Australia outside Canberra.[57]

The ALP's policy document for the Latrobe Valley was the only geographically specific policy statement released during the election campaign. It came a month after detailed polling had identified the concerns of voters – particularly swinging voters – in the valley. The commitment on Loy Yang B 3 and 4 was in a section entitled 'Jobs and the Economy', and was accompanied by a commitment to refurbish existing power station units and a general commitment that brown coal would continue to be the basis of Victoria's electricity generation. This policy document was carefully crafted to woo swinging voters. It addressed concerns over SECV employment and other issues (such as environmental protection) dear to the hearts of swinging voters but not considered important by committed voters.[58]

With the October election won narrowly by four seats, the government was then less specific on the fate of Loy Yang B in a ministerial statement in December 1988 made in response to the NREC report. No reference was made in this statement to construction beginning within three years. It indicated that: 'This commitment to Loy Yang B3 and B4 has been made with the confidence that joint SECV/Union studies and actions will ensure its cost competitiveness with other supply options'.[59] The government was thus using the promised continuity in construction employment as a lever in attempting to decrease manning levels and achieve other productivity gains in the operation of Latrobe Valley power stations.

Demand management and development planning

The government did not wait until after the election before implementing other aspects of the NREC recommendations. In June 1988 the Minister of Industry, Technology and Resources established the joint SECV–Department of Industry, Technology and Resources Demand Management Development Project. The project team realised early in its work that there was unlikely to be enough expertise in Victoria or even in Australia as a whole to help them with their work, and they therefore obtained ministerial approval to engage North American consultants with expertise in demand management and integrated resource planning. The project engaged Decision Focus Incorporated for integrated planning and modelling and Synergic Resources Corporation for demand management program design, development and evaluation and market planning and research. A staff member from a North American utility was also seconded to the project.

These consultants confirmed in their first visit that the SECV completely lacked any tools adequate for conducting integrated planning as its modelling work for planning was geared entirely to timing new additions of generating capacity to the system and the financial performance the SECV's business under a range of different futures.[60] Again, the SECV was found to be capable of only deterministic approaches to planning, despite the reforms of the early 1980s. The task force revealed that while the idealised depiction of the SECV approach to planning indicated a reiterative approach, 'the actual process applied tended to be more "once through" on an annual or biennial basis...'.[61] The planning approach had been almost unambiguously deterministic. High, median and low economic and demographic forecasts were combined with econometric and time series techniques to develop high, median and low forecasts for electricity demand and energy. The impact of conservation was then estimated and plant expansion and financial and business plans developed to meet the median forecast. Some minor flexibility was provided for future plant timings.[62]

As a result of the NREC inquiry and the Demand Management Development Project, a computer model was acquired that would permit a more dynamic approach to planning. The Generalised Equilibrium Modelling System (the proprietary version of the Tennessee Valley Authority's Strategic Analysis Model) was purchased from the project consultants DFI. Thus by 1989 the SECV had moved to a scenario approach to forecasting, which identified the potential benefits of DSM. Its forecast for the period 1989–90 to 2003–04 was in the range 1.4 to 2.7 per cent a year growth with zero DSM, and 0.4 to 1.4 per cent with aggressive DSM.[63] These forecasts not only made the uncertainty explicit, they were also substantially lower than those that had been placed before the NREC.

It was also decided to spend $55m over three years on twenty-nine demand management projects in line with the recommendations of the Demand Management Development Project.[64] The government engaged the American conservation expert, Amory Lovins, as a consultant.[65] Lovins argued that even conservative utilities in the US were spending 2 per cent of revenue on demand management, but the SECV was spending only 0.8 per cent, and the $55m three-year program was merely a pilot project. This amount was more than any other Australian utility, but only about a third of what it arguably should have been spending. Nevertheless, Jim Smith, Chairman of the SECV, argued that the recommendations of the Lovins Report were too financially risky.[66]

One problem that beset the Demand Management Development Project from the outset was the shadow cast by the existing overcapacity over the whole exercise. The project team recognised that very low short-run marginal costs would prevail for five years, 'driven by the capital costs that have been sunk into major capital programs; namely, the Loy Yang project and the major Plant Life Extension and Plant Improvement Programs at Hazelwood and Yallourn W'.[67] This factor should have led to SECV caution. However, it should also be noted that the utility clearly was not convinced that demand-side management constituted any advantage for itself because, in its submission to the Industry Commission Inquiry into Energy Generation and Distribution in 1990, it indicated that it considered such activities as merely part of its 'community service obligations'.[68]

The SECV had shown some willingness throughout the 1980s to respond to the conservation challenge. In April 1987 appliance labelling was introduced, and in June a joint SECV/DITR cogeneration promotion was launched, although it was limited to 150 MW.[69] But it seems clear that, while the government paid lip service to such approaches, the politics of development prevailed. In April 1987 the government published an industry plan, *Victoria – The Next Decade*, which included a flexible pricing package to attract energy-intensive industries and established an energy-intensive industry facilitation unit in the Department of Industry, Technology and Resources.[70] The SECV, understandably, supported this approach:

> The SEC has supported the Victorian Government's initiatives in the energy intensive industries area by continuing to offer electricity prices which are the lowest in Australia and among the lowest in the world for industries of their type.[71]

Whatever the reasons for the conservatism of the Demand Management Development Project team, its recommendations were criticised by the Conservation Council of Victoria, which had been provided with funding to consider and comment on work done in the project. The Conservation Council was particularly critical of the project's failure to incorporate consideration of pricing as a means of suppressing demand, but the project team defended this approach on the grounds that government policy viewed 'electricity pricing as a key means of facilitating economic development of Victoria'.[72] This statement gives a clear view of the relative importance of conservation and development in relation to electricity planning in Victoria. The Conservation Council also criticised what it saw as the poor treatment of externalities in the project and recommended the application of costing discounts to give credit for the absence of negative externalities for conservation options. The government ultimately accepted this recommendation.

The Minister for Manufacturing and Industry Development, David White, established an Electricity Development Strategy Consultative Panel in May 1990 to assist with the assessment of the SECV's first *Electricity Development Strategy Implementation Review* (EDSIR), which had been published in December 1989 in response to the recommendation in the NREC report.[73] This document did not present a new strategy but rather reviewed the implementation of the recommendations of the NREC inquiry.

The Brunswick to Richmond Powerline Review Panel had recommended in July 1989 that the EDSIR be published triennially, with annual implementation reviews. It also recommended that DITR conduct an external review of EDSIR and that a consultative panel be established to provide independent specialist advice on the content of the EDSIR and the consultative process appropriate to its public scrutiny.[74] MITR accepted these recommendations in October 1989, and the EDSIR was prepared as a basis for public consultations during 1990. The SECV established an Electricity Supply and Demand Consultative Group with which to discuss the shape of the EDSIR. The group consisted of government departments and agencies, trade unions, business and employer groups, and community and interest groups.

The EDSIR noted that the Production Improvement Program (PIP) launched in September 1986 had resulted in improvements in output from existing plant of some 20 per cent – or some 6 tWh.[75] The PIP included plant life extensions for Hazelwood and improvements at Yallourn W and Loy Yang, which were assisted greatly by labour mobility between stations permitted by the improvements in industrial relations. By now the SECV was also considering supply options other than brown coal. The SECV had in 1986 entered into a joint venture to explore the Golden Beach gas field 4 km off the Gippsland coast of eastern Victoria with a view to developing it to supply a 250–350 MW gas turbine or combined cycle peaking or intermediate load station. The EDSIR included provision for site banking for this option – early planning and development approvals to minimise lead times, but without the SECV or the government making a commitment to proceed with such a station.[76]

The government's commitment to Loy Yang B 3 and 4 as the next baseload power station had been made on the condition that its cost-competitiveness with black coal such as Oaklands could be demonstrated in a joint SECV Management/Union Loy Yang Cost Study, which had been initiated in 1987. However, the EDSIR had to report that the cost study had 'just been closed off without a successful outcome because a number of major proposals necessary for competitiveness could not be accepted'.[77]

The consultative panel was given the brief of assisting the department's consideration of the *Electricity Development Strategy Implementation Review* in order to provide an assessment of strategic issues affecting electricity planning. The 'department' in question changed its identity twice during the course of the panel's deliberations, first from Industry, Technology and Resources to Industry and then to Manufacturing and Industry Development. These changes signalled a declining emphasis for energy issues and a considerable retreat from the situation prevailing before the absorption of the Department of Minerals and Energy into the Department of Industry, Technology and Resources after the 1985 state election.

The consultative panel released a Guide to Consultation and an Issues Paper in September 1990, and conducted numerous public consultations before producing a Draft Final Report in March 1991. It both sought the views of the public on the EDSIR and made recommendations on how accountability and consultation could be incorporated into future planning processes. Such niceties were, however, to be overshadowed by factors associated with the decline of the Cain Government, the partial sale of the Loy Yang B power station and the downsizing of the SECV. In the midst of this turbulence the government did, however, both defer approving any further capacity and see through significant reform of the SECV, including the adoption of further conservation measures.

The government sought to bring together the various initiatives on energy reform in various sectors in a draft strategy or Green Paper on Renewable Energy Conservation in February 1990 and, after considerable public consultation, released an Energy Efficiency Strategy in June 1991.[78] One significant initiative announced by the minister in this document was a study (to be completed by the end of 1992) into ways of incorporating externalities into the planning process. As an interim measure, the minister announced that a 10 per cent cost advantage would be granted to conservation and renewable energy resource options. While this commitment came rather late in the piece, it did indicate that the government was becoming more serious about conservation.

The government was simultaneously coming to realise that it could not continue to hold out hope that Loy Yang B 3 and 4 could be constructed, given concerns over the level of the state's indebtedness and the absence of sufficient demand to justify such a further expansion. Concern over debt was signalled from a number of quarters. At the May 1989 meeting of the Loans Council Victoria's public sector borrowings were reduced by 25 per cent in nominal terms.[79] The Economic and Budget Review Committee's inquiry into limits of debt in Victoria's electricity, water and gas authorities reported to parliament in September 1990. Also in 1990 the credit ratings of the SECV were downgraded from AAA by both Moody's (to Aa+) and Australian Ratings (to AA+).[80] These ratings were downgraded further in 1991.[81] The concerns over debt were to lead to the sale of a share of Loy Yang B 1 and 2 in the face of a hostile reception from the left of the Labor Party and the power unions. This asset sale was particularly painful for the unions because it necessitated the efficient operation of the station and this, as well as the threat of competition from the likely establishment of a South-east Australia Electricity Grid, required further job losses in the SECV. The grid proposal arose out of the Industry Commission's recommendations for the establishment of a competitive national market, which would pit Latrobe Valley brown coal against New South Wales black coal as a source of generation in an interconnected system.

We have already seen the government's 'flip-flopping' over Loy Yang B before and after the 1988 election. Its public pronouncements from then on were increasingly negative. Premier John Cain stated in July 1989 that the government was reviewing the timing of the construction of Loy Yang B on the grounds of finance and greenhouse gas considerations.[82] By late 1989 the original timing of first power from Loy Yang B Unit 3 of November 1998 could only be justified by a scenario of high economic growth, none of the planned demand management, no further extensions to the plant life of Hazelwood and no gas-fired plant. Indeed, that unit could have been needed between 1997 and 2014, depending on market conditions and the SECV's response.[83] Minister David White stated in June 1990 that Loy Yang B 3 and 4 would have to be delayed on environmental grounds, as the government would not meet its targets for greenhouse gas reduction if the units went ahead on schedule.[84] Then, in January 1991, White and new Premier Joan Kirner (who succeeded Cain after his resignation in August 1990) indicated that conservation could delay the need for Loy Yang B 3 and 4 until beyond the turn of the century.[85] Kirner then stated in April 1991 that Loy Yang B 3 and 4 were being reconsidered because of the greenhouse effect after White had foreshadowed a gas-fired station being built in Gippsland by about 1995, with the cancellation of Loy Yang B 3 and 4.[86]

Restructuring, downsizing and privatisation

The SECV outlined its achievements to that point in its submission to the Industry Commission inquiry in August 1990.[87] It had reduced its controllable operating costs (other than depreciation and finance charges) by 40 per cent in real terms, reduced staff numbers by 21 per cent and increased sales by 42 per cent in the five years to 1989–90 (including, of course, sales to the Portland smelter). It had also improved the available capacity factor for its brown coal plant from 59 per cent in 1985–86 to 69 per cent in 1989–90, decreased reserve plant margins from 45–50 per cent to 25–30 per cent and reduced prices by 3 per cent a year in real terms. Its claims on reserve plant margin reductions were just a little bold, considering that the Portland smelter had been commissioned during this period and, as a large interruptible load, decreased the reserve plant requirements substantially without any SECV action being necessary.

While the SECV had not been able to achieve the level of agreement with unions on workplace reform it considered necessary to make future brown coal developments competitive, during 1989 it began a process of substantial industrial and organisational reform, aimed at increasing productivity and achieving a flatter organisational structure. The original aim had been to reduce the size of the workforce by 20 per cent,[88] but staff numbers were to be cut almost in half over the next four years, from about 21 000 to fewer than 12 000. These cuts included a 50 per cent reduction in employment in the Latrobe Valley, from a high of about 10 000 in 1985 to a little more than 5000 in 1993.

While most of these reductions were achieved with voluntary redundancies and early retirements, there was some evidence that the SECV had been rather heavy-handed in achieving its downsizing. In March 1991 a memorandum entitled 'The Power Grid Development Department Strategy for Personnel Reductions' dated 25 October 1990 was leaked to the media.[89] This memorandum argued that downsizing objectives would be difficult to achieve if departure options remained voluntary. It therefore set out a plan of demoralisation to achieve departures, including fostering rumours of further job cuts, forcing people into positions for which they were not suited so as to increase the attractiveness of the voluntary redundancy package, and keeping all non-essential staff together in one area, giving them no meaningful work and limited access to a telephone. An SECV spokesman denied that the plan had been implemented and attributed it to the personal views of one manager.

The reforms resulted in considerable friction between the ALP State Government and its union power base. The Trades Hall Council and the Gippsland Trades and Labour Council (acting on behalf of Victoria's power industry unions) wrote to Premier Joan Kirner in November 1990 calling for the removal from office of the Minister for Industry and Economic Planning (David White) and the Chairman of the SECV (Jim Smith), claiming that the SECV was in chaos.[90] The issues concerning the unions were the indications of further job losses and the push by the SECV to sell Loy Yang B into private ownership. The commissioning of Loy Yang B was about to add $3b to the utility's $8b level of indebtedness, and the SECV had looked to private ownership as a means of debt reduction.

The subsequent Cabinet decision to partially privatise Loy Yang B also caused problems for the government, provoking an angry response from the ALP caucus, as it went against party policy. Latrobe Valley member of parliament Keith Hamilton (left-wing member for Morwell) described the option to sell 40 per cent of the station as 'rape' and an option to sell the entire station as 'murder'.[91] Hamilton had earlier stated that the leftist caucus had elected Kirner as its candidate for Premier on the understanding that there would be no sale of public utilities.[92] At one stage wholesale privatisation of the electricity sector had been considered as a response to the state's considerable debt burden, but Treasurer and Socialist Left faction member Tony Sheehan assured the faction in March 1991 that the government had abandoned its push to privatise the SECV.[93] Kirner had given the power unions an assurance that the decision would be made by the government and the ALP, not by the SECV. However, the power unions believed that any decision should be dictated by the findings of an ALP caucus committee set up to look into the matter.[94] While privatisation by the ALP was unlikely, reform was seemingly inevitable. In 1991 the Parliamentary Public Bodies Review Committee conducted an inquiry into the appropriate form for corporatising the SECV.

The SECV had already undertaken a significant restructuring. In 1989 it had restructured itself into three '**ring-fenced**' strategic business units dealing with generation, transmission and customer services (or distribution), linked not by strong organisational ties but by transfer pricing. Each developed business and strategic plans with performance measures and targets, and within them a number of business centres, supplying SECV and other customers in competition with private sector suppliers, were also established. Moves were made to flatten the organisational structure, and at the time staff levels were reduced in 1989–90. These reductions included first the downsizing of the Design and Construction section and then its disestablishment. With no additional capacity beyond the already-designed Loy Yang B Units 3 and 4 in the utility's planning horizon, the 791-strong Design and Construction group was disbanded in late 1991.

Throughout this period of reform progress continued towards implementing demand-side management in Victoria, but it was progress that was painstakingly slow. Its thrust was undermined by the restructuring into business units. During 1991–92 a review of the Demand Management Action Plan was undertaken in response to the many changes in the electricity industry since the plan had begun in 1989 and 'slower than expected progress in the implementation of and response to the 3-Year Plan'.[95] As a result of this review the plan was extended for a further two years to 1995.[96] The SECV noted that customer awareness and interest were taking time to develop, and decided to introduce some 'structural changes' to the incentive packages to improve participation.[97] These incentives were little and late when compared with those introduced in our Canadian case studies. A Higher Efficiency Motor Rebate Scheme (for example) was introduced only in July 1992.

The SECV's enthusiasm for demand management was blunted by the existing surplus capacity. It noted that there was 'likely to be a continuing surplus of power generation in south-eastern Australia, and little need for either Demand Management or new generation to supplement existing resources before the turn of the century'.[98] The SECV failed to spend the $55m it had budgeted for DSM, spending only $20.9m of a budgeted $30m on non-capital expenditure. This expenditure was estimated to have reduced retail revenue by $37m (or 1.35 per cent), producing long-term benefits with a net present value of $47m.[99]

The delay in spending this money was attributed to longer than expected time to design, prepare and launch programs,[100] but it is clear that the utility had made no great effort to put the program in place. Its annual reports reveal that only five staff were appointed to run the Demand Management program in 1989.[101] This number was increased to eleven by 1991,[102] twelve by 1992[103] and seventeen by 1993,[104] which does not indicate great enthusiasm for demand management. This observation is confirmed by the absence of any strong corporate goal involving conservation. The only demand management performance measure was a target of off-peak to peak load ratio of not less than 80 per cent, and this target was abandoned as no longer relevant in 1992.

The seventeen staff in the Demand Management program in 1993 were located in the Customer Services Group, and the separation of retailing from production – particularly in the light of surplus generating capacity – was threatening to obscure the potential benefits of conservation for generation planning. Transactions between strategic business units were on a strictly commercial basis, and the SECV decided that in 1993–94 there would be an increasingly commercial focus for DM activities 'to ensure that the Customer Service Group derives a greater benefit from Demand Management expenditure'.[105] And after the Demand Management Action Plan was completed in 1995, the Customer Services Group was to 'focus only on activities with a direct commercial benefit'.[106]

Conclusion

In October 1992 the ALP was swept from power and replaced by a Liberal–National Party coalition headed by Jeffrey Kennett. This government promptly increased the share of Loy Yang B to be sold from 40 to 51 per cent and began further reforms aimed at selling the SECV into private ownership. These further reforms cannot be discussed in any detail here as they were still being played out at the time of writing. However, as we have seen, the establishment of separate business units had already begun to separate the potential benefits of DSM for generation planning from the generation 'company', and there is considerable controversy over the implications of private ownership for conservation. We shall return briefly to this point in the next chapter.

While the reform process continues in Victoria, however, the case history up to the point at which the ALP lost office tells us much about institutions and electricity planning, and about reverse adaptation and the processes involved in reversing it. First, we can see clearly the significance of distributive politics, reflected in a consistent preference for the use of within-state resources from the time the SECV was established through to decisions in favour of brown coal when its economic advantage for electricity generation was at least questionable. Distributive politics can also be seen to be significant in driving the scale of expansion of the system, as well as its nature. This triumph of distributive politics – so clearly evident in the bipartisan approach to Portland and Loy Yang – is not just the result of federal competition, as it was evident in our New Zealand case, although it has been observed elsewhere in a federal context.[107]

Moreover, it must be stressed that *political* factors determined the reform processes. The SECV was expansionary because it was encouraged to be so by successive governments from both sides of politics. It began on the path to reform to risk-sensitive planning and conservation because it was required to do so by the reformist Cain Labor Government elected in 1982. It failed to pursue these directions of reform not because it was able to throw off the political shackles but because the government was giving it contradictory directions, wanting it both to continue the reform process and to become a brown-coal-driven version of the HEC in Tasmania: a vehicle for industrial development based on low-cost public electricity. This pursuit of divergent goals simultaneously by governments is not uncommon[108] and is probably an important feature of the way governments respond to new demands. In the absence of strong pressure in favour of conservation, the distributive politics of development swamped most of the efforts at conservation-oriented regulatory reform. But once it became clear that, regardless of how much support there might be in the Latrobe Valley for such a course, further large-scale brown coal development could not be justified, conservation was accorded greater prominence – just in time to be displaced by privatisation as the dominant reform issue.

There was a certain dialectical flavour to this process. Competition from black coal at Oaklands was a significant factor in overriding the preference for within-state energy sources. However, the most important one was the belated establishment of a *de facto* south-east Australian power grid as the result of the spare capacity built into the Portland transmission line. Excessive ambition to build a four potline smelter there brought about the physical development that allowed economic rationality to prevail over political since – with the establishment of something resembling a market – brown coal could no longer compete with black when there was excess generating capacity in New South Wales.

This short-run economic rationality, of course, was the artefact of the politics that resulted in both the Portland transmission line and the excess capacity in New South Wales being built. However, regardless of its origins, it spelled the end for the era of brown coal development in the Latrobe Valley – and serious problems, too, for conservation, which will have to compete for some time to come with electricity at very low short-run marginal cost. Again, this is the result of political factors, not of the machinations of technocrats seeking to subvert their political master. The market-oriented institutions supplanting those of reverse adaptation are less than perfect when it comes to realising environmental or social goals but they are at least subject to further contestation rather than being predetermined by the technology employed or the technicians who employ it.

CHAPTER 7

Institutions and
electricity planning

'Politicians are the same the world over – they promise a
bridge, even when there is no river.'
Attributed to Nikita Kruschev

The cases we have examined here all point to the importance of distributive patterns of politics in supporting the reverse adaptation of electric
utilities and the significance of regulatory policies and agencies in bringing about reform. We shall shortly examine this conclusion in greater
detail, but an immediate question that comes to mind is whether we can
safely make such generalisations – whether our cases here are typical of
other utilities. While space does not permit us to probe other cases too
deeply, we can both confirm that the cases studied in depth here are not
atypical and briefly survey some other comparable utilities. At the same
time, this will allow us to examine some issues relating to demand-side
management before moving on to consider in some detail the nature of
reverse adaptation and some issues in institutional reform.

In the Canadian context we can point to similar patterns in distributive politics driving electricity planning in the provinces of Manitoba,
Saskatchewan and Alberta.[1] The starkest example of an unreconstructed
utility persisting in its distributive form is probably Hydro Quebec, where
the enormous hydroelectric potential of James Bay has been developed
largely for markets in the United States. Concern in the United States
over the impact of these developments on the environment and on
indigenous peoples has helped to transform the distributive regime
somewhat, and Hydro Quebec is moving to make public consultation a
permanent part of its planning process after finding that consultation
improved its 1993 development plan considerably.[2] There is hope of

160

reform, perhaps, even in Quebec, but there is also support for our observations in developments thus far.

In Australia, New South Wales was also caught up in the enthusiasm of Prime Minister Fraser's resources boom in the late 1970s with plans for the Lochinvar and Tomago aluminium smelters, expansion of the Kurri Kurri smelter and related power station construction at several sites in the state's Hunter Valley. Again, the pattern is one of distributive politics rather than of unchecked technocratic expansion. The state electrical utility, the Electricity Commission of New South Wales (or Elcom) initially was reluctant to implement the government's planned expansion program, but was *directed* to do so by the government.[3] This program called for the bringing forward of the commissioning of the 4×660 MW Eraring Power Station by one year to 1984 and the progressive commissioning of the 4×660 MW Bayswater and 2×660 MW Mount Piper stations by 1988. The government also directed that a 660 MW unit be installed at Tallawarra (near Wollongong) to maintain employment in that region.

As it happened, the 1980 forecast of 6 per cent load growth did not eventuate, the Lochinvar smelter proposal was cancelled and the construction program was slowed. The commissioning of Bayswater was not completed until 1987, and Mount Piper was deferred until 1992. Both were commissioned at a time of considerable surplus, despite the decommissioning of old capacity at Pyrmont, White Bay and Vales Point No 1 stations. The 1985 Elcom forecast showed a surplus of 8000 GWh in 1987 – about the capacity of Mount Piper.[4] Despite this surplus, Elcom argued in 1986 for a new 660 MW unit at a new site by the mid 1990s. Instead, the government established a Commission of Inquiry into Electricity Generation Planning. The commission's findings signalled the end of the developmental phase for Elcom since it led to an appreciation that the fifteen-year range of error in the utility's forecasts was about the output of one of its 4×660 MW stations – at a capital cost of about $2b. This was about the cost of the overinvestment in 1988.[5] Elcom would thus appear to have been as heavily reverse-adapted as the other utilities studied here, and this situation seems to have resulted from factors related to distributive politics.

Moreover, politics has been able to achieve reform. By 1991 Elcom had been restructured, and commissioners with a strong non-engineering background had been appointed.[6] The State Government had decided to establish three competitive generating groups and a ring-fenced transmission grid organisation within the ambit of a corporatised commission, which was named the Pacific Power Corporation of NSW Ltd. Each generating group would be free to sell power into a pool in open competition with IPPs. Between June 1988 and June 1991 Elcom had reduced its workforce from 10 600 to 6700. It had decommissioned inefficient plant at Wallerawang, Vales Point and Munmorah.[7]

An Electricity Council of New South Wales, established in 1987 to coordinate initiatives within the New South Wales electric supply industry, was working together with Elcom in 1991 to develop a DSM strategy relevant to New South Wales conditions.[8] Under expected load growth projections no new base-load plant was required in the New South Wales system until about 2005.[9] The privatisation of Pacific Power was deferred after the government failed to win an outright majority in the 1991 state election, but the government increased its revenues from the utility's earnings with a vengeance from $150m to $700m a year.[10] Again, distributive politics lay behind the expansionary phase, and regulatory politics was able to put an end to the reverse adaptation.

A similar pattern of distributive politics driving electricity planning was also evident in Queensland in the 1980s. There, it was decided to build the 4×350 MW Tarong Power Station, the 2×350 MW Callide B Power Station and 4×350 MW Stanwell Power Station to cater for a four-potline Boyne Island smelter to be built at Gladstone by Comalco and its partners, and a smelter proposed by Alcan for a site at Bundaberg. In the event Comalco built two rather than the planned four potlines at Boyne Island, and Alcan cancelled all three. The resulting overcapacity weakened considerably the government's bargaining position in the sale of electricity to Comalco and others. The rationale was that it was better to sell the capacity and receive some income than receive none at all.[11]

What has been absent in Queensland up to the time of writing has been any strong political push for reform. There has been some change, with the Gladstone power station sold into private ownership, but even that act can be seen as a continuation of distributive policy. The station was purchased by Comalco to supply an expanded Boyne Island smelter. However, while the sale might have been stimulated in part by moves towards the establishment of a south-east Australian grid, with open access for private generators, Comalco was given very favourable terms by the government in order to secure the smelter development. Further, government guarantees for the sale of electricity in excess of smelter demand were sought by Comalco's financiers and granted by the Queensland Government, thus undermining the move towards the establishment of a competitive market.

Similar guarantees were provided in the sale of the Loy Yang B power station to Mission Energy in Victoria. They were also sought in Western Australia where the government aimed to interest private investors in building a new coal-fired station. Plans for a privately owned $2 billion Collie power station all but collapsed after the Western Australian

Government maintained it would not make any form of guarantee.[12] One consortium failed to find finance at acceptable rates, leaving Asea Brown Boveri as the sole players, but they ran into similar problems and the banking community constantly pushed for concessions the ALP State Government found unacceptable. The incoming Liberal–National Coalition Government later cancelled the project, replacing it instead with a $500m 300 MW station to be owned by State Energy Commission but run by the private sector.[13] These events reflected distributive politics dominating the electricity planning process, however, with the employment benefits accruing from coal-fired developments distorting government decisionmaking, but with the government seeking to involve the private sector.[14]

South Australia has been less afflicted by reverse adaptation in its electricity planning than the other Australian states, thanks to the relative paucity of its energy resources. It was tempted in the mid 1980s to rely on its difficult and expensive indigenous subbituminous coals for future electricity supply, but the excess capacity in the Victorian system was eventually to prevent that. The excess transmission capacity to supply the Portland smelter meant that the Victorian and South Australian systems were very close to being interconnected, and the logical step to intertie the two systems (and provide South Australia with purchased imports) was taken. Because the New South Wales and Victorian systems were interconnected through the Snowy Mountains hydroelectric scheme, this resulted in the interconnection of the three south-eastern states for the first time.

The interconnection of the power supply helped to break down barriers between the states that had been quite deliberately maintained so as to favour within-state sources of generation. One is reminded here of a similar lack of resolve to deal with the rail gauge problem in Australia,[15] since such barriers to free trade were functional for states in a federation in which tariff was prohibited. The highly centralised nature of the Australian states can also be seen to have contributed to the absence of interconnection, since transmission lines tended to run towards capital cities where the load was concentrated and away from state borders. Following an inquiry by the Industry Commission in 1991, and in a new spirit of cooperation among the states fostered by then Prime Minister Bob Hawke, agreement to establish a south-eastern Australia grid was reached. The grid will be transparent, and open competition between generators will be possible for the first time. One immediate consequence has been the end of future plans for capacity expansion in Victoria in the face of the considerable overcapacity in New South Wales. Another has been to hasten the drive to reform in Victoria.

All of this raises questions about the effects of these moves towards the imposition of market discipline on Australian utilities. It is too early to do little more than speculate on the outcome, but the effect on Victoria has been significant. In addition to transferring its transmission assets to National Electricity, the Victorian Government decided to split the SECV into Generation Victoria and Electricity Services Victoria in 1993.[16] The government's plans are for the SECV's generating capacity to remain under a single umbrella, but each generating unit will trade independently in a relatively lightly regulated market and might ultimately be privatised as individual companies.[17] The transmission grid will remain state-owned, but there will be five regionally based distribution companies, which will own and operate the low-voltage lines. Line and energy charges will be separated to give customers access to the different entities.

But reform in Australia has been patchy. In New South Wales the privatisation of Pacific Power has been deferred, while the incoming Liberal Government in South Australia merged the Electricity Trust of South Australia and the Engineering and Water Supply Department rather than privatise either.[18] In Western Australia the Liberal Government decided to separate the gas and electricity arms of the State Energy Commission.

This raises some interesting questions about the fate of demand-side management in such restructured institutions. While there is some controversy over whether DSM should be pursued by utilities, it does appear to offer both reductions in uncertainty costs and a means of addressing global problems of energy use (such as acid rain and the greenhouse effect) by reducing fossil fuel consumption. While it is by no means a panacea, the fate of such an approach in the face of market-oriented reforms should be of concern to policymakers.

One issue with DSM is how the costs of programs should be apportioned when energy uses such as space heating might be provided by different sources. Should an electric utility fund conservation measures (such as insulation) that might impact on gas demand *or* electricity demand? Or should it confine such programs to energy uses (such as lighting or motors) that can be met only by electricity? If we accept that markets alone are the appropriate institutional mechanisms for making social choices, we are likely to hold the latter position; if we consider that markets have imperfections, and that some costs and benefits cannot be captured by markets, we are likely to hold that there is a case for electric utilities fostering conservation even when the benefits might lead to lower gas consumption rather than lower uncertainty costs for the electric utility. The old energy commission in Western Australia at least allowed sector-wide issues to be considered. As we have seen in the

Victorian case, the establishment of separate business units has already resulted in the demand management benefits of reducing uncertainty costs being turned into externalities for the distribution group and beyond the control of the generation planners.

The relationship between ownership and conservation in electric utilities is problematic. Private ownership is capable of redressing some of the worst excesses of the old reverse-adapted electric utilities, but it should not be seen as a solution to *all* the issues that pertain to electricity. While least-cost utility planning and open competitive access to electricity grids will lead to efficiencies, market-based solutions are going to result in high rates of discount being used in evaluations. This will favour (and has favoured in the United Kingdom) gas over coal, hydro and nuclear capacity, and will skew the pattern of future generation. This will extend to choices on the demand side as well as the supply side, as was recognised in the Victorian context by the Demand Management Development Project:

> The significant difference in the required rate of return on new investment by private industry and private individuals compared with the SECV for its core business activities explains why there is a significant amount of energy saving potential which is cost-effective from a societal perspective. Direct public sector investment in the installation of energy efficient equipment must therefore be seriously considered.[19]

In a nutshell, society cares more about posterity than do private investors. Society rightly cares about whether gas supplies in one nation might be depleted over fifteen years, but capital is largely indifferent to results that far into the future, and it will happily move on to investments in other sectors (or even other nations) if no further opportunities exist. The same point applies to issues such as global warming resulting from the combustion of fossil fuels. No market can capture societal concern over issues relating to the global commons.

Nevertheless, there has been a tendency for approaches such as that in the Industry Commission report in Australia to ignore differences in perspective between society, industry and individual consumers. The Industry Commission report attributed the failure of consumers to adopt conservation to ignorance and recommended education programs. This attitude ignores research indicating that consumers apply high discount rates to the savings flowing from investments in conservation technology.[20] A neoclassical economic prescription that there ought not be differences between the discount rates of individuals, private firms and society appears to have taken precedence over research indicating that there are such differences – and, ironically, the notion that consumers best know their own interests has been overturned in the process. The Industry Commission approach also ignores research indicating the predominance of social factors such as lifestyle over economic factors in energy use decisions.[21]

Least-cost planning would, therefore, appear to have a place in electric utilities regardless of their ownership structure, but there is some controversy over the future for demand-side management programs – both whether there is a need for them and whether they are effective. As we have seen, there is a justification for DSM if one lacks confidence that markets are adequate as social choice mechanisms, and, while some doubts have been raised about their effectiveness, such programs seem to have acceptance even at the commercial level for utilities in reducing uncertainty costs. After some DSM programs showed good short-run returns, followed by some disappointing results, some of the innovative programs were slowed considerably or stopped entirely.

Nevertheless, DSM is still seen as having considerable potential that has not yet been tapped,[22] and most of the savings so far have been in capacity rather than energy. DSM programs in the US have produced peak demand reductions of about 5 per cent but energy savings of only about 0.6 per cent. Interestingly, the cost of achieving these savings has been less for public utilities than for investor-owned utilities.[23] Even so, the consensus among US utility executives seems to be that DSM produces significant savings and is worthwhile financially.[24]

The benefits of DSM will continue to be debated. Let us now move on to consider what we can learn from our study about reverse adaptation and the process of institutional reform.

Reverse adaptation

Winner has argued that five features characterise what we might call the aggregate patterns of reverse adaptation. We can use these five features as a basis for an initial discussion of our five case studies.

The first characteristic of reverse adaptation Winner identifies is that '*The system controls markets relevant to its operations*'.[25] For Winner, the combination of planning and vertical integration can reduce the capacity of consumers for independence of action, especially by suspending the market through contract. As J.K. Galbraith has noted, sophisticated technologies such as those involved in modern electricity generation increase the time between the beginning of a task and its completion, require great amounts of capital, bring an inflexible commitment of resources, and require specialised staff and a highly developed organisation. As a result planning assumes a central importance, and all possible steps must be taken to 'insure that what is ultimately foreseen eventuates in fact'.[26] What develops is what Galbraith termed a 'technostructure', which by various means 'controls both supply and demand and thereby eliminates the sordid perils of the market'.[27]

We can point here to the extent of vertical integration of electricity supply in Tasmania, clearly the most reverse-adapted of the utilities studied. There, the HEC controlled generation, transmission and distribution and was able to control not just forecasts of future demand but also for many years the actual demand, by means of contracts for bulk industrial sales on terms very favourable to industry. This use of contracts to control markets, particularly to improve load factors, has long been important in the expansion of electric systems,[28] and the sales (or anticipated sales) to aluminium smelters were significant factors in the New Zealand and Victorian cases. In British Columbia, where Alcan supplied its Kitimat smelter from its own generating capacity, it was the province's pulp and paper industry that constituted the significant group of industrial consumers. It might be that the somewhat lesser energy-intensiveness of that industry facilitated reform to end reverse adaptation. We should also note that Ontario Hydro neither controlled retail distribution nor made significant bulk industrial sales, although it could also be argued that for many years it represented those distribution interests.

Nevertheless, leaving aside the question of electricity-intensive industry, the monopoly generating and transmission position of the utilities in question allowed them to structure tariffs in such a way as to encourage demand growth to match supply, usually by means of cross-subsidies between classes of consumers. Thus high prices were often charged to those with inelastic demand and lower prices for those with elastic demand. Even so, we cannot get very far in attempting to explain the historical performance of Ontario Hydro, for example, in terms of vertical integration and market control.

Winner's second characteristic of reverse adaptation is that *'The system controls or strongly influences the political processes that ostensibly regulate its output and operating conditions'.* Winner notes that 'the best examples of this genre come from public agencies able to write their own tickets, for example, the [United States] Army Corps of Engineers'.[29] It is clear that the autonomy and political influence of the HEC, SECV, BC Hydro and Ontario Hydro were significant factors in the adaptation of those utilities to growth. But how then do we explain the New Zealand Electricity Department, which operated under full ministerial responsibility? It might be argued that the NZED and the supply authorities were able to use their control over technical knowledge to minimise the ability of the politicians to scrutinise the electricity planners. However, this argument can be countered by saying that the inherent dangers in the planners' ambition were highlighted in the view of other government agencies (the Commission for Energy Resources, Treasury and Department of Statistics). These danger signs were not heeded by politicians because they preferred not to see them and instead favoured development.

The third characteristic of reverse adaptation is that *'The system seeks a "mission" to match its technological capabilities'*. In Winner's words, 'Unlike the fabled Alexander, therefore, it does not weep for new worlds to conquer. It sets about creating them'.[30] This description best fits the HEC, which would often make claims that its 'team' should be kept intact. It even loaded the thermal option with the cost of the redundancy payments associated with not keeping the team together. In New Zealand the civil engineering construction workforce was in a different agency, the Ministry of Works and Development, and this argument was not so apparent. With the SECV, BC Hydro and Ontario Hydro it was no more than implicit. The argument to 'Give the system something to do'[31] was thus not always articulated explicitly, but it was implicit in the SECV case at least in the desire to ensure employment continuity in the Latrobe Valley.

Next, Winner argues, reverse adaptation exists when *'The system propagates or manipulates the needs it also serves'*.[32] Most of the utilities we have studied here have been involved to some extent in the active marketing of their product, although clearly those having vertical integration with retail distribution have been more so. There is, of course, little wrong with this unless one subscribes to the view that advertising can promote false needs, but there is very definitely a problem when this characteristic is combined with the next: *'The system discovers or creates a crisis to justify its own further expansion'*.[33] Winner uses the case of electric utilities promoting electricity use and then 'discovering' a shortage that must be met as 'double reverse adaptation'.[34] We have seen here that many of the utilities studied exhibited triple, quadruple or even quintuple reverse adaptation. Winner argues that, regardless of whether a real shortage exists, the important thing is that the system

> command a virtual monopoly of information concerning the situation and can use this monopoly for self-justification. Persons and groups outside usually do not have access to or interest in the information necessary to scrutinise the 'need' in a critical way.[35]

This situation is most apparent in those systems (such as in Tasmania) where the utility dominates the forecasting process. The danger is greatest where forecasts are produced only when an attempt is being made to justify a particular development proposal rather than on an annual (or some other regular) basis. Yet, again, New Zealand had annual published forecasts and did not escape reverse adaptation, so what are we to make of this feature? The key to avoiding reverse adaptation (and achieving reform) would seem to lie in Winner's remark that outsiders 'do not have access to *or interest in* the information necessary to scrutinise the "need" in a critical way' (emphasis added).

The participation of outsiders in the forecasting and planning process is an issue to which we shall return presently, but we should first note the general issue of which this qualification is subsidiary. The point is that the five features of reverse adaptation alone are not enough to explain fully the patterns revealed in our five cases, both the past patterns of behaviour and the reform processes. In short, Winner tends to ignore the politics and some organisational factors that support reverse adaptation. These are factors that determine whether there will be interest in scrutinising the forecasts and plans of electric utilities.

The key to understanding the patterns of utility performance in our case studies – and how change was possible – is to appreciate that each enjoyed strong political support, and reverse adaptation is probably not possible without such political support. And the fact that reforms to end reverse adaptation were possible when politicians decided such were needed reinforces this point. What we have with the utilities we have examined, therefore, is not so much a case of technological determinism (or autonomous technology) but a set of institutions adapted to particular ends – reverse-adapted, yes, but only because of the support embedded deeply in the politics of development and able to be redeemed through changes in the supporting political apparatus. A cross-sectional study of a number of reverse-adapted institutions would be unlikely to pick up this perspective, since the importance of political factors in sustaining the reverse adaptation would be only implicit. It is made more obvious in our present study because it is a longitudinal study of change, so the factors supporting the *status quo* and producing change are much more apparent.

In chapter 1 we saw that Fischer posed the question of whether it was possible to build genuinely democratic institutions in a technological society, whether it is 'possible to establish a public community capable of engendering a political conversation between the rulers and the ruled?'[36] Our cases suggest that we could answer this question with at least a 'perhaps'. Participation is, indeed, one key to this process, as is changing the nature of the agencies themselves. Let us now turn to examine these key political factors.

Politics and reverse adaptation

Winner concedes the point that a reverse-adapted system relies on political support. He notes that such a system 'requires its own means: the resources, freedom, and social power to continue its work. It needs, among other things, an atmosphere of laws and regulations to facilitate rather than limit its ability to act'.[37] The point has also been made by Thomas Hughes who notes, in his study of the economic history of the electricity industry, that the momentum of these sociotechnical systems (which led to technical and social conservatism) stemmed from 'their institutionally structured nature, heavy capital investments, supportive legislation, and the commitment of know-how and experience'.[38]

The clear picture that emerges from our case studies here is not one of technological determinism nor of autonomous technology but rather one of strong support for reverse adaptation resulting from the distributive politics that favour development. In each case there was a tendency, to a greater or lesser extent, for politicians to see expansion of the electric system as a means of fostering the development of their state, province or nation.

Tasmania lies at one extreme, with both the industries attracted by cheap power and the dam-building process itself serving this role. In New Zealand the attractions of large development projects were enough to overwhelm institutional arrangements that we might have expected to guard against reverse adaptation. In this case federalism was not a factor, indicating that the peripheral location in the world economy of both New Zealand and the Australian states might be more significant than interstate competition in explaining developmental politics in Australia. (We might include Canada here also, since Quebec was successful in attracting smelter investment from the French company Pechiney, which had also been a player in New Zealand, Victoria and New South Wales; footloose Alusuisse also wandered the political landscape of Victoria, New South Wales and New Zealand looking for a home.) Politics in British Columbia was also driven by the desire to foster development, particularly of the province's forest resources, while in Ontario the program of nuclear expansion served both the Ontario uranium industry and the national ambition to develop CANDU technology. In Victoria the government's continued perception throughout the 1980s that the state's ability to provide cheap electricity provided an important policy instrument to attract industry was the factor that limited the extent of reform.

As we saw in chapter 1, Theodore J. Lowi has provided an analytical framework that is useful in understanding these issues because it relates the politics of development to the features of agencies involved in such policymaking – in this case, the electric utilities. To recap, Lowi holds that pursuing distinctively different policies requires distinctive kinds of agencies so that the change in policy from one type to another will be accompanied – and will have to be accompanied – by a change in administrative regime.[39] Each distinctive kind of policy will thus generate a distinctive arena of power. In Lowi's terms, developmental policies of subsidy and public works (or 'pork barrel') are 'distributive' whereas those involving the balancing of development goals with environmental or other values are 'regulatory'. Each will give rise to distinctive agency characteristics.

Recall that Lowi suggests that distributive agencies have few integrative rules of conduct because the type of policies they deal with do not require consistency, and they are affected by this 'absence of responsibility for imposing authoritative rules'.[40] Common professional training is relied on to provide consistency in the absence of rules requiring consistency and dealing with the problem of coordination. Reliance is placed on decision rules rather than formal legal procedure (in comparison to regulatory agencies), and the top management positions are therefore likely to be filled by technical specialists. The archetypal distributive agency is that described by Kaufman (1960) in his classic study of the US forest service.[41] In the US Forest Service the common professional training of foresters was significant; with electric utilities it is engineering. Galbraith has made a similar point in noting that in the 'technostructure' cooperation is achieved because of the similar training of the technocrats, which produces 'technical soul brothers'.[42]

An example of the importance of common training comes from France where the Planning Bureau mediates between the forecasts of Electricité de France and the Ministry of Finance and other large public sector energy suppliers, 'But the quarrel remains entirely within the family of graduates from the élite engineering schools'.[43] Few nations have training institutions that quite parallel the *grandes écoles* in France. However, the dominance of engineers in the managerial ranks of utilities, and in many cases on their governing boards, is indicative of the distributive agency type in which little reliance is placed on external accountability mechanisms because little reliance is needed when the agency is serving widely accepted development goals.

Traditionally, there has been a considerable element of subsidisation in most publicly owned utilities as a result of their access to public resources (such as rivers for hydro capacity, or brown coal), subsidised capital, government guaranteed loans and exemptions from various taxes.[44] 'Such subsidies obviously conflict with energy conservation goals.'[45] In reforming utilities so as to require them to pay attention to conservation and other environmental factors, or to economic risks, politicians are imposing regulatory policies that override the old distributive operating rationales. This requires a different kind of agency – one that operates in accordance with external rules and that requires procedural rather than technical expertise. The imposition of the discipline of the market can be (and has been) one way of imposing this external regulation.[46]

Regulatory agencies, Lowi maintains, are responsible for applying 'rules imposing obligations on individuals, and providing punishment for non-compliance'.[47] This requires that administrators know the rules and share interpretations about when and how to apply them. The need for consistency among cases makes administrative precedent important. Such agencies will be rule-bound rather than being bound by tradition, authority, status or hierarchy. It is no coincidence, then, that Roberts and Bluhm found greater receptiveness to environmental regulation in utilities in which lawyers rather than engineers occupied the executive heights.[48]

What Lowi's perspective suggests is that an end to reverse adaptedness among utilities will require an end to engineering dominance and the introduction of new modes of rationality – especially procedural and economic rationality. The treatment of electricity forecasting and planning as a technical matter, to be approached by methods such as statistical projection, rather than one subject to uncertainty, social construction and contestation by competing interests, is a key component of reverse adaptation. Recognition of the latter components, and the imposition of different modes of rationality, is an important component of reform. This might, as Baumgartner and Midttun note, explain the somewhat better track record of energy forecasting in the United States, where the process is open and contested, and often subject to market discipline, rather than being undertaken by agencies with a monopoly not just of supply but also of forecasting expertise.[49]

We have seen that the reforms at BC Hydro and Ontario Hydro involved the replacement of engineering dominance by organisational forms that privileged other disciplinary skills backgrounds such as economics and business. This kind of change was less marked at the SECV, where the extent of reform was correspondingly less marked (until the new changes following the change of government in 1992). We should note also that the regulatory pressures brought to bear in each of the Canadian cases was price regulation rather than rate-of-return regulation, which the Averch–Johnson hypothesis tells us will lead to gold-plating or overbuilding.

All of this suggests that the key to reforming electric utilities lies in the imposition of market discipline on utilities, or the imposition of some kind of effective regulatory control – or both. As we have seen earlier, there are some difficulties in accepting that markets can be relied on totally to achieve conservation and other environmental and social objectives – at least without substantial corrections for market failures associated with externalities and utility and consumer myopia over the benefits of conservation. Not that market-based reforms and regulation are necessarily mutually exclusive options, but if regulation is to prevail over the seductive distributive attractions of development, how is such reform to be achieved? As alluded to earlier, opening the institutions of electricity planning up to outside participation appears to be one key possibility.

A model of organisational change has been suggested by Mazmanian and Nienaber in their study of an engineering agency, the US Army Corps of Engineers, in responding to the imposition of environmental constraints – a shift from distribution to regulation closely analogous with our cases here.[50] They argue that organisations exist in equilibrium and need to move to a new equilibrium point 'in keeping with changing public needs and wishes'.[51] They suggest that the cycle of change begins when sovereigns, clientele groups or others important to an agency voice new demands. No organisation is totally homogeneous so some insiders will become sensitive to the need for change, particularly since they will see change as a means of survival.

We might add that those who are disgruntled by the *status quo* are more likely to be receptive to change since those who are in entrenched positions will fear loss of power or position from any change. There are limits to how far we can take this explanation of resistance to change in organisations because it assumes that those in positions of authority have reached their zenith or will not benefit further from change. The significant point for Mazmanian and Nienaber's cycle, however, is that there is likely to be an increase in conflict between members of the organisation. (Their expression is 'overt tension', but conflict is probably a more common response.)

At this stage those seeking change must 'emancipate' the organisation from the tangle of rules and regulations that hold it in its present structure. First, however, the agents of change must establish trust on the part of their colleagues that they will respect the traditional values and missions of the organisation, not embarrass their superiors and colleagues, and not reflect poorly on the organisation. Unless this trust is established, Mazmanian and Nienaber maintain, 'attempts to change will invariably be subverted from within, irrespective of the formal authority of the change-seekers'.[52]

The change-seekers must then identify their goals with a process-related concept in an open planning process. A catchphrase or buzzword will help in this process of communicating the goals. 'The message to those inside and outside the organisation is clear: the organisation is seriously rethinking its traditional missions and is searching for goals more compatible with the needs of its changing external environment.'[53] LCUP and DSM can provide the 'process-related concepts' necessary for change, but so too can the language of the market.

What is required next is reorganisation to disrupt traditional patterns of behaviour. Reorganisation will disrupt the established chain of command, the status ordering and the patterns of communications existing in the organisation. Such reorganisation can also disrupt the unofficial constraints that make up the informal systems of power and communication, which are otherwise hard to manipulate. External recruitment of new staff who can be socialised into the new organisation can also be helpful here.

There is little prospect of change within the organisation persisting, however, unless the forces in the external environment that helped sustain the previous organisation are altered. This is, therefore, the stage at which the organisation seeks new client groups in the private sector as consumers and in the public sector as potential beneficiaries of the new services. Mazmanian and Nienaber see a major difference between public and private agencies in this process because, unlike private agencies, public agencies must contend with those who actually or potentially are opposed to their activities. 'For public agencies, then, part of the change effort rests on public participation and citizen input as major strategies.'[54] Focus on public input can be to placate previously hostile groups or to provide broad-based support for the new mission – or to establish agency credibility and legitimacy. The price for this support is a basic reformulation of its decisionmaking processes, with less centralised control over decision processes as a result.

Finally, 'Once the new missions are identified and new groups are granted access to agency decisions, a new equilibrium, albeit often uneasy, is established'.[55] This is not to say that all controversies have been resolved, simply that a new level of accommodation has been achieved. This dynamic process of readjustment occurs repeatedly and is simply 'the process of mutual adjustment that occurs between an agency and its attentive publics in a changing world'.[56]

The experience in British Columbia and Ontario suggests that utility regulation, and the access to the forecasting and planning processes it provided, played a crucial role in aligning the two electric utilities to the new priorities of environmental quality and conservation. It also made them aware of the uncertainty costs of overcapacity and the role of energy options other than large, centralised generating capacity in reducing these costs by reducing lead times.

The regulatory process was helpful in realigning BC Hydro to the new uncertain environment, although it was by no means a sufficient cause of the changes. But the Ontario experience suggests that neither is effective formal utility regulation a necessary cause of utility responsiveness. What does appear to be common to both cases, however – and this is borne out by Mazmanian and Nienaber – is the importance of opening up the decisionmaking processes to the public in bringing about agency realignment. This was supported by the views of Ontario Hydro staff expressed to the author. The extensive public consultation undertaken by Ontario Hydro – even if it was intended only to legitimise plans for further nuclear capacity – for the first time brought the utility's system planners into contact with the public, and the engineers found their assumptions open to challenge and debate. They gained some idea of what the public thought and were somewhat surprised by it.

The Site C decision in British Columbia was a more dramatic shock for the planners there because the Utilities Commission found that it could not accept the forecast of demand and the recommendation that consumers should pay for a large dam rather than lower-cost conservation. Denial of the opportunity to build Site C brought BC Hydro's reverse adaptation to a juddering halt. Ontario Hydro took somewhat longer to stop, perhaps because being larger it had more momentum, partly because there was no sudden denial of authorisation to construct, but mainly because of the gradual overwhelming of its plans by political and demand growth realities it could no longer control. Ontario Hydro had been under almost relentless siege by groups such as Energy Probe for two decades. In Victoria, there was not the same concerted pressure brought to bear by the more significant environmental groups. None even made submissions to the NREC inquiry to counter the developmental mentality that amounted to an only slightly weaker version of Tasmania's hydroindustrialisation.

Roberts and Bluhm have suggested that 'outsiders trying to coerce an organisation, especially one with a weak control system, may have to threaten its very survival if their external pressure is to be effectively transmitted to individual decision makers'.[57] There is nothing like a crisis to bring about change, but Roberts and Bluhm note that it is not certain how large a crisis is required and what kind of changes will result. Moreover, because of the time constraint inherent in crisis, such a set of circumstances can 'produce an *increased* reliance on traditional habits of mind and rules of thumb, for both cognitive and psychodynamic reasons'.[58] Substantive changes to the structure of the organisation might follow only after the crisis has passed.

Despite these reservations, all the utilities studied here underwent sweeping reform only after they encountered substantial threats to their existence. In New Zealand the reforms were part of a sweeping program of market-based reform across the public sector. The New Zealand Electricity Department ceased to exist. In Tasmania the HEC was reformed because it was no longer the authoritative development agency it had been; its forecasts and its credibility were in tatters. BC Hydro ran up against unfavourable regulation at a time of fiscal restraint, which reinforced the Utilities Commission's decision. Reform here was sudden, swift and fundamental. The SECV underwent radical change only when the prospect of the emergence of national competition meant that future power stations would not be able to compete with surplus capacity in New South Wales. It also faced mounting debt. Until then, the thrust for reform was limited by the government's belief that cheap electricity was a reliable tool of industrial development. Ironically, Ontario Hydro was turned around with less organisational trauma than most other utilities studied, largely because the absence of real demand growth rather than some regulatory agency thwarted its plans.

Directions for reform

Electric utility regulation can be seen as having assisted in the development of flexible strategic planning by BC Hydro and Ontario Hydro. The process of conducting open public hearings, with widely dispersed rights of intervention both in setting rates and in deciding on capital expansion, would appear to be useful even if (as in the case of the Ontario Energy Board) regulation is not effective in a formal sense.

While this contrasts with the traditional view that effective regulation is usually thwarted by agency capture, there have been other favourable reports about the effectiveness of regulation in North America.[59] California is one state in which regulation has played an important role in aiding the shift towards giving conservation a role in strategic planning.[60] But regulatory commissions can discourage sound planning by insisting on historical cost recovery rather than marginal cost pricing in rate setting, and often they have threatened to penalise utilities to force them to meet reliability criteria, usually in the absence of least cost planning methodologies.[61] 'The regulatory response to these new strategies has, for the most part, been one of uncertainty, with inconsistent actions by different regulatory bodies.'[62]

It is clear from our cases that provision for meaningful public involvement in the process of strategic planning has a vital role to play in ensuring the responsiveness of electrical utilities. This participation will become increasingly important, not just because of higher uncertainty costs in their planning horizons but also because of new constraints, such as the need to meet public demands for energy conservation and higher environmental quality, and related questions, such as limiting total emissions of greenhouse gases. Utilities in Australia generally appear to be some distance behind their Canadian counterparts in public involvement in planning, in responsive and environmentally responsible strategic planning, and in pursuing conservation and non-conventional energy sources as a means of coping with a number of challenges, including long lead times under conditions of uncertainty and greenhouse gas emissions.

The Australian states have moved rapidly to place their utilities on a more commercial footing, with some limited privatisation, but (as we have seen) there is no guarantee that either private utilities or private consumers will make socially optimal choices about energy consumption and conservation. Indeed, the two most notable examples of privatisation (the sale of the Gladstone power station in Queensland and the partial sale of Loy Yang B in Victoria) have both proceeded only after the conclusion of agreements (at the insistence of financiers) whereby the government guarantees the purchase of their output. Many market-oriented reforms do coincide with the ending of reverse adaptation. However, it would be simplistic to assume that the market can do it all, especially when important factors of production are not included as market goods and there are issues at stake that extend well beyond the concern of any market.

Market mechanisms form part – but only part – of the institutional repertoire for reform, and there are several other institutional issues that need to be addressed. One such problem is the question of whether one utility (electric, for example) should 'purchase conservation' when the reduction in energy use might be felt most in another utility's sphere of activity, for example, when gas is used for domestic space heating. There are numerous possible ways of dealing with the problem, including coordination (and funding) by a central policy agency or (more radically) the approach of energy service companies, such as those that have operated in France for more than fifty years.[63] Under this arrangement the company contracts with the consumer to provide specified levels of energy service – heating, lighting or traction, for example – and then provides that service at least cost. The incentive to achieve conservation is built into the firm's structure. Competition between energy service companies for profits and market share can result in an institutional bias towards conservation and the selection of appropriate energy sources and technology that exists neither with traditional utility arrangements nor with the regional distribution monopolies proposed for Victoria in 1994.

Such an arrangement might seem rather radical, but the fact remains that 'consumers do not really buy electricity – they buy light, heat for cooking their meals, hot water for bathing, comfort through air conditioning or heating, and what it takes to run a host of different kinds of appliances and machines'.[64]

Kennedy has suggested that one way for utilities to deal with alternative energy sources and conservation is to enter these markets themselves, as BC Hydro and Ontario Hydro have done. Utilities could become active in marketing conservation, but the problem would still remain that the social and environmental benefits of conservation would not coincide with the benefits for each utility. Further, rebates and subsidies on energy-efficient appliances could come to be used as marketing devices to increase market share for each utility.

It would be preferable to establish institutions capable of providing both public scrutiny of energy prices and the costs of energy conserved, and measuring the cost of 'negawatts' (including social and environmental costs and uncertainty costs) against additions to capacity. Such institutions must also make available to governments (independently of the gas and electricity utilities) options allowing social choices about the level of socially and environmentally desirable conservation, rather than the level that is in the best interests of each utility to pursue. Such institutions could provide for public contributions to the strategic planning process and could assess options for governments on matters such as tariffs and additions to capacity – and on which energy sources should be encouraged for particular purposes. What is needed is a set of institutions that will clarify the choices involved rather than – as has usually been the case – institutions that obscure the assumptions and preferences embedded deeply in their forecasting and planning approaches. As Louis Puiseux has pointed out, 'The real role of the expert planner should be . . . to propose possible alternatives from which one can choose through a political process'.[65]

Contesting the future

Langdon Winner has argued that to ignore the demands of crucial technological systems that provide essential goods and services, or to leave them insufficiently fulfilled, 'is to attack the very foundations on which modern social order rests'.[66] Louis Puiseux concurs, arguing that:

> The demand for transparency in energy forecasting is part of the more general problem of the social control of technological development ... Yesterday, the struggle was over the division of the productivity gains. What is at stake today is nothing less than control over the content of modernity.[67]

These are bold claims, and Puiseux in particular is undoubtedly describing an example *in extremis* in France, with the nuclear ambitions of EdF. However, they are claims that have a ring of truth even when we are talking about electricity systems that rely heavily on energy sources as long-standing and relatively benign as hydraulic energy. Michael Pusey, for example, has argued that the prestige of the Australian state relies 'on images of huge infrastructural engineering, energy, and resource projects of the Snowy Mountains Authority, and, more problematically, on the centrally driven social reforms and interventions of the early 1970s'. Further, he argues, 'Prestige of this kind is bound up with ideas of modernity and modernisation that are increasingly problematic'.[68]

Modernism was earlier seen as positivistic, technocentric and rationalistic, and was identified with the belief in linear progress, absolute truths, the rational planning of ideal social orders and the standardisation of both knowledge and production.[69] That description fits the image of the traditional electric utility like a glove; indeed, electricity is a creature of the modern age. Harvey sees a new postmodern regime of accumulation, resting on flexibility of labour processes, labour markets, products and patterns of consumption, and characterised by new sectors of production, new markets and 'greatly intensified rates of commercial, technological and organisational innovation'.[70] This age of uncertainty has brought the old approaches to electricity planning undone as well as providing the technology to meet this need for flexibility. Technological advances on the supply side have overcome the difficulties of high uncertainty costs resulting from large generating units, and allowed a role for small independent power producers, often utilising waste energy. Demand-side technology has offered alternatives to new generation with lower uncertainty costs and, therefore, often lower total costs than traditional demand-side responses. And planning technology facilitated by advances in information processing has both made possible approaches such as LCUP and democratised the planning process by, for example, providing utility critics with the capacity to verify, and in some cases undermine, utility forecasts and economic evaluations.

As we noted in chapter 1, it has been argued that the engineering profession has served only the dominant class in society – the capitalist class.[71] It was pointed out, however, that this is but one of four models of technocracy. The others are 'benevolent technocracy', rule by a self-interested élite and an 'autonomous technology' model.[72] We have tended here to reject the notion of technology existing beyond political support and control and, while there is ample evidence that the engineering élite in most utilities has been self-interested and often far from benign, the picture that emerges in relation to electric utilities is one of 'servants of power'. Whether or not one sees – as do Noble and Christie[73] – power residing with the capitalist class, this is an image of a technocracy subject (at least in principle) to control by political institutions. As we have seen, such control is problematic and tenuous, but at least it is open to contest, so that the image (applied to Ontario Hydro in the 1920s) of electric utilities as 'political Frankensteins', beyond the control of their masters, is not entirely adequate.

If what is at stake is control over the content of modernity, then (as this study shows) we must go beyond the technological dimension to examine the context created by the economic, social and political institutions that support the existing system. For, as Hughes has noted,

> Attempting to reform technology without systematically taking into account the shaping context and the intricacies of internal dynamics may well be futile. If only the technical components of a system are changed, they may snap back into their earlier shape like charged particles in a strong electromagnetic field.

The field must be attended to; values may need to be changed, institutions reformed, or legislation recast.[74]

Robert Paehlke has argued that this concern with the content of technology – with the technological shape of future society – is what distinguishes environmental politics from other progressive movements with which it has some affinity.[75] The task for environmentalists, then, is to design and construct institutions that will not promote high levels of energy consumption where conservation is not only possible but also often cheaper, and which will not lead inexorably to the reliance of societies on centralised electric power systems – systems that ultimately will necessitate nuclear technology or will pay little regard to issues such as global warming.

Continuing Hughes' analogy, our ability as a society to influence choices about what kind of future we share will depend crucially on our ability to develop a kind of institutional 'quantum mechanics' so as to be able to alter the arrangement of institutional particles by rearranging the political field. This study has done no more than identify some of the particles and a few of the forces.

Glossary and abbreviations

ALP   Australian Labor Party.

assessed system average capacity   The expression used to refer to the 'firm' energy capacity of a hydroelectric or mixed hydrothermal system; the level of demand that can reliably be supplied in the long term.

average long-term hydro energy output   The average annual non-firm energy output of a hydroelectric system or the hydroelectric component of a mixed hydrothermal system; cannot necessarily be supplied in all years without a thermal station providing a firming role.

avoided cost   Particularly in demand-side management and the supply of electricity from independent power producers, the cost that does not have to be paid by the utility, against which the benefits of the DSM or IPP can be measured.

baseload generation   A term applied to the generation that occurs by generating plant operating most of the time to meet the invariable base of demand (see **peak load**).

BC Hydro   British Columbia Hydro and Power Authority.

BCUC   British Columbia Utilities Commission.

black ban   A union ban on work on a project or in an industrial plant, likely to be extended to any contractor or worker who ignores the ban.

BPA   Bonneville Power Administration.

CANDU   Canadian Deuterium Uranium (heavy water) nuclear reactor.

capacity factor   The ratio, expressed as a percentage, of the average load a generating unit or station is capable of meeting over a year to the peak load it is capable of meeting.

CEO   chief executive officer.

c/kWh   cents per kilowatt-hour.

cogeneration   The generation of electricity in conjunction with steam-raising for direct industrial application, or in order to utilise waste heat from some industrial process.

combined cycle   A technique for increasing substantially the conversion efficiency of using gas for electricity generation; it involves first using the gas to fuel a combustion turbine and then recovering exhaust heat for application to a steam turbine.

combustion turbine (CT)   A machine that, like a jet engine, uses the expansions of burnt gases to turn a turbine for electricity generation; also referred to as 'gas turbine'.

COO   Chief Operating Officer.

CPI   Consumer Price Index.

CRPR   Committee to Review the Power Requirements.

demand management (DM)   See **demand-side management**.

demand-side management (DSM)   The use of the active marketing of energy conservation in order to reduce peak capacity requirements (and thus improve system operating economics) or defer the requirement for capacity additions as part of least-cost utility planning.

demarketing   The active promotion of conservation by provision of information or attempts to change the attitudes of consumers.

deterministic planning   A planning approach that involves finding the least-cost way of meeting the most likely load forecast scenario, which is accepted as beyond the ability of the planner to change.

distribution   A term used to describe the low-voltage reticulation of electricity for retail sale.

DITR   Department of Industry, Technology and Resources.

DSOS   demand/supply options study.

ECNSW (or **Elcom**)   Electricity Commission of New South Wales.

ESAA   Electric Supply Authorities Association.

EdF   Electricité de France.

EDS   Environmental Defence Society.

EDSIR   Electricity Development Strategy Implementation Review.

firm energy   That which can be supplied regardless of exigencies such as drought (in a hydro system).

footloose   A term used to describe industries, such as aluminium smelting, which are not tied to a specific geographical location through a need to locate close to sources of raw materials.

Fordism   A system of production (developed by US industrialist Henry Ford (1863–1947)) involving mass production techniques of standardised, deskilled production lines.

gold-plating   The overinvestment in physical plant by utilities, according to the Averch–Johnson hypothesis, usually in response to regulation that sets allowed prices at some rate of return on capital. It can lead to beneficial environmental effects, such as a willingess to invest in pollution control capital.

GWh   gigawatt-hours – one thousand megawatt hours (or a million kWh).

HEAT   Hydro Employees Action Team.

HEC   Hydro Electric Commission of Tasmania.

hydraulic plant   A generating unit which uses falling water passing over a turbine to generate electricity.

IPP   independent power producers.

integrated resource planning (IRP)   An approach to electricity planning that involves integrating supply and demand curves in a more reactive sense than with deterministic planning, so that the effects of supply costs or other constraints (environmental, for example) on demand in various end-uses can be examined.

interconnection (or **intertie**)   The connection of two or more transmission grids to allow sharing of reserve plant or sales of electricity on an opportunistic basis or through long-term contracts for firm energy.

kilowatt (kW)   A measure of electrical power, or the ability to perform work; one thousand watts (a basic measure, but one too small to be useful for practical purposes).

kilowatt hour (kWh)   The basic measure of electrical energy, which is ordinarily used for retail billing; one kilowatt applied for a period of one hour.

least-cost utility planning (LCUP)   An approach to electricity planning that incorporates the costs of uncertainty by assessing the total costs of a future system containing combinations of all supply-side and demand-side measures under a range of demand scenarios, each of which has been assigned a probability of occurrence (contrast **deterministic planning**).

load factor   The ratio, expressed as a percentage, of the average load on a system or one of its components to the peak load.

load shifting   A demand management device aimed at moving consumption from a period of peak demand to a period of lower demand in order to reduce the capital cost of the system.

megawatt (MW)   A measure of electrical power, or the ability to perform work; one million watts (see **kilowatt**). Power is the rate of supplying or using energy.

megawatt average (MWav)   An often useful way of expressing the energy delivered by a power station, demand on a system or demanded by a large consumer. If maintained over a year, it amounts to 8760 megawatt hours.

MIL   major industrial load.

MOE   Ministry of Energy.

MWD   Ministry of Works and Development.

NDP   New Democratic Party.

negawatts   An expression coined by Amory Lovins to describe the 'capacity' available to utilities by pursuing conservation – in contrast to the megawatts of traditional capacity.

NREC   Natural Resources and Environment Committee.

NUG   non-utility generation.

NZED   New Zealand Electricity Department.

OEB   Ontario Energy Board.

Ontario Hydro   Hydro-electric Power Corporation of Ontario.

PCEPD   Planning Committee on Electric Power Development.

peak clipping   A demand management device used to limit capital costs of the system by achieving reductions in peak demand by conservation or load-shedding.

peak load   The highest load placed on a system or one of its components at any point in time.

peak load generation   Generation that occurs periodically during the course of a day to meet the peak load occurring on the system.

PFUC   Planning and Finance Utilisation Committee.

PIP   Production Improvement Program.

potline   A series of 'pots' in which aluminium oxide (alumina) is reduced to produce aluminium metal by means of the application of large quantities of electricity.

PURPA   Public Utility Regulatory Policies Act of 1978 (USA).

regulatory interventionism   The active encouragement of demand-side management or least-cost utility planning by regulatory policies or regulatory agencies which encourage or do not discourage expenditure on such programs in rate-setting decisions.

reserve margin   An excess of generating capacity designed to ensure the continuation of reliable electricity supply in the event of a sudden loss of a generator. It usually comprises **spinning reserve** and **stationary reserve**. Large interconnected systems can achieve cost reductions by pooling reserve requirements, and large interruptible loads (such as aluminium smelters) can provide reserve margins.

reverse adaptation   The tendency for inflexible sociotechnical systems to adapt ends to suit the means at their disposal.

ring-fenced   A situation in which transactions between business units occur on a commercial basis; goods and services provided by one to the other are charged for, rather than being provided *gratis* as continues to occur within the 'fence'.

RPM   Resource Planning Model

SECV   State Electricity Commission of Victoria.

site banking   A technique for dealing with the costs of uncertainty in electricity planning by reducing the lead time for power station construction; it involves engaging in planning and design work – including obtaining environmental clearances – but stopping short of commencing construction.

spinning reserve   Commonly a reserve margin equal to the capacity of the largest generating unit on the system that can be met immediately if that largest unit should fail or become disconnected from the system. It is usually provided by hydraulic capacity or by underloading steam turbine units.

stationary reserve   A reserve margin, often equal to the size of the second largest generating unit on the system, which can be brought into service in 1–3 minutes.

steam plant   A generating unit that uses the passage of (superheated) steam across a turbine to generate electricity. The steam might be produced by burning a fossil fuel such as oil or coal, by nuclear fission, or as a result of cogeneration.

thermal firming   The use of thermal capacity to provide greater reliability in a hydroelectric system by using thermal plant when water yields in catchments are low.

tpa   tonnes per annum.

transmission   The conveyance of electricity at high voltage from generating stations to substations for subsequent retail distribution or high-voltage industrial uses.

TVA   Tennessee Valley Authority.

tWh   terawatt-hours – a thousand million kWh.

valley filling   A demand management device that aims to improve plant (and thus capital) utilisation rates by selling electricity during off-peak periods.

W   Watts.

Notes

Introduction

1 Thomas Baumgartner and Atle Midttun, 'Modelling and forecasting in self-reactive policy contexts: Some meta-methodological comments' in Thomas Baumgartner and Atle Midttun (eds), *The Politics of Energy Forecasting*, Clarendon Press, Oxford, 1987, p. 290.

2 Clegg, Stewart R., *Modern Organizations: Organization Studies in the Postmodern World*, Sage, London, 1990, p. 177.

3 Ibid., p. 178.

4 David Harvey, *The Condition of Postmodernity: An Enquiry into the Origins of Cultural Change*, Basil Blackwell, Oxford, 1989, p. 9.

5 Ibid., p. 44.

6 Ibid., pp. 338–42.

7 Donald A. Schon, *Beyond the Stable State*, Penguin, Harmondsworth, 1971.

8 Some notable examples are covered in the case studies that follow, but there have been similar cases in other nations in which power scheme construction led to considerable conflict, for example, the Alta River project in Norway. See Thomas Mathiesen, 'Civil disobedience at 70° north', *Contemporary Crises* 7 (1983) pp. 1–11. Baumgartner and Midttun have argued that energy forecasting became part of the political process only when challenges to the planners' forecasts emerged in the 1970s, but this is true only if we have a restricted view of the realm of politics, which excludes the dominance of development values described here. See Thomas Baumgartner and Atle Midttun, 'Energy forecasting and political structure: Some comparative notes' in Thomas Baumgartner and Atle Midttun (eds), *The Politics of Energy Forecasting*, Clarendon Press, Oxford, 1987, p. 267.

9 Langdon Winner, *Autonomous Technology: Technics-out-of-control as a Theme in Political Thought*, MIT Press, Cambridge, MA.,1977, p. 229.

10 See, for example, D. Victor Anderson, *Illusions of Power*, Praeger, New York, 1985.

11 World Bank, *The World Bank's Role in the Electric Power Sector: Policies for Effective Institutional, Regulatory, and Financial Reform*. World Bank, 1993 (a World Bank policy paper), Washington, DC, p. 44.

12 Baumgartner and Midttun, 'Energy forecasting and political structure', p. 273.

13 World Bank, op. cit., p. 44.

14 Baumgartner and Midttun, 'Energy forecasting and political structure', p. 273. The problem of overcapacity was not confined to the developed world. It was estimated in 1989 that in developing countries the investment in capacity in excess of that necessary to provide prudent margins was $50 billion; much of it existed because of poor maintenance. See World Bank, op. cit., p. 37.

15 Louis Puiseux, 'The ups and downs of electricity forecasting in France: Technocratic élitism' in Baumgartner and Midttun, *The Politics of Energy Forecasting*, Clarendon Press, Oxford, 1987.

16 Baumgartner and Midttun, 'Modelling and forecasting in self-reactive policy contexts', pp. 295–7.

17 Baumgartner and Midttun, 'Energy forecasting and political structure', p. 268.

18 Ibid., p. 272.

19 World Bank, op. cit., p. 42.

20 Baumgartner and Midttun, 'Energy forecasting and political structure', pp. 284–5.

21 World Bank, op. cit., p. 42.

22 Clegg, op. cit., p. 181.

23 G. Stevenson, *Mineral Resources and Australian Federalism*, Research Monograph No. 17, Centre for Research on Federal Financial Relations, ANU, Canberra, 1976.

24 See: John Beggs, 'Australia: One day in the sunshine' in Merton J. Peck (ed.), *The World Aluminium Industry in a Changing Energy Era*, Resources for the Future, Washington, DC, 1988; Jim Falk and Peter Murphy, 'New aluminium proposals and Australian energy policy', *Australian Quarterly* 53 (1981) pp. 141–58; and Ann Hodgkinson, 'Structural changes in the world aluminium industry and implications for Australia', *Journal of Australian Political Economy* 14 (1983) pp. 34–58.

25 B.J. Galligan, 'Federalism and resource development in Australia and Canada', *Australian Quarterly* 54 (1982) pp. 236–51. See also Aynsley Kellow, 'Federalism, development and the environment', *Regional Journal of Social Issues* 18 (1986) pp. 75–84.

26 Galligan, B., Aynsley Kellow and C. O'Faircheallaigh, 'Minerals and energy policy' in B. Galligan (ed.), *Comparative State Policies*, Longman Cheshire, Melbourne, 1988.

27 For a discussion of these methodological issues, see Aynsley Kellow, 'Australian federalism: The need for New Zealand (as well as Canadian) comparisons', *Australian–Canadian Studies* 6 (1988) pp. 59–72.

28 See Arendt Lijphart, 'Comparative politics and the comparative method', *American Political Science Review* 65 (1971) pp. 682–93.

29 There has inevitably been an element of selectivity since each of the cases could sustain – and perhaps merits – a book in itself, and there must of necessity be some theoretical 'line' employed in researching and writing each case for a comparative survey.

30 See: F.W. Eggleston, *State Socialism in Victoria*, King, London, 1932; W. Pember Reeves, *State Experiments in Australia and New Zealand*, Macmillan, Melbourne, 1969; N.G. Butlin, A. Barnard and J.J. Pincus, *Government and Capitalism in Australia*, Allen & Unwin, Sydney, 1982.

31 See Brian Head (ed.), *State and Economy in Australia*, Oxford University Press, Melbourne, 1983.
32 It should be noted that New South Wales has established a Pricing Tribunal and the Victorian Government intends putting in place a regulatory regime to accompany a proposed privatised industry structure.
33 World Bank, op. cit., p. 43.
34 Ibid., p. 44–5.
35 P. McKay, *Electric Empire: The Inside Story of Ontario Hydro*, Between the Lines, Toronto, 1983; see also Lawrence Soloman, *Power at What Cost?* Energy Probe Research Foundation, Toronto, 1984.

1 Institutions and electricity planning

1 See, for example, Thorstein Veblein, *The Engineers and the Price System*, A.M. Kelly, New York, 1921.
2 See Thomas P. Hughes, *Networks of Power: Electrification in Western Society 1880–1930*, Johns Hopkins University Press, Baltimore, 1983.
3 This, as we shall see later, was the exact expression used by critics of Ontario Hydro in 1934.
4 For a discussion of institutions in relation to natural resources, see Oran Young, *Natural Resources and the State*, University of California Press, Berkeley, 1981.
5 By way of example I have a financial calculator, intended for business use, that discounts cash flows. It has presumably been designed to be adequate for private business use, yet it does so only for eighteen years. The periods over which electricity planners must operate are very much in the distant future for private business.
6 Swan, Peter L., 'The economics of QANGOs: SECV and ELCOM' in *The Economics of Bureaucracy and Statutory Authorities*, CIS Policy Forums No. 1, 1983, p. 28.
7 E. Oatman and J.L. Plummer, 'The meaning of strategic planning in regulated and unregulated firms' in J.L. Plummer, E. Oatman, and P.K. Gupta (eds), *Strategic Management and Planning for Electric Utilities*, Prentice-Hall, Englewood Cliffs, 1985, p. 2.
8 Ibid., p. 2.
9 See D. Victor Anderson, *Illusions of Power*, Praeger, New York, 1985.
10 Richard F. Hirsh, *Technology and Transformation in the American Electric Utility Industry*, Cambridge University Press, Cambridge, 1989.
11 R.R. Booth, 'Optimal generation planning considering uncertainty', *IEEE Transactions on Power Apparatus and Systems*, Vol *PAS–91* No. 1, pp. 70–7 (Jan–Feb 1972).
12 Herman Daly, 'Energy demand forecasting: Prediction or planning?' *Journal of the American Institute of Planners* 42 (1976) pp. 4–15. For this reason, Robinson has advocated that we use 'backcasting' rather than forecasting in energy planning. See J.B. Robinson, 'Energy backcasting: A proposed method of policy analysis', *Energy Policy* 10 (1982) pp. 337–44.
13 Oatman and Plummer, op. cit., p. 3.
14 Christopher Hood, *The Limits of Administration*, Wiley, London, 1976, p. 81. One might add that Hood exhibits considerable faith that the chances of a 'fix' in a horse race are unrelated to the stakes, but his underlying point remains valid.

15 Oedipus, on hearing the predictions of the oracles that he would murder his father and commit incest with his mother, went into self-exile and created the very conditions that permitted the prophecy to be fulfilled, since he no longer recognised either parent when he later encountered them.

16 Robert Formaini, *The Myth of Scientific Public Policy*, Transaction, New Brunswick, 1990, p. 24. See also Aaron Wildavsky and Mary Douglas, *Risk and Culture*, University of California Press, Berkeley, 1981.

17 Renfrew Christie has concluded from his study of the electricity industry in South Africa that: 'The explicit goals of electrical engineers and their controllers from 1905 to the present have been to "save labour", thereby increasing profitability … Capitalists and the state facilitated this entire process in South Africa in the twentieth century by ensuring the provision of public supplies of cheap power'. Renfrew Christie, *Electricity, Industry and Class in South Africa*, Macmillan, London, 1984, p. 204.

18 Dominic M. Geraghty, 'Strategic planning methods and objectives for utilities' in J.L. Plummer, E. Oatman and P.K. Gupta (eds), *Strategic Management and Planning for Electric Utilities*, Prentice-Hall, Englewood Cliffs, 1985, p. 15.

19 Marvin Shaffer, 'Electricity planning under conditions of uncertainty', Seminar Paper, Department of Economics, Latrobe University, 3 May 1985.

20 Geraghty, op. cit., p. 21.

21 Clark W. Gellings, Pradep C. Gupta and Ahmad Faruqui, 'Strategic implications of demand-side planning' in J.L. Plummer, E. Oatman and P.K. Gupta (eds), *Strategic Management and Planning for Electric Utilities*, Prentice-Hall, Englewood Cliffs, 1985, p. 139.

22 Shaffer, op. cit.

23 Andrew Ford, 'Short-lead-time technologies as a defense against demand uncertainty' in J.L. Plummer, E. Oatman and P.K. Gupta (eds), *Strategic Management and Planning for Electric Utilities*, Prentice-Hall, Englewood Cliffs, 1985, p. 128.

24 See Shaffer, op. cit.; E.G. Cazalet, C.E. Clark and T.W. Keelin, 'Costs and benefits of over/undercapacity in electric power system planning', *EPRI Research Project EA-972*, Electric Power Research Institute, Pasadena, CA, October 1978; Booth, op. cit.; J.H. Drinnan and K.R. Spafford, 'A stochastic resource planning model', Paper Presented at the Generation and System Planning and Operation Subsection, CEA Spring Meeting, Vancouver, March 1987; Cyrus K. Motlagh, *Structuring Uncertainties in Long-range Power Planning*, Michigan State University Public Utilities Papers, East Lansing, 1976. For accounts of the application of these approaches, see Howard S. Geller, 'Implementing electricity conservation programs: Progress towards least-cost energy services among U.S. utilities' in Thomas B. Johansson, Brigit Bodlund and Robert H. Williams (eds), *Electricity: Efficient End-use and New Generation Technologies and Their Planning Implications*, Lund University Press, Lund, 1989; or J.L. Plummer, E. Oatman and P.K. Gupta (eds), *Strategic Management and Planning for Electric Utilities*.

25 All references to prices are in the currency of the country to which the example refers.

26 'The notion of *gold-plating* is that of a regulated firm adding completely nonproductive capital to its rate base.' Frederic H. Murphy and Allen L. Soyster, *Economic Behaviour of Electric Utilities*, Prentice-Hall, Englewood Cliffs, NJ, 1983, p. 37.

27 H. Averch and L.L. Johnson, 'Behaviour of the firm under regulation constraint', *American Economic Review* 52 (December 1962).

28 Murphy and Soyster, op. cit., p. 1.
29 See Marc J. Roberts and Jeremy Bluhm, *The Choices of Power: Utilities Face the Environmental Challenge*, Harvard University Press, Cambridge, MA, 1981, p. 34.
30 L. De Alessi, 'Managerial tenure under private and government ownership in the electric power industry', *Journal of Political Economy* 82 (May–June), pp. 645–53.
31 Ibid., p. 647.
32 Murphy and Soyster, op. cit., p. 7. See also A. Sanghvi and D. Limaye, 'Planning for electrical generation capacity in the Pacific Northwest: A decision analysis of the costs of over- and under-building', *Energy Policy* 7 (1979), and Cazalet, Clark and Keelin, op. cit.
33 Paul L. Joskow and Richard Schmalensee, *Markets for Power: An Analysis of Electric Utility Deregulation*, MIT Press, Cambridge, MA, 1983, pp. 106–7.
34 Frederic H. Murphy and Allen L. Soyster, *Economic Behaviour of Electric Utilities*, Prentice-Hall, Englewood Cliffs, NJ, 1983, p. 118.
35 An interesting topic for further research would be to see whether the adoption of this technique was earlier in those utilities subject to price regulation than in those subject to rate-of-return regulation.
36 US Congress 1980, The Pacific Northwest Electric Power Planning and Conservation Act, PL No 96-501.
37 Anderson, op. cit.
38 See David Shapiro, *Generating Failure: Public Power Policy in the Northwest*, University Press of America, Lanham, 1989.
39 Ibid., p. 35.
40 The Northwest Planning Council has eight members, two nominated by the governor of each participating state. Plans must be approved by a majority that includes at least one voting member from each state, or by at least six members. See Shapiro, op. cit., p. 43.
41 Geller, op. cit., p. 756.
42 See, for example, A.K. Meier and J. Whittier, 'Consumer discount rates implied by consumer purchases of energy-efficient refrigerators', *Energy* 8 (1983), pp. 957–62.
43 Geller, op. cit., p. 755.
44 Ibid., p. 756.
45 Ibid., p. 743.
46 Barbara R. Barkovich, *Regulatory Interventionism in the Utility Industry: Fairness, Efficiency and the Pursuit of Energy Conservation*, Quorum Books, New York, 1989.
47 See Geller, op. cit., p. 756.
48 See Robert H. Williams, 'Innovative approaches to marketing electric efficiency' in Johansson, Bodlund and Williams (eds), *Electricity: Efficient End-use and New Generation Technologies and Their Planning Implications*.
49 Hood, op. cit., pp. 77–8.
50 Ibid., p. 77.
51 Ibid., p. 75.
52 Ibid., p. 78.
53 David Elliott and Ruth Elliott, *The Control of Technology*, Wykeham, London, 1976, p. 55.
54 Langdon Winner, *Autonomous Technology: Technics-out-of-control as a Theme in Political Thought*, MIT Press, Cambridge, MA, 1977.
55 Roberts and Bluhm, op. cit., pp. 37–8.

56 Peter Pringle and James Spigelman, *The Nuclear Barons*, Michael Joseph, London, 1982, p. x.
57 Leon Festinger, *A Theory of Cognitive Dissonance*, Stanford University Press, Stanford, CA, 1957.
58 Festinger's approach seems particularly well suited to forecasting since the thinking behind the development of his theory of cognitive dissonance was probably influenced by his earlier work looking at responses to failed prediction, albeit religious prediction. See Leon Festinger, Stanley Schachter and Henry W. Rieken, *When Prophecy Fails*, Harper & Row, New York, 1964 (originally published 1956).
59 Herbert Marcuse, *One Dimensional Man*, Beacon Press, Boston, 1964.
60 Frank Fischer, *Technocracy and the Politics of Expertise*, Sage, Newbury Park, CA, 1990, p. 45.
61 Jurgen Habermas, *Knowledge and Human Interests*, Beacon Press, Boston, 1971.
62 Fischer, op. cit., p. 45.
63 Formaini, op. cit.
64 Fischer, op. cit., p. 47.
65 Ibid., p. 48.
66 Pringle and Spigelman, op. cit., pp. x–xi.
67 Incrementalism was developed in Charles E. Lindblom, 'The science of "muddling through"', *Public Administration Review* 19 (1959), pp. 79–88, and developed further in Charles E. Lindblom, 'Still muddling, not yet through', *Public Administration Review* 39 (1979), pp. 517–26.
68 P.D. Henderson, 'Two British errors: Their probable size and some possible lessons' in C. Pollitt, L. Lewis, J. Negro and J. Patten (eds), *Public Policy in Theory and Practice*, Hodder & Stoughton, London, 1979, p. 244.
69 Ibid., pp. 244–5.
70 J.S. Anderson, 'The seer-sucker theory: The value of experts in forecasting', *Technology Review* 83 (1980), pp. 18–24.
71 David F. Noble, *America by Design*, Alfred A. Knopf, New York, 1977, p. 34.
72 Noble, op. cit., p. 324.
73 Elliott and Elliott, op. cit., p. 53.
74 Fischer, op. cit., p. 31.
75 Theodore J. Lowi, 'American business, public policy, case studies, and political theory', *World Politics* 16 (1964), pp. 677–715; Theodore J. Lowi, 'Decision making vs policy making: Towards an antidote for technocracy', *Public Administration Review* 30 (1970), pp. 314–25; Theodore J. Lowi, 'Four systems of policy, politics and choice', *Public Administration Review* 33 (1972), pp. 298–310.
76 Aynsley Kellow, 'Promoting elegance in policy theory: Simplifying Lowi's arenas of Power', *Policy Studies Journal* 16 (1988), pp. 713–24.
77 Theodore J. Lowi, 'The state in politics: The relation between policy and administration' in Roger G. Noll (ed.), *Regulatory Policy and the Social Sciences*, University of California Press, Berkeley, 1985, p. 92.
78 Lowi, 'The state in politics', p. 92.
79 Herbert Kaufman, *The Forest Ranger*, Johns Hopkins University Press, Baltimore, 1960.
80 Lowi, 'The state in politics', p. 82.
81 Ibid., p. 86.
82 Ibid., p. 86.
83 Roberts and Bluhm, op. cit., p. 35.
84 Anthony Downs, 'Why the budget is too small in a democracy', *World Politics* 12 (1960), pp. 541–63.

85 Lowi, 'The state in politics', p. 85.
86 Ibid., pp. 88–91.
87 Ibid. Interestingly, Lowi developed his schema out of a study of bureaucracy (in New York City government), but for twenty years concern with interest groups, legislative politics and the like dominated its applications.
88 Richard B. Riley, 'Public policy and the electric power industry in Canada: A comparative political analysis of power development in three western provinces', unpublished PhD dissertation, Duke University, Durham, NC, 1975, p. 337.
89 G.D. McColl, *The Economics of the Electricity Supply Industry in Australia*, Melbourne University Press, Melbourne, 1976.
90 Leslie Hannah, *Electricity Before Nationalisation*, Macmillan, London, 1979, p. 173.
91 Eric M. Uslaner, 'Energy, issue agendas, and policy typologies' in Helen M. Ingram and R. Kenneth Godwin (eds), *Public Policy and the Natural Environment*, JAI Press, Greenwich, CT, 1985.
92 Lowi, 'The state in politics', p. 72.
93 Roberts and Bluhm, op. cit.

2 Tasmania: The means justify the ends

1 HEC, *Report on the Gordon River Power Development Stage Two*, Hobart, 1979.
2 Doug Lowe, *The Price of Power*, Macmillan, Melbourne, 1984, p. 8.
3 See B.W. Davis, 'Waterpower and wilderness: Political and administrative aspects of the Lake Pedder controversy', *Public Administration (Sydney)* 31 (1972), pp. 21–42.
4 For discussion of hydroindustrialisation and the political economy of Tasmania see: P. Thompson, *Power in Tasmania*, Australian Conservation Foundation, Melbourne, 1981; A. Kellow, 'Electricity planning in Tasmania and New Zealand: Political processes and the technological imperative', *Australian Journal of Public Administration*, 45 (1986), pp. 2–17; and B.W. Davis, 'Tasmania: The political economy of a peripheral state' in B. Head (ed.), *The Politics of Development in Australia*, Allen & Unwin, Sydney, 1986.
5 This brief account will focus only on the main features of the case relevant to electricity planning at the state level. A brief overview that includes both the wilderness and federal dimensions can be found in Aynsley Kellow, 'The dispute over the Franklin River and south-west wilderness area in Tasmania, Australia', *Natural Resources Journal* 29 (1) 1989, pp. 129–46, on which this summary is based.
6 See R.A. Herr and B.W. Davis, 'The Tasmanian parliament, accountability and the Hydro Electric Commission: The Franklin River controversy' in J.R. Nethercote (ed.), *Parliament and Bureaucracy*, Hale & Iremonger, Sydney, 1982.
7 For an overview of the history of conflict over the south west, see B.W. Davis, 'The struggle for south-west Tasmania' in R. Scott (ed.), *Interest Groups and Public Policy: Cases From the Australian States*, Macmillan, Melbourne, 1980.
8 With subsequent investigation, the output of the Gordon Below Franklin was increased to 181 MWav.
9 For a description of the machinations within the Labor Party and a history of the ALP in Tasmania see R. Davis, *Eighty Years' Labor*, Sassafras Books, Hobart, 1983.

10 For a discussion of the implications of Lowi's theory of policy types in Westminster systems of government see Aynsley Kellow, 'The policy roles of bureaucrats and politicians in New Zealand', *Politics* 19 (1984), pp 43–53.

11 Lowe, op. cit.

12 For a description of the Tasmanian political system, see W.A. Townsley, *The Government of Tasmania*, University of Queensland Press, St Lucia, 1976.

13 Such a motion was not strictly admissible because it constituted a negativing of the intent of the bill. A ruling to this effect was given by the president of the Legislative Council, but the committee chairman put a motion dissenting from the president's ruling and the motion was passed. This was the first time in the history of the council that a considered ruling by a president had been overturned.

14 See Terry Newman, 'Tasmanian referenda since Federation', Appendix T of the *Report of the Royal Commission into the Constitution Act 1934*, Government Printer, Hobart, 1982.

15 See G. Smith, 'The Tasmanian House of Assembly elections, 1982', *Politics* 17 (1982), pp. 81–8.

16 The Liberal Party held office as a minority government from 1969 to 1972 with the support of a minor party.

17 See P.J. Tighe, 'Hydroindustrialisation and conservation policy in Tasmania' in K.J. Walker (ed.), *Australian Environmental Policy*, University of New South Wales Press, Kensington, 1992; see also P. Read, *The Organisation of Electricity Power in Tasmania*, University of Tasmania, Hobart, 1986, and A.W. Knight, 'The development of hydroelectric power in Tasmania' in H.G. Raggatt (ed.), *Fuel and Power in Australia*, Cheshire, Melbourne, 1969.

18 See Lowe, op. cit., pp. 9–10.

19 Ibid., p. 9.

20 Ibid., p. 17.

21 Ibid., pp. 19–20.

22 See Tighe, op. cit., p. 135.

23 HEC, *Report on Further Power Developments 1970–1980 with Reference to Second Generating Set, Bell Bay Power Station and Pieman River Power Development*, Hobart, 1970.

24 Ibid., p. 7.

25 Ibid., p. 7–8. The HEC confirmed this approach in 1983, stating that it has, 'consistently made provision in its forecasts for major industrial load growth over and above any contractural commitments'. HEC, *Load Forecast*, November 1983, p. 2.

26 See also HEC, *Annual Report*, 1973–74, p. 3.

27 HEC, *Report on Further Power Developments 1970–1980*, p. 9.

28 HEC, *Annual Report*, 1973–74, p. 3.

29 Kellow, 'Electricity planning in Tasmania and New Zealand', p. 9.

30 HEC, *Report on Further Power Developments 1970–1980*, pp. 12–14.

31 HEC, *Annual Report*, 1989, p. 5.

32 Energy Policy and Analysis Pty Ltd, *A Review of the Hydro Electric Commission's Most Recent Financial Analysis on the Gordon Below Franklin Scheme*, Report for the Business Association for Economical Power, May 1982.

33 HEC, *Pieman River Power Development Capital Cost*, 6 November 1984.

34 Kellow, 'Electricity planning in Tasmania and New Zealand', p. 9; this offer came in a letter from the HEC to Comalco on 1 February 1974.

35 HEC, *Report on the Gordon River Power Development Stage Two*, Appendix 2: *The Forecast of Demand*, Hobart, 1979, p. 47.

36 HEC, *Forecast of Demand*, p. 33.
37 Tighe, op. cit., p. 136.
38 Report of the Directorate of Energy to the Coordination Committee on Future Power Development, May 1980, p. 227.
39 Senate Select Committee on South-West Tasmania, Transcripts of Evidence, 21 May 1982, p. 3222.
40 Ibid., pp. 3274–5.
41 HEC, *Load Forecast*, November 1983, p. 36.
42 HEC, Submission to the Senate Select Committee on South-West Tasmania, 1982, p. 36.
43 See Aynsley Kellow, 'A neglected option in Tasmania's power debate', *Search* 14 (1983–84), pp. 306–8.
44 HEC, *Annual Report 1983–84*, p. 25.
45 HEC, *Annual Report 1984–85*, p. 5.
46 HEC, *Annual Report 1983–84*, p. 7.
47 HEC, *Annual Report 1984–85*, p. 6.
48 HEC, *Annual Report 1987–88*, p. 19.
49 HEC, *Annual Report 1986–87*.
50 HEC, *Annual Report 1987–88*, pp. 6–7.
51 HEC, *Annual Report 1988–89*, p. 20.
52 HEC, *Annual Report 1989–90*, p. 21.
53 HEC, ibid., p. 12.
54 HEC, ibid., p. 22.
55 HEC, *Annual Report 1992*, p. 40.
56 HEC, ibid., p. 3.
57 *Age*, 11 December 1985.
58 *Australian*, 29 July 1993.
59 *Australian*, 23 August 1993.
60 *Australian*, 21 December 1993.
61 McColl, G.D., *Economics of the Electricity Supply Industry in Australia*, Melbourne University Press, Melbourne, 1976, p. 149.
62 Aynsley Kellow, 'Public project evaluation in an Australian state: Tasmania's dam controversy', *Australian Quarterly* 55(3), 1983, pp. 263–77.

3 New Zealand: The triumph of distributive politics

1 Rosslyn Noonan, *By Design*, Ministry of Works and Development, Wellington, 1975, p. 262. Sir Julius Vogel was a New Zealand statesman and prime minister (1873–75 and 1876).
2 The Wakefield system involved selling land to pay for assisted passages for immigrants.
3 Noonan, op. cit., p. 264.
4 Murray D. Kennedy, 'When the rain stopped falling', *Public Utilities Fortnightly* 131 (16), 1993, pp. 21–4.
5 For a discussion of the adoption and implementation of the Water and Soil Conservation Act see Aynsley Kellow, 'Making policies and prescribing placebos: Pollution control in New Zealand', New Zealand Institute of Public Administration, *Public Sector Research Papers* IV (3), Wellington, 1983.
6 The pace of the construction program in the 1950s and 1960s sometimes necessitated the engagement of international contractors.
7 The electricity for the smelter was sold to Comalco Power Ltd, but the smelter itself was operated by New Zealand Aluminium Smelters, owned 50 per cent

by Comalco and 25 per cent each by the Japanese companies Sumitomo Chemical and Showa Denko. It is popularly known as Comalco.

8 The Campaign Against Foreign Control in New Zealand in 1977 published a cartoon booklet, 'The amazing adventures of NZ's no. 1 power junky: The true story of Comalco in NZ', in which the 0.17 c price was claimed. After the quadrupling of the price in 1977 the revenue for sales to all bulk industries in the early 1980s was about 1 c/kWh. Since the smelter price can be assumed to be lower than the average, the 0.17 c figure appears to be reasonable. (The Minister of Energy confirmed the quadrupling on 14 March 1985; see *New Zealand Parliamentary Debates* for that day, p. 3664.)

9 Details of the ensuing campaign to preserve Lake Manapouri within its natural limits can be found in Les Cleveland, *Anatomy of Influence*, Hicks Smith, Wellington, 1972, ch 3.

10 An account of the Marsden B decision has been published previously as part of Aynsley J. Kellow, 'The policy roles of bureaucrats and politicians in New Zealand', *Politics* 19, November 1984, pp. 43–53.

11 The decision not to raise Lake Manapouri also limited the amount of storage available in the South Island hydro system, as did the decision in 1973 to preserve Lake Wanaka within its natural levels.

12 Committee to Review the Power Requirements, *Report*, 1974, p. 4. While the demand forecast was not published until 1974, it served as the justification for building Marsden B when it was announced in August 1973.

13 Environmental impact reports were required for public projects from April 1974 under the Environmental Protection and Enhancement Procedures, a set of administrative procedures that drew their authority from a Cabinet decision, but were later given statutory recognition in the controversial *National Development Act 1979.*

14 Ministry of Works and Development, Submission on the Marsden B Environmental Impact Report, 8 July 1974.

15 Planning Committee on Electric Power Development, *Report*, 1975, p. 9; emphasis added.

16 M. Desai has observed that, in planning in India, 'typically more is known about the future than about the present or the past'. Cited by P.D. Henderson, 'Two British errors: Their probable size and some possible lessons' in C. Pollitt, L. Lewis, J. Negro and J. Patten (eds), *Public Policy in Theory and Practice*, Hodder & Stoughton, London, 1979, p. 242.

17 A discussion of this planning process was earlier published in Aynsley Kellow, 'Electricity planning in Tasmania and New Zealand: Political processes and the technological imperative', *Australian Journal of Public Administration* 45 (1986), pp. 2–17.

18 PCEPD Annual Report, Appendix to the Journals of the House of Representatives D6B 1974, p. 4.

19 Cited in *National Business Review*, 'NBR Outlook', August 1984, p. 11.

20 See *New Zealand Times*, 14 November 1982.

21 Cited in *National Business Review*, 'NBR Outlook', August 1984, p. 29.

22 The origins of the 'Think Big' program were described by Richard Kennaway in 'International aspects of New Zealand's energy resources', Paper presented at the 1982 Australasian Political Studies Association Conference, Perth.

23 Geoffrey Bertram, *Electricity in New Zealand: Is There a Surplus to Sell?*, Development Information Group, Wellington, 1980.

24 *Otago Daily Times*, 30 September 1983.

25 See Paul Powell, *Who Killed the Clutha?*, John McIndoe, Dunedin, 1979.

26 *Age*, 18 April 1980.

27 The economics of the smelter were criticised by economics professor Paul van Moeseke in 1980 in two unpublished reports, 'Aluminium smelting in New Zealand: An economic appraisal' and 'Aluminium and power: the second smelter report'.

28 The review process included: an interdepartmental committee (1967–72); the Clutha Valley Liaison Committee (1972–73); the Clutha Valley Development Commission (1973–74); Environmental Impact Report and Audit (1975); and the Clutha Advisory Committee (1976).

29 MWD on behalf of NZED, *Environmental Impact Report on Design and Construction Proposal, Clutha Valley Development*, December 1977, pp. 7 and 22.

30 See, for example, *New Zealand Times*, 4 March 1984.

31 See *Otago Daily Times*, 14 May 1982. The title case judgment was *Gilmore & Ors v National Water and Soil Conservation Authority & Anor*, High Court (Administrative Division) M183/81, 13 May 1982.

32 The government waited until the tribunal decision on the rehearing of the water rights application before announcing funding for the study – too late to stop the works from closing on 1 September with the loss of 600 jobs. See *Otago Daily Times*, 2 September 1982.

33 *Otago Daily Times*, 15 June 1982.

34 Ministry of Energy, *Report of the Electricity Sector Planning Committee*, Wellington, 1981, p. 11.

35 Earlier use of private contractors had occurred when MWD was fully committed or, in the case of the Manapouri scheme, which involved tunnelling and excavation deep underground, lacked expertise.

36 Ministry of Energy, *Report of the Electricity Sector Planning Committee*, Wellington, 1980, p. 16.

37 Electricity Division, Ministry of Energy, *Report of the Ministry of Energy, Electricity Division, to the Select Committee Considering the Clutha Development (Clyde Dam) Empowering Bill*, October 1982, p. 3.

38 Ibid., p. 13.

39 Ibid., p. 17.

40 Ibid., p. 17.

41 Ibid., p. 17.

42 John Culy, *Electricity Restructuring: Towards a Competitive Wholesale Market*, NZ Institute of Economic Research (NZIER Discussion Paper), Wellington, 1992, p. 28. At the time of commissioning in 1994 the cost of the Clyde Dam was $1700m.

43 Ibid., p. 11.

44 Ibid., p. 12.

45 NZ Treasury, *Economic Management* (briefing document released 30 August 1984).

46 *Auckland Star*, 20 September 1983.

47 For a review of these developments, see Michael Johnson and Stephen Rix (eds), *Powering the Future: The Electricity Industry and Australia's Energy Future*, Pluto Press, Sydney, 1991, pp. 74–5.

48 Roderick S. Deane, 'Reforming the public sector' in Simon Walker (ed.), *Rogernomics: Reshaping New Zealand's Economy*, GP Books, Wellington, 1989, p. 134.

4 British Columbia: Winning reform after losing the Peace

1 BC Hydro, *Annual Report 1980–81*, p. 3.
2 Constance Brissenden, 'Powersmart makes US inroads', *Public Utilities Fortnightly* 131(21), 1993, pp. 46–51.
3 Ted Flanigan and Alex Fleming, 'BC Hydro flips a market', *Public Utilities Fortnightly* 131(15), 1993, pp. 20–22 and 34.
4 See N.A. Swainson, *Conflict Over the Columbia: The Background of an Historic Treaty*, McGill-Queens University Press, Montreal, 1979.
5 Aidan Vining, 'Provincial hydro utilities' in Allan Tupper and G. Bruce Doern (eds), *Public Corporations and Public Policy*, Institute for Research on Public Policy, Montreal, 1981, p. 164.
6 Ibid., p. 166.
7 BC Hydro, *Annual Report 1978–79*, p. 15.
8 BC Hydro, *Annual Report 1980–81*, p. 19.
9 BC Hydro and Power Authority, *Energy Blueprint 1980*, Vancouver, 1980.
10 BC Hydro, *Annual Report 1980–81*, p. 19.
11 While the dam would have inundated some forest, wildlife habitat and heritage resources, most of the land to be flooded was agricultural. Some 2000 ha were to have been flooded, and the annual loss of production was estimated at $60m.
12 See W.R. Derrick Sewell, 'Energy in British Columbia', *British Columbia: Its Resources and its People*, University of Victoria, Department of Geography (Western Geographical Series Vol. 24), Victoria, BC, 1986.
13 BC Hydro, *Annual Report 1981–82*, p. 22.
14 Ibid., p. 7.
15 Ken Peterson, Manager, Load Forecast, BC Hydro, interview with the author, June 1987.
16 BC Hydro, *Annual Report 1980–81*, p. 3.
17 For a description of the model see J.H. Drinnan and K.R. Spafford, 'A stochastic resource planning model', Paper presented at the Generation and System Planning and Operation Subsection, CEA Spring Meeting, Vancouver, March 1987.
18 ICF Incorporated, *The Economic Costs of an Electricity Supply-Demand Imbalance*, Report Prepared for British Columbia Hydro and Power Authority, February, 1982.
19 BC Hydro, Systems Planning Division, *Financial Risks of Resource Planning*, Report Prepared for the BC Utilities Commission, March 1987, p. 1.
20 BC Utilities Commission, *Site C Report: Report and Recommendations*, Victoria, BC, 29 September 1983.
21 Marvin Shaffer, 'The benefits and costs of two BC Hydro construction projects', in Robert C. Allen and Gideon Rosenbluth (eds), *Restraining the Economy*, Economic Policy Institute, Vancouver, BC, 1986.
22 See Irving K. Fox, 'BC power development: Are we going the way of WHOOPS?', Occasional Paper, Westwater Research Center, University of British Columbia, Vancouver, 1983.
23 See Robert C. Allen and Gideon Rosenbluth (eds), *Restraining the Economy*, Economic Policy Institute, Vancouver, BC, 1986, and Warren Magnusson, William K. Carroll, Charles Doyle, Monika Langer and R.B.J. Walker (eds), *The New Reality: The Politics of Restraint in British Columbia*, New Star Books, Vancouver, 1984.
24 BC Hydro, *Annual Report 1983–84*, p. 10.

25 See BC Hydro, *Annual Report 1984–85*, pp. 15 and 23.
26 BC Hydro, *Annual Report 1983–84*, pp. 11–12.
27 BC Hydro, *Annual Reports 1984–85*, p. 6; *1985–86*, p. 3.
28 Peterson interview.
29 Transfers were made from export income to the domestic side via a rate stabilisation account, created in accordance with a Utilities Commission ruling made on 30 March 1982.
30 BC Hydro, *Annual Report 1991*, pp. 40–1. Later annual reports provide staffing levels for the early 1980s in the electricity side of the operation only after the sale of the gas and rail undertakings in 1989.
31 Peterson interview.
32 BC Hydro, Systems Planning Division, op. cit., Appendix 1.
33 Cited in ibid., p. 7.
34 BC Hydro, *Demand Side Management: A Progress Report*, Report to the BC Utilities Commission, March 1987.
35 BC Hydro, *Twenty Year Resource Plan*, 1989, p. 39.
36 See Peter L. Swan, 'The economics of QANGOs: SECV and ELCOM' in *The Economics of Bureaucracy and Statutory Authorities*, CIS Policy Forums No. 1, Sydney, 1983.
37 See Paul Sabatier, 'Social movements and regulatory agencies: Toward a more adequate and less pessimistic theory of clientele capture', *Policy Science* 6 (1975), pp. 301–42.
38 BC Hydro, *Annual Report 1980–81*, p. 30.
39 A deputy minister in the Canadian system is the chief administrator – or what was once called a permanent head.
40 See BC Hydro, *Annual Report 1978–79*.
41 In several cases the incumbent was an engineer redeployed within the organisation, but the key point is that the position did not require the incumbent to hold engineering credentials.
42 BC Hydro, *Annual Report 1989*, p. 23.
43 Ibid., p. 26.
44 BC Hydro, *Annual Report 1990*, p. 17.

5 Ontario: The decline and fall of the Electric Empire

1 In 1984 Soloman estimated the cost of Hydro's 1979 expansion plans at $67 billion. Lawrence Soloman, *Power at What Cost?*, Energy Probe Research Foundation, Toronto, 1984, p. 46.
2 P. McKay, *Electric Empire: The Inside Story of Ontario Hydro*, Between the Lines, Toronto, 1983.
3 Ontario Hydro, *Sustainable Development: The Economy and the Environment*, Background Paper, February 1993.
4 See W.R. Plewman, *Adam Beck and the Ontario Hydro*, Ryerson Press, Toronto, 1947.
5 For the early history of Ontario Hydro see: H.V. Nelles, *The Politics of Development: Forests, Mines and Hydro-electric Power in Ontario 1849–1941*, Macmillan, Toronto, 1974; H.V. Nelles, 'Public ownership of electrical utilities in Manitoba and Ontario 1906–30', *Canadian Historical Review* 57 (1976), pp. 461–85; Merrill Denison, *The People's Power: The History of Ontario Hydro*, McClelland & Stewart, Toronto, 1960.
6 John H. Dales, *Hydroelectricity and Industrial Development: Quebec 1898–1940*, Harvard University Press, Cambridge, MA, 1957, p. 167.

7 See R.P. Bolton, *An Expensive Experiment: The Hydro-electric Power Commission of Ontario*, Baker & Taylor, New York, 1913. Bolton, an engineer, was particularly strident in his criticisms of Hydro – witness the following passage: 'The citizens and taxpayers of the state of New York, confronted with a proposal for the expenditure of their money in an evidently ill-considered and distinctly ill-informed scheme of Governmental speculation in the electrical industry, fomented by radical and interested politicians under the guise of advocating conservation, turned to a sister Province, for information as to the workings therein, of a Governmental experiment of the character proposed for their own adoption, and in its managers, exponents and advocates in the press, found:

'The same lofty disregard of plain figures and facts, the same wordy generalizations, the same assumption of being the sole savior of the people's interests, all covering:

'The same private greed on the part of manufacturing interests, and the same insistent demand for cheap conveniences on the part of those who can best afford to pay for them' (p. 3).

8 James Mavor, *Niagara in Politics*, E.P. Dutton, New York, 1925, p. 240.

9 'Paid-for propaganda? Who instigates attacks on Ontario Hydro? Important facts brought to public attention by the Hydro-Electric Power Commission of Ontario', Toronto, 1934, p. 7. For a somewhat more prosaic defence of Hydro, see the earlier pamphlet, 'The Hydro-Electric Power Commission of Ontario: Its origin, administration and achievements', Toronto, 1928.

10 'Paid-for propaganda?', p. 6.

11 *Power Corporations Act 1970.*

12 See Marc J. Roberts and Jeremy Bluhm, *The Choices of Power: Utilities Face the Environmental Challenge*, Harvard University Press, Cambridge, MA, 1981, p. 166.

13 Ontario, Royal Commission on Electric Power Planning (Porter Commission), *Report*, Toronto, 1980.

14 Nuclear Cost Inquiry (Ralph F. Brooks, Chairman), *Report to the Minister of Energy*, 31 January 1989.

15 Ontario Nuclear Safety Review (F. Kenneth Hare, Commissioner), *The Safety of Ontario's Nuclear Power Reactors: A Scientific and Technical Review; Report to the Minister*, 29 February 1988.

16 McKay, op. cit.; see also Soloman, op. cit., Energy Probe Research Foundation, Toronto, 1984.

17 Canada in turn has about a quarter of the world's uranium reserves.

18 McKay, op. cit., pp. 208–9.

19 Denison, op. cit., p. 279.

20 See Roberts and Bluhm, op. cit., p. 175.

21 The crisis was met by imports and occasional load-shedding at industrial plants, but no brown-outs or black-outs occurred.

22 Roberts and Bluhm, op. cit., p. 176.

23 Ibid., p. 176.

24 Ibid., p. 180.

25 Ibid., p. 182.

26 Ibid., p. 183.

27 Ibid., p. 183.

28 McKay, op. cit., pp. 208–9.

29 Roberts and Bluhm, op. cit., p. 184.

30 Terence J. Downey, 'The development of Ontario's uranium industry' in
    J. Angrand and C. Rabier (eds), *Natural Resources and the Politics of Development*,
    Laurentian University Press, Sudbury, Ont., 1986.
31 Ontario Hydro, *Annual Report 1986*, p. 41.
32 Ontario, Select Committee on Energy, *Final Report on Toward a Balanced
    Electricity System*, July 1986, Appendix H, p. 3. Atomic Energy of Canada and
    the provincial government jointly contributed $258m to the construction and
    operation of units 1 and 2 at Pickering station; see Ontario Hydro, *Statistical
    Yearbook 1985*, p. 41.
33 Jack O. Gibbons, *The Cost of Not Implementing Marginal Cost Pricing*, Energy
    Probe Research Foundation, Toronto, 1980. See also: Glenn P. Jenkins,
    'Public utility finance and economic waste', *Canadian Journal of Economics* 18
    (1985), pp. 484–98; Jean-Thomas Bernard and Robert D. Cairns, 'On public
    utility pricing and foregone economic benefits', *Canadian Journal of Economics*
    20 (1987), pp. 152–63. Jenkins argues that the economic losses generated by
    the Canadian provincial power utilities in the late 1970s were about $2–2.5b
    a year.
34 Soloman, op. cit., p. 48.
35 Michael Agrell, project leader, Demand/Supply Option Study, Ontario
    Hydro, interview with the author, June 1987.
36 McKay, op. cit., p. 183. See also C.A. Hooker, R. MacDonald, R. van Hulst and
    P. Victor, *Energy and the Quality of Life: Understanding Energy Policy*, University of
    Toronto Press, Toronto, 1981.
37 The fixed charge ratio is given by earnings before interest and taxes plus
    expense addback over interest payments.
38 Aidan Vining, 'Provincial hydro utilities' in Allan Tupper and G. Bruce Doern
    (eds), *Public Corporations and Public Policy*, Institute for Research on Public
    Policy, Montreal, 1981, p. 157.
39 Soloman, op. cit., pp. 55–6.
40 Ibid., pp. 39–40.
41 Ontario Hydro, *Statistical Yearbook 1985*, p. 56.
42 Ontario Hydro, *Providing the Balance of Power*, 1989, p. 10.
43 Vining, op. cit., p. 157.
44 Agrell interview.
45 Ontario Hydro, *Annual Report 1982*, p. 14.
46 Ontario Hydro, *Annual Report 1983*, p. 20.
47 Quoted by Soloman, op. cit., p. 44.
48 Ontario, Select Committee on Energy, *Toward a Balanced Electricity System*, July
    1986.
49 Ontario Hydro, System Planning Division, *Meeting Future Energy Needs: Draft
    Demand/Supply Planning Strategy* (Report 666 SP), December, 1987.
50 Agrell interview.
51 Vining, op. cit., p. 157.
52 Ontario Hydro, *Annual Report 1986*, p. 29.
53 R. Higgin, 'Regulation of the Crown-owned electric utility in Ontario', Paper
    presented to the 4th Annual CAMPUT Regulatory Educational Conference,
    Lake Louise, Alberta, 1990.
54 Ontario Hydro, System Planning Division, *Meeting Future Energy Needs*, p. s–1.
55 Roberts and Bluhm, *Choices of Power*, p. 196.
56 Ontario Hydro, System Planning Division, *Meeting Future Energy Needs*, p. 9-1.
57 Ontario, Select Committee on Energy, 'Report on Darlington Nuclear Gener-
    ating Station', December 1985.

58 Ontario, Select Committee on Energy, *Final Report on Toward a Balanced Electricity System*, July 1986.
59 Ontario Hydro, System Planning Division, *Meeting Future Energy Needs*, pp. 9–15.
60 Ontario, Select Committee on Energy, *Report on Ontario Hydro Draft Demand/ Supply Planning Strategy* (2 Vols), January 1989.
61 Ontario, *Review by Government Ministries of Ontario Hydro's Draft Demand/Supply Planning Strategy*, Report to the Minister of Energy, 15 July 1988. Twelve ministries participated in the review.
62 Ontario, *Review of Ontario Hydro's Draft Planning Strategy*, Report of the Electricity Planning Technical Advisory Panel to the Minister of Energy, 15 July 1988.
63 Ibid., p. 21.
64 Ibid., p. 47.
65 Ibid., pp. 47–8.
66 Ibid., p. 48. This subsequent inquiry, also chaired by Ralph Brooks, found Hydro's estimates to have an acceptable level of accuracy. See Ontario, Nuclear Cost Inquiry, *Report to the Minister of Energy*.
67 There are obviously many pitfalls in marketing conservation. For example, when Ontario Hydro ran a promotion on high-efficiency electric motors, dealers did not stock them. Rather than ordering efficient motors, dealers were matching the incentives and supplying low-efficiency motors.
68 Details of the public consultation process are provided in Ontario Hydro, *Final Report: Public/Government Review and Input into Ontario Hydro's Demand/ Supply Planning Process*, November 1991.
69 Ontario Hydro, *Annual Report 1988*, p. 11.
70 Ontario Hydro, *Annual Reports 1986* and *1991*.
71 Ontario Hydro, *Annual Report 1986*, p. 19.
72 Ontario Hydro, *Annual Report 1989*, p. 24.
73 Ontario Hydro, *Annual Report 1989*, pp. 28 and 49; BC Hydro, *Annual Report*, 1989.
74 Ontario Hydro, *Annual Report 1989*, p. 28.
75 See *Toronto Star*, 13 October 1991.
76 Ann Shortell, 'Electrical storm', *Toronto Life*, October 1991, pp. 25–34.
77 Ibid., p. 25.
78 The deputy minister is the chief executive of the agency.
79 Ontario Hydro, *Annual Report 1991*, pp. 40–1.
80 Ontario Hydro, *Providing the Balance of Power: Update 1992*.
81 Ibid., pp. 11–14.
82 Indeed, Strong is reported to oppose subsidising conservation on the grounds that the utility should not need to pay people to do what is good for them. The problem with this approach, as we have seen, is that the perceptions of economic signals about appropriate levels of conservation diverge for society, utility and individuals.
83 Maurice Strong, *The New Ontario Hydro*, Statement to Employees, 14 April 1993.
84 This number of fourteen included two on special leave.

6 Victoria: Uncertain reform

1 George Bates, Chief General Manager, SECV, 'Electricity generation and distribution: The future', Paper prepared for presentation at the conference, 'Managing Microeconomic Reform in a Public System', Monash University, Melbourne, 19 April 1991.

2 For a historical account of the SECV see the official history by Cecil Edwards, *Brown Power: A Jubilee History of the State Electricity Commission of Victoria*, SECV, Melbourne, 1969.

3 Bruce Hartnett, 'Newport: A conflict over power' in Sol Encel, Peter Wilenski and Bernard Schaffer (eds), *Decisions*, Longman Cheshire, Melbourne, 1981, p. 167.

4 G.D. McColl, *The Economics of the Electricity Supply Industry in Australia*, Melbourne University Press, Melbourne, 1976.

5 SECV, *Latrobe Valley Power Station Siting (Task Force Report Vol 1)*, May 1980, p. 4. In 1993 demand was about half this forecast for 1999–2000.

6 See Hartnett, op. cit., p. 179.

7 John Alford, 'Industrial relations: Labor's special but difficult relationship' in M. Considine and B. Costar (eds), *Trials in Power: Cain, Kirner and Victoria 1982–92*, Melbourne University Press, Melbourne, 1992, p. 157.

8 These details of the Portland deal were contained in documents obtained by the *Age* newspaper and published on 10 September 1981.

9 *Age*, 10 September 1981.

10 Ibid.

11 *Age*, 19 April 1980.

12 *Age*, 11 May 1981.

13 *Age*, 16 April 1980.

14 J.K. Stanley and V.J. Martin, *Aluminium Smelting: A Cost-benefit Analysis*, Premier's Department, Victoria (Discussion Paper No. 4), September 1979; Postscript January 1980.

15 Having peaked at about $US2300/tonne in the March quarter of 1980, the spot price for aluminium was only about $US1500/tonne in August 1981 and fell to about $US1000/tonne by June 1982.

16 *Age*, 4 December, 1981.

17 *Age*, 5 December 1981.

18 Part of the load at Alcoa's Point Henry smelter was met from the company's power station at Anglesea – the only privately owned station in the state.

19 *Age*, 25 November 1981.

20 *Financial Review*, 24 November 1981.

21 Rosenthal, S., and Peter Russ, *The Politics of Power: Inside Australia's Electric Utilities*, Melbourne University Press, Melbourne, 1988, pp. 140–1.

22 Ibid., p. 145.

23 SECV, *Annual Report*, 1983–84, p. 55.

24 John Cain, 'Achievements and lessons for reform governments' in M. Considine and B. Costar (eds), *Trials in Power: Cain, Kirner and Victoria 1982–92*, Melbourne University Press, Melbourne, 1992, pp. 270–1.

25 *Age*, 30 March 1981.

26 *Financial Review*, 18 April 1983.

27 SECV, *Report to the Government on Proposed Extension to the State Generating System – Loy Yang Project*, February 1976.

28 SECV, *Report on Loy Yang Project Costs*, November 1982, p. 15.

29 *Age*, 16 December 1980.

30 *Age*, 6 September 1980.

31 *Australian*, 16 December 1981.

32 Victoria, Department of Management and Budget, Committee of Review, *Cost Estimates of the Loy Yang Power Station Project*, Submitted by Rheinbraun Consulting Australia Pty Ltd, December 1982.

33 *Age*, 2 October 1981.

34 *Age*, 25 April 1981.

35 *Financial Review*, 8 December 1981. Alcoa's price at Point Henry had already been cut by 6 per cent.

36 SECV, *Report on Loy Yang Project Costs*, November 1982; Victoria, Committee of Enquiry into Loy Yang Costs, Report by Professor F.K. Wright to Dr Peter Sheehan, Director-General, Department of Management and Budget, 9 December 1982; Victoria, Department of Management and Budget, Committee of Review, *Cost Estimates of the Loy Yang Power Station Project*, Submitted by Rheinbraun Consulting Australia Pty Ltd, December 1982; Victoria, Department of Management and Budget, Committee of Review into Loy Yang Costs, *Report on O&M Costs, Overheads: Capital Costs*, Ernst & Whinney, 9 December 1992; Victoria, Department of Management and Budget, Committee of Review, Cost Estimates and Management of the Loy Yang Power Station by the State Electricity Commission of Victoria. *Report by Fluor Australia Pty Ltd*, 10 December 1982.

37 SECV, *Review of Electricity Supply Situation in Victoria 1982–84*, August 1982.

38 Victoria, Department of Minerals and Energy, *Electricity Pricing 1982–83*. August 1982; Victoria, Department of Minerals and Energy, *Gas Pricing 1982–83*, September 1982.

39 Victoria, Department of Minerals and Energy, *Energy Pricing Principles and Policies 1983–84*, Information Paper, June 1983; Victoria, Latrobe Valley Ministerial Council, *Strategy Planning for Victoria's Brown Coal – What the Government Will Do*, July 1982; Victoria, Public Service Board, *Report Recommending Arrangement to Strengthen the Relationships Between the State Electricity Commission and the Government*, 20 October 1982.

40 J. Falk, R. Badham and G. Smith, *Public Accountability and Electricity Planning in Victoria*, Victorian Energy Planning Program, Consultant's Report No. 4, April 1984.

41 SECV, *Electricity Supply and Demand to the Mid 1990s: Draft Government Energy Policy*, October 1984; see also SECV, *Electricity Supply and Demand to the Mid 1990s: Review of the Timing of Loy Yang B Units 1 and 2*, July 1986. The order of the words, *supply* and *demand* in the titles of SECV reports might well be an interesting reflection of reverse adaptation.

42 See SECV, *Electricity Development Strategy Implementation Review*, December 1989, p. 18.

43 NREC, *Report on Electricity Supply and Demand Beyond the Mid 1990s*, April 1988, pp. 21–2.

44 Details of then-existing demand management programs are contained in SECV/DITR, Demand Management Development Project, *3 Year Demand Management Action Plan*, Information Paper No. 5, December 1989.

45 SECV, *Annual Report*, 1986–87, p. 14.

46 NREC, op. cit., p. 1.

47 SECV, *Electricity Supply and Demand Beyond the Mid 1990s – Planning and Approval Processes*, August 1986.

48 SECV, *Annual Report*, 1986–87, p. 83.

49 The inquiry commissioned several reports that dealt with issues such as LCUP, DSM, plant refurbishment and so on. See, for example: P.M. Garlick and Associates, *Power Plant Availability Issues*, NREC Background Paper, November 1987; G. McColl, *The Economic Framework for Considering Options for Electricity Supply in Uncertain Environments and Review of Evidence Presented to the Inquiry into Electricity Supply and Demand Beyond the Mid 1990s*, NREC Discussion Paper, November 1987.

50 SECV, *Annual Report*, 1987–88, p. 73.

51 Ibid., p. 73.
52 McColl, op. cit., p. 101.
53 G.D. McColl, *The Economics of the Electricity Supply Industry in Australia*, Melbourne University Press, Melbourne, 1976.
54 McColl, *Electricity Supply and Demand Beyond the Mid 1990s*, p. xxv.
55 Powerline Review Panel, *Final Report to the Victorian Government*, July 1989.
56 Australian Labor Party, *The La Trobe Valley: The Next Four Years*, September 1988, p. 3.
57 Department of the Parliamentary Library, *Statistics on Electoral Districts: McMillan*, Canberra, 1987.
58 For a discussion of these techniques, which were crucial to the narrow victories for the ALP in Victoria in 1985 and 1988, see Stephen Mills, *The New Machine Men*, Penguin, Melbourne, 1986.
59 Ministerial Response to the Report of the Natural Resources and Environment Committee, 'Electricity Demand and Supply Beyond the Mid 1990s', by the Hon. Evan Walker MLC, Minister for Industry, Technology and Resources, 9 December 1988.
60 SECV/DITR, Demand Management Development Project, *Status Report*, Information Paper No. 1, February 1989.
61 SECV/DITR, Demand Management Development Project, *Integrated Resource Planning*, Information Paper No. 4, December 1989.
62 SECV/DITR, Demand Management Development Project, *Status Report*, Information Paper No. 1, February 1989, p. 30.
63 SECV, *Annual Report*, 1988–89, p. 81.
64 Department of Industry, *Annual Report*, 1989–90, p. 49. The recommended strategy was contained in SECV/DITR, Demand Management Development Project, *3 Year Demand Management Action Plan*, Information Paper No. 5, December 1989.
65 Amory Lovins, *Report to the Minister for Industry and Economic Planning on Matters Pertaining to Victorian Energy Policy*, November 1990.
66 *Age*, 27 December 1990.
67 SECV/DITR, Demand Management Development Project, *Status Report*, Information Paper No. 1, February 1989, p. 22.
68 SECV, *Submission to the Industry Commission Inquiry into Energy Generation and Distribution*, August 1990. See also Industry Commission, *Energy Generation and Distribution (3 Vols)*, 1991.
69 SECV, *Annual Report*, 1986–87, p. 52.
70 See ibid., p. 51.
71 SECV, *Annual Report*, 1987–88, p. 51.
72 SECV/DITR, Demand Management Development Project, *Final Report*, January 1990, p. 17.
73 SECV, *Electricity Development Strategy Implementation Review*, December 1989.
74 Ibid., p. 6.
75 Ibid., pp. 16–17.
76 Ibid., p. 21.
77 Ibid., p. 42.
78 Victoria, Department of Manufacturing and Industry Development, *Victoria's Energy Efficiency Strategy*, June 1991.
79 SECV, *Electricity Development Study Implementation Review*, December 1989, p. 31.
80 SECV, *Annual Report*, 1989–90, p. 25.
81 SECV, *Annual Report*, 1990–91, p. 27.

82   *Age*, 13 July 1989.
83   SECV, *Electricity Development Study Implementation Review*, December 1989, pp. 54–5.
84   *Age*, 18 June 1990.
85   *Age*, 26 January 1991.
86   *Age*, 23 April 1991.
87   SECV, *Submission to the Industry Commission Inquiry into Energy Generation and Distribution*. August 1990, p. 37.
88   SECV, *Annual Report*, 1988–89, p. 86.
89   *Age*, 5 March 1991.
90   *Age*, 23 November 1990.
91   *Age*, 13 June 1991.
92   *Age*, 6 February 1991.
93   *Age*, 14 March 1991.
94   *Age*, 16 March 1991.
95   SECV, *Annual Report*, 1991–92, p. 68.
96   SECV, *Demand Management Annual Report*, 1991–92.
97   SECV, *Annual Report*, 1991–92, p. 69.
98   SECV, *Annual Report*, 1991–92, p. 68.
99   SECV, *Demand Management Annual Report*, 1991–92.
100 SECV, *Annual Report*, 1991–92, p. 70. The same excuses were still being made a year later.
101 SECV, *Annual Report*, 1989–90, p. 131.
102 SECV, *Annual Report*, 1990–91, p. 134.
103 SECV, *Annual Report*, 1991–92, p. 124.
104 SECV, *Annual Report*, 1992–93, p. 148.
105 Ibid., p. 92.
106 Ibid.
107 See Richard B. Riley, 'Public policy and the electric power industry in Canada: A comparative political analysis of power development in three western provinces', unpublished PhD dissertation, Duke University, 1975.
108 Aaron Wildavsky, 'If planning is everything, maybe it is nothing', *Policy Sciences* 4(1973), pp. 127–53.

7 Institutions and electricity planning

1   Richard B. Riley, 'Public policy and the electric power industry in Canada: A comparative political analysis of power development in three western provinces', unpublished PhD dissertation, Duke University, 1975.
2   Richard Drouin, 'Planning for the future of electricity', *Public Utilities Fortnightly* 131(7), 1993, pp. 13–14.
3   S. Rosenthal and P. Russ, *The Politics of Power: Inside Australia's Electric Utilities*, Melbourne University Press, Melbourne, 1988, p. 51.
4   Ibid., p. 54.
5   NSW Audit Commission, *Focus on Reform: Report on the State's Finances*, August 1988.
6   Electricity Commission of NSW, *Annual Report 1991*, p. 5.
7   Ibid., p. 15.
8   Ibid., p. 55.
9   Ibid., p. 52.
10 *Age*, 29 May 1993.

11 Details of this concessionary sale of electricity were contained in Cabinet documents obtained by the *National Times* and published in its 21–27 June 1985 edition.

12 *Financial Review*, 7 October 1992.

13 *Australian*, 4 August 1993.

14 Frank Harman, 'Gas, coal and politics: Making decisions about power stations', *IPA Backgrounder* 4(3), 1992.

15 Garth Stevenson, *Rail Transport and Australian Federalism*, Research Monograph No. 48, Centre for Research on Federal Financial Relations, Australian National University, Canberra, 1987.

16 *Age*, 8 October 1993. See also *Financial Review*, 11 August 1993.

17 *Age*, 5 February 1994.

18 *Australian*, 18 May 1993.

19 SECV/DITR, Demand Management Development Project, *Short-Term Demand Management Objectives*, Information Paper No. 2, June 1989, p. 16.

20 A.K. Meier and J. Whittier, 'Consumer discount rates implied by consumer purchases of energy-efficient refrigerators', *Energy* 8 (1983), pp. 957–62.

21 P.C. Stern and E. Aronson (eds), *Energy Use: The Human Dimension*, W.H. Freeman, New York, 1984.

22 Michael A. Laros and Brian J. Daly, 'Demand-side management: Surviving in the '90s', *Public Utilities Fortnightly* 130(3), 1992, pp. 16–18. For review of DSM experience in the United States, see the special issue of *Public Utilities Fortnightly* on the subject: Vol 131 (9), 1993.

23 Eric Hirst, 'Electric utility DSM programs through the year 2000', *Public Utilities Fortnightly* 130(4) 1992, pp. 11–14, p. 11.

24 See the forum on the topic in *Public Utilities Fortnightly*, 131(11), 1993, pp. 46–63.

25 L. Winner, *Autonomous Technology: Technics-out-of-control as a Theme in Political Thought*, MIT Press, Cambridge, MA, 1977, p. 242.

26 J.K. Galbraith, *The New Industrial State*, New American Library, New York, 1967, p. 28.

27 Ibid., p. 164.

28 Thomas P. Hughes, *Networks of Power: Electrification in Western Society 1880–1930*, Johns Hopkins University Press, Baltimore, 1983.

29 Winner, op. cit., p. 243.

30 Ibid., p. 244.

31 Ibid., p. 245

32 Ibid., p. 246.

33 Ibid., p. 249.

34 Ibid., p. 250.

35 Ibid.

36 F. Fischer, *Technocracy and the Politics of Expertise*, Sage, Newbury Park, CA, 1990, p. 31.

37 Winner, op. cit., p. 259.

38 Hughes, op. cit., p. 465.

39 Theodore J. Lowi, 'The state in politics: The relation between policy and administration' in Roger G. Noll (ed.), *Regulatory Policy and the Social Sciences*, University of California Press, Berkeley, 1985.

40 Ibid., p. 92.

41 Herbert Kaufman, *The Forest Ranger: A Study in Administrative Behavior*, Johns Hopkins University Press, Baltimore, 1960.

42 Galbraith, op. cit., p. 165.
43 Thomas Baumgartner and Atle Midttun, 'Energy forecasting and political structure: Some comparative notes' in Thomas Baumgartner and Atle Midttun (eds), *The Politics of Energy Forecasting*, Clarendon Press, Oxford, 1987, p. 272.
44 Paul L. Joskow and Richard Schmalensee, *Markets for Power: An Analysis of Electric Utility Deregulation*, MIT Press, Cambridge, MA, 1983, p. 106.
45 Ibid., p. 107.
46 Michael Pusey has noted similar changes within the upper echelons of the Australian public service with the replacement of technical specialists by economists. He argues: 'The criterion that these exceptionally intelligent people use to judge the intellectual abilities of their peers is the agility and speed with which they can conjure up abstract models of a very particular kind ... It is this which distinguishes these intellectuals from the technocrats and social reformers of earlier times for whom intellectual virtuosity was measured against the more narrowly instrumental capacity of professionals of all kinds – educationists, medical experts, engineers and town planners – to find goals and means appropriate to needs and contexts of action – in schools and education systems, in water resource management or whatever. Instead what counts in the new order is the elegance, speed and agility with which one can create a formal, *transcontextual* commensurability of reference across goals that are turned into *objects* of decisions that will be made on extrinsic criteria.' Michael Pusey, *Economic Rationalism in Canberra: A Nation Building State Changes Its Mind*, Cambridge University Press, Melbourne, 1991, p. 176.
47 Lowi, op. cit., p. 85. Halligan and Power have made a similar disctinction to Lowi's between 'technicist' and 'administrationist' regimes; see John Halligan and John Power, *Political Management in the 1990s*, Oxford University Press, Melbourne, 1992, pp. 16–17.
48 Marc J. Roberts and Jeremy Bluhm, *The Choices of Power: Utilities Face the Environmental Challenge*, Harvard University Press, Cambridge, MA, 1981.
49 Baumgartner and Midttun, op. cit., pp. 284–5.
50 D.A. Mazmanian and J. Nienaber, *Can Organizations Change? Environmental Protection, Citizen Participation and the Army Corps of Engineers*, Brookings Institution, Washington, 1979, pp. 191–4.
51 Ibid., p. 192.
52 Ibid.
53 Ibid., pp. 192–3.
54 Ibid., p. 193.
55 Ibid.
56 Ibid., p. 194.
57 Roberts and Bluhm, op. cit., p. 34.
58 Ibid., p. 43.
59 Douglas D. Anderson, *Regulatory Politics and Electric Utilities: A Case Study in Political Economy*, Auburn House, Boston, 1981, p. 182.
60 Barbara R. Barkovich, *Regulatory Interventionism in the Utility Industry: Fairness, Efficiency and the Pursuit of Energy Conservation*, Quorum Books, New York, 1989.
61 E. Oatman and J.L. Plummer, 'The meaning of strategic planning in regulated and unregulated firms' in J.L. Plummer, E. Oatman and P.K. Gupta (eds), *Strategic Management and Planning for Electric Utilities*, Prentice-Hall, Englewood Cliffs, 1985, p. 4.

62 James Lehr Kennedy, 'The role of regulators in electric utility strategic planning' in Plummer, Oatman and Gupta, *Strategic Management and Planning*, p. 199.

63 See Robert H. Williams, 'Innovative approaches to marketing electric efficiency' in Thomas B. Johansson, Brigit Bodlund and Robert H. Williams (eds), *Electricity: Efficient End-use and New Generation Technologies and Their Planning Implications*, Lund University Press, Lund, 1989.

64 Kennedy, op. cit., p. 199.

65 Louis Puiseux, 'The ups and downs of electricity forecasting in France: Technocratic élitism', in Baumgartner and Midttun, *Politics of Energy Forecasting*, p. 201. On French energy service companies see Olivier de la Morinière, 'Energy service companies: The French experience' in Johansson, Bodlund and Williams, *Electricity*.

66 Winner, op. cit., p. 259.

67 Puiseux, op. cit., p. 202.

68 Pusey, op. cit., p. 32.

69 David Harvey, *The Condition of Postmodernity: An Enquiry into the Origins of Cultural Change*, Basil Blackwell, Oxford, 1989.

70 Ibid., p. 147.

71 David F. Noble, *America by Design*, Alfred A. Knopf, New York, 1977, p. 324.

72 David Elliott and Ruth Elliott, *The Control of Technology*, Wykeham, London, 1976, p. 53.

73 Renfrew Christie, *Electricity, Industry and Class in South Africa*, Macmillan, London, 1984.

74 Hughes, op. cit., p. 465.

75 In Paehlke's words: 'Environmental politics is about choosing technologies, about the criteria for such choices, and about their unintended effects'. Robert C. Paehlke, *Environmentalism and the Future of Progressive Politics*, Yale University Press, New Haven, 1989, p. 189.

Bibliography

Primary sources

Age, Melbourne.

Auckland Star, Auckland.

Australia, Senate Select Committee on South West Tasmania, Transcripts of Evidence.

Australia, Department of the Parliamentary Library, *Statistics on Electoral Districts: McMillan*, Canberra, 1987.

Australia, Industry Commission, *Energy Generation and Distribution (3 Vols)*, 1991.

Australian Labor Party, *The La Trobe Valley: The Next Four Years*, September 1988.

British Columbia Hydro and Power Authority, *Annual Reports*.

British Columbia Hydro and Power Authority, *Energy Blueprint 1980*, Vancouver, 1980.

British Columbia Hydro and Power Authority, Systems Planning Division, *Financial Risks of Resource Planning*, Report Prepared for the BC Utilities Commission, March 1987.

British Columbia Hydro and Power Authority, *Demand Side Management: A Progress Report*, Report to the BC Utilities Commission, March 1987.

British Columbia Hydro and Power Authority, *Twenty-year Resource Plan*, 1989.

British Columbia Utilities Commission, *Site C Report: Report and Recommendations*, Victoria, BC, 29 September 1983.

Energy Policy and Analysis Pty Ltd, *A Review of the Hydro-electric Commission's Most Recent Financial Analysis on the Gordon Below Franklin Scheme*, Report for the Business Association for Economical Power, May 1982.

Falk, J., R. Badham and G. Smith, *Public Accountability and Electricity Planning in Victoria*, Victorian Energy Planning Program, Consultant's Report No. 4, April 1984.

P. M. Garlick and Associates, *Power Plant Availability Issues*, NREC Background Paper, November 1987.

ICF Incorporated, *The Economic Costs of an Electricity Supply–Demand Imbalance*, Report Prepared for British Columbia Hydro and Power Authority, February 1982.

Lovins, Amory, *Report to the Minister for Industry and Economic Planning on Matters Pertaining to Victorian Energy Policy*, November 1990.

McColl, G., *The Economic Framework for Considering Options for Electricity Supply in Uncertain Environments and Review of Evidence Presented to the Inquiry into Electricity Supply and Demand Beyond the Mid 1990s*, NREC Discussion Paper, November 1987.

National Business Review, Wellington.

New South Wales, Commission of Inquiry into Electricity Generation Planning in New South Wales, *Report*, June 1986.

New South Wales, Audit Commission, *Focus on Reform: Report on the State's Finances*, August 1988.

New South Wales, Electricity Commission of NSW, *Annual Reports*.

New Zealand Times, Wellington.

New Zealand, Committee to Review the Power Requirements, *Report*, Appendices to the Journal of the House of Representatives, D6A, 1970–79.

New Zealand, Electricity Division, Ministry of Energy, *Report of the Ministry of Energy, Electricity Division, to the Select Committee Considering the Clutha Development (Clyde Dam) Empowering Bill*, October 1982.

New Zealand, Planning Committee on Electric Power Development, *Report*, Appendices to the Journal of the House of Representatives, D6B, 1970–79.

New Zealand, Ministry of Works and Development, Submission on the Marsden B Environmental Impact Report, 8 July 1974.

New Zealand, *Parliamentary Debates (Hansard)*.

New Zealand, Ministry of Works and Development on behalf of New Zealand Electricity Department, *Environmental Impact Report on Design and Construction Proposal: Clutha Valley Development*, December 1977.

New Zealand, Treasury, *Economic Management*, briefing document released 30 August 1984.

Ontario, Hydro Electric Power Commission, *The Hydro Electric Power Commission of Ontario: Its Origin, Administration and Achievements*, Toronto, 1928.

Ontario, Ontario Hydro, *Annual Reports*.

Ontario, Ontario Hydro, *Statistical Yearbooks*.

Ontario, Ontario Hydro, *Sustainable Development: The Economy and the Environment*, Background Paper, February 1993.

Ontario, Ontario Hydro, System Planning Division, *Meeting Future Energy Needs: Draft Demand/Supply Planning Strategy* (Report 666 SP), December 1987.

Ontario, Ontario Hydro, *Final Report: Public/Government Review and Input into Ontario Hydro's Demand/Supply Planning Process*, November 1991.

Ontario, Ontario Hydro, *Providing the Balance of Power: Update 1992*.

Ontario, Royal Commission on Electric Power Planning, *Report*, Toronto, 1980.

Ontario, Nuclear Cost Inquiry (Ralph F. Brooks, Chairman), *Report to the Minister of Energy*, 31 January 1989.

Ontario, Nuclear Safety Review (F. Kenneth Hare, Commissioner), *The Safety of Ontario's Nuclear Power Reactors: A Scientific and Technical Review*, Report to the Minister, 29 February 1988.

Ontario, *Review of Ontario Hydro's Draft Planning Strategy*, Report of the Electricity Planning Technical Advisory Panel to the Minister of Energy, 15 July 1988.

Ontario, *Review by Government Ministries of Ontario Hydro's Draft Demand/Supply Planning Strategy*, Report to the Minister of Energy, 15 July 1988.

Ontario, Select Committee on Energy, *Report on Darlington Nuclear Generating Station*, December 1985.

Ontario, Select Committee on Energy, *Final Report on Toward a Balanced Electricity System*, July 1986.

Ontario, Select Committee on Energy, Report on Ontario Hydro Draft Demand/
    Supply Planning Strategy (2 Vols), January 1989.
Otago Daily Times, Dunedin.
Strong, Maurice, *The New Ontario Hydro*, Statement to Employees, 14 April 1993.
Tasmania, Directorate of Energy, *Report to the Coordination Committee on Future
    Power Development*, May 1980.
Tasmania, Hydro Electric Commission, *Report on Further Power Developments 1970–
    1980 With Reference to Second Generating Set, Bell Bay Power Station and Pieman
    River Power Development*, Hobart, 1970.
Tasmania, Hydro Electric Commission, *Report on the Gordon River Power Develop-
    ment Stage 2*, Hobart 1979.
Tasmania, Hydro Electric Commission, Submission to the Senate Select Com-
    mittee on South West Tasmania, 1982.
Tasmania, Hydro Electric Commission, *Load Forecast*, Hobart, November 1983.
Tasmania, Hydro Electric Commission, *Pieman River Power Development Capital
    Cost*, 6 November 1984.
Tasmania, Hydro Electric Commission, *Annual Reports*.
Toronto Life, Toronto.
Toronto Star, Toronto.
Victoria, Department of Industry, *Annual Report*, 1989–90.
Victoria, Department of Management and Budget, Committee of Review, *Cost
    Estimates of the Loy Yang Power Station Project*, Submitted by Rheinbraun
    Consulting Australia Pty Ltd, December 1982.
Victoria, Department of Management and Budget, Committee of Enquiry into
    Loy Yang Costs, *Report by Professor F. K. Wright to Dr Peter Sheehan, Director-
    General, Department of Management and Budget*, 9 December 1982.
Victoria, Department of Management and Budget, Committee of Review into Loy
    Yang Costs. *Report on O&M Costs, Overheads: Capital Costs*, Ernst & Whinney,
    9 December 1992.
Victoria, Department of Management and Budget, Committee of Review, Cost
    Estimates and Management of the Loy Yang Power Station by the State Elec-
    tricity Commission of Victoria, *Report by Fluor Australia Pty Ltd*, 10 December
    1982.
Victoria, Department of Manufacturing and Industry Development, *Victoria's
    Energy Efficiency Strategy*, June 1991.
Victoria, Department of Minerals and Energy, *Electricity Pricing 1982–83*, August
    1982.
Victoria, Department of Minerals and Energy, *Gas Pricing 1982–83*, September
    1982.
Victoria, Department of Minerals and Energy, *Energy Pricing Principles and Policies
    1983–84*, Information Paper, June 1983.
Victoria, Latrobe Valley Ministerial Council, *Strategy Planning for Victoria's Brown
    Coal – What the Government Will Do*, July 1982.
Victoria, Ministerial Response to the Report of the Natural Resources and
    Environment Committee, *Electricity Demand and Supply Beyond the Mid 1990s*,
    by the Hon. Evan Walker MLC, Minister for Industry, Technology and
    Resources, 9 December 1988.
Victoria, Parliament, Natural Resources and Environment Committee, *Report on
    Electricity Supply and Demand Beyond the Mid 1990s*, April 1988.
Victoria, Powerline Review Panel, *Final Report to the Victorian Government*, July
    1989.

Victoria, Public Service Board, *Report Recommending Arrangement to Strengthen the Relationships Between the State Electricity Commission and the Government*, 20 October 1982.

Victoria, State Electricity Commission, *Annual Reports*.

Victoria, State Electricity Commission, *Report to the Government on Proposed Extension to the State Generating System – Loy Yang Project*, February 1976.

Victoria, State Electricity Commission, *Latrobe Valley Power Station Siting (Task Force Report Vol 1)*, May 1980.

Victoria, State Electricity Commission, *Review of Electricity Supply Situation in Victoria 1982–84*, August 1982.

Victoria, State Electricity Commission, *Report on Loy Yang Project Costs*, November 1982.

Victoria, State Electricity Commission, *Electricity Supply and Demand to the Mid 1990s: Draft Government Energy Policy*, October 1984.

Victoria, State Electricity Commission, *Electricity Supply and Demand to the Mid 1990s: Review of the Timing of Loy Yang B Units 1 and 2*, July 1986.

Victoria, State Electricity Commission, *Electricity Supply and Demand Beyond the Mid 1990s: Planning and Approval Processes*, August 1986.

Victoria, State Electricity Commission, *Electricity Development Strategy Implementation Review*, December 1989.

Victoria, State Electricity Commission, *Submission to the Industry Commission Inquiry into Energy Generation and Distribution*, August 1990.

Victoria, State Electricity Commission, *Demand Management Annual Report*, 1991–92.

Victoria, State Electricity Commission and Department of Industry, Technology and Resources, Demand Management Development Project, *Status Report*, Information Paper No. 1, February 1989.

Victoria, State Electricity Commission and Department of Industry, Technology and Resources, Demand Management Development Project, *Short-term Demand Management Objectives*, Information Paper No. 2, June 1989.

Victoria, State Electricity Commission and Department of Industry, Technology and Resources, Demand Management Development Project, *Integrated Resource Planning*, Information Paper No. 4, December 1989.

Victoria, State Electricity Commission and Department of Industry, Technology and Resources, Demand Management Development Project, *3-Year Demand Management Action Plan*, Information Paper No. 5, December 1989.

Victoria, State Electricity Commission and Department of Industry, Technology and Resources, Demand Management Development Project, *Final Report*, January 1990.

Secondary sources

Alford, John, 'Industrial relations: Labor's special but difficult relationship' in M. Considine and B. Costar (eds), *Trials in Power: Cain, Kirner and Victoria 1982–92*, Melbourne University Press, Melbourne, 1992.

Anderson, Douglas D., *Regulatory Politics and Electric Utilities: A Case Study in Political Economy*, Auburn House, Boston, 1981.

Anderson, D. Victor, *Illusions of Power*, Praeger, New York, 1985.

Anderson, J.S., 'The seer-sucker theory: The value of experts in forecasting', *Technology Review* 83 (1980), pp. 18–24.

Anderson, O.D., *Forecasting Public Utilities*, North Holland, Amsterdam, 1980.

Anon, 'Paid-for Propaganda? Who Instigates Attacks on Ontario Hydro? Important Facts Brought to Public Attention by the Hydro-Electric Power Commission of Ontario', Toronto, 1934.

Atkinson, Michael M. and Marsha A. Chandler (eds), *The Politics of Canadian Public Policy*, University of Toronto Press, Toronto, 1983.

Averch, H., and L.L. Johnson, 'Behaviour of the firm under regulation constraint', *American Economic Review* 52 (December 1962), pp. 1052–69.

Baden, John, and Richard L. Stroup (eds), *Bureaucracy vs Environment: The Environmental Costs of Bureaucratic Governance*, University of Michigan Press, Ann Arbor, 1981.

Bailey, Elizabeth E., *Public Regulation: New Perspectives on Institutions and Policy*, MIT Press, Cambridge, MA, 1987.

Baldwin, John R., *The Regulatory Agency and the Public Corporation*, Ballinger, Cambridge, MA, 1975.

Ballin, H.H., *The Organisation of Electricity Supply in Britain*, Electrical Press, London, 1946.

Banbright, J.C., *Principles of Public Utility Rates*, Columbia University Press, New York, 1961.

Barkovich, Barbara R., *Regulatory Interventionism in the Utility Industry: Fairness, Efficiency and the Pursuit of Energy Conservation*, Quorum Books, New York, 1989.

Battle, Ellen F., Gordon S. Gislason and Gordon W. Douglas, *Potential Benefits and Costs of Canadian Electricity Exports*, Canadian Energy Research Institute, Calgary, 1983.

Bauer, John, *Public Organization of Electric Power*, Harper & Brothers, New York, 1949.

Bauer, John, *Effective Regulation of Public Utilities*, Arno Press, New York, 1976 (originally published 1925).

Baughman, Martin L., Paul L. Joskow and Dilip P. Kamat, *Electric Power in the United States: Models and Policy Analyses*, MIT Press, Cambridge, MA, 1979.

Baumgartner, Thomas and Atle Midttun (eds), *The Politics of Energy Forecasting*, Clarendon Press, Oxford, 1987.

Beeche, H.J., *Electrical Development in New Zealand: The Story of the Generation and Distribution, Use of, and Dependence on, Electrical Energy in New Zealand*, Neville Graham Dunning for the Electric-power Boards and Supply Authorities' Association of New Zealand, Wellington, 1950.

Beggs, John, 'Australia: One day in the sunshine' in Merton J. Peck (ed.), *The World Aluminium Industry in a Changing Energy Era*, Resources for the Future, Washington, DC, 1988.

Bernard, Jean-Thomas, and Robert D. Cairns, 'On public utility pricing and foregone economic benefits', *Canadian Journal of Economics* 20 (1987), pp. 152–63.

Bertram, Geoffrey, *Electricity in New Zealand: Is There a Surplus to Sell?*, Development Information Group, Wellington, 1980.

Boehm, E.A., 'The impact of electricity', *Economic Record* 31 (1955), pp. 61–76.

Bolton, R.P., *An Expensive Experiment: The Hydro-electric Power Commission of Ontario*, Baker & Taylor, New York, 1913.

Booth, R.R., 'Optimal generation planning considering uncertainty', *IEEE Transactions on Power Apparatus and Systems*, Vol PAS-91 No. 1, pp. 70–7 (Jan–Feb 1972).

Butlin, N.G., A. Barnard and J.J. Pincus, *Government and Capitalism in Australia*, Allen & Unwin, Sydney, 1982.

Cain, John, 'Achievements and lessons for reform governments' in M. Considine and B. Costar (eds), *Trials in Power: Cain, Kirner and Victoria 1982–92*, Melbourne University Press, Melbourne, 1992.

Caldwell, Lynton K., 'Energy and the structure of social institutions', *Human Ecology* 4 (1976): 31–46.

Caldwell, Lynton K., Lynton R. Hayes and Isabel M. MacWhirter, *Citizens and the Environment: Case Studies in Popular Action*, Indiana University Press, Bloomington, IN, 1976.

Campen, James T., *Benefit, Cost and Beyond: The Political Economy of Benefit–Cost Analysis*, Ballenger, Cambridge, MA, 1986.

Cazalet, E.G., C.E. Clark and T.W. Keelin, 'Costs and benefits of over/ undercapacity in electric power system planning', *EPRI Research Project EA-972*, Electric Power Research Institute, Pasadena, CA, October 1978.

Chandler, Marsha A., 'State enterprise and partisanship in provincial politics', *Canadian Journal of Political Science* 15 (1982), pp. 711–40.

Christie, Renfrew, *Electricity, Industry and Class in South Africa*, Macmillan, London, 1984.

Clegg, Stewart R., *Modern Organizations: Organization Studies in the Postmodern World*, Sage, London, 1990.

Cleveland, Les, *Anatomy of Influence*, Hicks Smith, Wellington, 1972.

Cose, Ellis, *Decentralizing Energy Decisions: The Rebirth of Community Power*, Westview, Boulder, CO, 1983.

Crabb, Peter, 'Hydro power on the periphery: A comparison of Newfoundland, Tasmania and the South Island', *Alternatives* 10(4) 1982, pp. 12–20.

Crew, Michael, A. (ed.), *Regulating Utilities in an Era of Deregulation*, Macmillan, London, 1987.

Culy, John, *Electricity Restructuring: Towards a Competitive Wholesale Market*, Institute of Economic Research (NZIER Discussion Paper), Wellington, NZ, 1992.

Dales, John H., *Hydroelectricity and Industrial Development: Quebec 1898–1940* Harvard University Press, Cambridge, MA, 1957.

Daly, Herman, 'Energy demand forecasting: Prediction or planning?', *Journal of the American Institute of Planners* 42 (1976), pp. 4–15.

Davis, Bruce W., 'Waterpower and wilderness: Political and administrative aspects of the Lake Pedder controversy', *Public Administration (Sydney)* 31 (1972), pp. 21–42.

Davis, Bruce W., 'Professional values and accountability in government: The case of Australian public investment' in Patrick Weller and Dean Jaensch (eds), *Responsible Government in Australia*, Drummond, Richmond, Vic., 1980.

Davis, B.W., 'The struggle for South West Tasmania' in R. Scott (ed.), *Interest Groups and Public Policy: Cases From the Australian States*, Macmillan, Melbourne, 1980.

Davis, B.W., 'Tasmania: The political economy of a peripheral state' in B. Head (ed.), *The Politics of Development in Australia*, Allen & Unwin, Sydney, 1986.

Davis, Peter V., 'Selling saved energy: A new risk role for the utilities' in Dorothy S. Zinberg (ed.), *Uncertain Power: The Struggle for a National Energy Policy*, Pergamon Press, New York, 1983.

Davis, R., *Eighty Years' Labor*, Sassafras Books, Hobart, 1983.

De Alessi, L., 'Managerial tenure under private and government ownership in the electric power industry', *Journal of Political Economy* 82 (May–June 1974), pp. 645–53.

De Souza, Glenn R., *Energy Policy and Forecasting: Economic, Financial and Technological Dimensions,* D.C. Heath, Lexington, MA, 1981.

Deane, Roderick S., 'Reforming the public sector' in Simon Walker (ed.), *Rogernomics: Reshaping New Zealand's Economy,* GP Books, Wellington, 1989.

Denison, Merrill, *The People's Power: The History of Ontario Hydro,* McClelland & Stewart, Toronto, 1960.

Dillon, Robert John, *Reality and Value Judgment in Policymaking: A Study of Expert Judgments About Alternative Energy Technologies,* Arno, New York, 1979.

Douglas, Mary, *How Institutions Think,* Routledge & Kegan Paul, London, 1987.

Douglas, Mary, and Aaron Wildavsky, *Risk and Culture,* University of California Press, Berkeley, 1982.

Downey, Terence J., 'The development of Ontario's uranium industry', in J. Angrand and C. Rabier (eds), *Natural Resources and the Politics of Development,* Laurentian University Press, Sudbury, Ont., 1986.

Downs, A., 'Why the budget is too small in a democracy', *World Politics* 12 (1960), pp. 541–63.

Drinnan, J.H., and K.R. Spafford, 'A stochastic resource planning model', Paper Presented at the Generation and System Planning and Operation Subsection, CEA Spring Meeting, Vancouver, March 1987.

Drouin, Richard, 'Planning for the future of electricity', *Public Utilities Fortnightly* 131(7) 1993, pp. 13–14.

Ducsik, Dennis W., *Public Involvement in Energy Facility Planning,* Westview Press, Boulder, 1986.

Edwards, Cecil, *Brown Power: A Jubilee History of the State Electricity Commission of Victoria,* SECV, Melbourne, 1969.

Eggleston, F.W., *State Socialism in Victoria,* King, London, 1932.

Elliott, David, and Ruth Elliott, *The Control of Technology,* Wykeham, London, 1976.

Falk, Jim and Peter Murphy, 'New aluminium proposals and Australian energy policy', *Australian Quarterly* 53 (1981), pp. 141–58.

Fenn, Scott, *America's Electric Utilities: Under Seige and in Transition,* Praeger, New York, 1984.

Ferrar, Terry A., Frank Clemente and Robert G. Uhler, *Electric Energy Policy Issues,* Ann Arbor Science, Ann Arbor, MI, 1979.

Festinger, Leon, *Theory of Cognitive Dissonance,* Stanford University Press, Stanford, CA, 1957.

Festinger, Leon, Stanley Schachter and Henry W. Rieken, *When Prophecy Fails,* Harper & Row, New York, 1964 (originally published 1956).

Fischer, Frank, *Technocracy and the Politics of Expertise,* Sage, Newbury Park, CA, 1990.

Formaini, Robert, *The Myth of Scientific Public Policy,* Transaction, New Brunswick, 1990.

Fox, Irving K., 'BC power development: Are we going the way of WHOOPS?', Occasional Paper, Westwater Research Center, University of British Columbia, 1983.

Galbraith, J.K., *The New Industrial State,* New American Library, New York, 1967.

Galligan, Brian, 'Federalism and resource development in Australia and Canada', *Australian Quarterly* 54 (1982), pp. 236–51.

Galligan, Brian, Aynsley Kellow and Ciaran O'Faircheallaigh, 'Minerals and energy policy' in B. Galligan (ed.), *Comparative State Policies,* Longman Cheshire, Melbourne, 1988.

Geller, Howard S., 'Implementing electricity conservation programs: Progress towards least-cost energy services among US utilities' in Thomas B. Johansson, Brigit Bodlund and Robert H. Williams (eds), *Electricity: Efficient End-use and New Generation Technologies and Their Planning Implications*, Lund University Press, Lund, 1989.

Gibbons, Jack O., *The Cost of Not Implementing Marginal Cost Pricing*, Energy Probe Research Foundation, Toronto, 1980.

Gordon, Richard L., *Reforming the Regulation of Electric Utilities*, Lexington Books, Lexington, MA, 1982.

Gormley, William T. Jr, *The Politics of Public Utility Regulation*, University of Pittsburgh Press, Pittsburgh, 1983.

Habermas, Jurgen, *Knowledge and Human Interests*, Beacon Press, Boston, 1971.

Halligan, John and John Power, *Political Management in the 1990s*, Oxford University Press, Melbourne, 1992.

Hannah, Leslie, *Electricity Before Nationalisation*, Macmillan, London, 1979.

Hannah, Leslie, *Engineers, Managers and Politicians: The First Fifteen Years of Nationalised Electricity Supply in Britain*, Macmillan, London, 1982.

Harman, Frank, 'Gas, coal and politics: Making decisions about power stations', *IPA Backgrounder* 4(3) 1992.

Hartnett, Bruce, 'Newport: A conflict over power' in Sol Encel, Peter Wilenski and Bernard Schaffer (eds), *Decisions*, Longman Cheshire, Melbourne, 1981.

Harvey, David, *The Condition of Postmodernity: An Enquiry into the Origins of Cultural Change*, Basil Blackwell, Oxford, 1989.

Hawkins, W.E., *Electrifying Calgary: A Century of Public and Private Power*, University of Calgary Press, Calgary, 1987.

Head, Brian (ed.), *State and Economy in Australia*, Oxford University Press, Melbourne, 1983.

Hellman, Richard, *Government Competition in the Electric Utility Industry: A Theoretical and Empirical Study*, Praeger, New York, 1972.

Henderson, P.D., 'Two British errors: Their probable size and some possible lessons' in C. Pollitt, L. Lewis, J. Negro and J. Patten (eds), *Public Policy in Theory and Practice*, Hodder & Stoughton, London, 1979.

Henderson, R.C., 'The evolution of public involvement in project planning at Ontario Hydro' in Dennis W. Ducsik (ed.), *Public Involvement in Energy Facility Planning: The Electric Utility Experience*, Westview Press, Boulder, CO, 1986.

Herr, R.A., and B.W. Davis, 'The Tasmanian Parliament, accountability and the Hydro Electric Commission: The Franklin River controversy' in J.R. Nethercote (ed.), *Parliament and Bureaucracy*, Hale & Iremonger, Sydney, 1982.

Higgin, R., 'Regulation of the Crown-owned electric utility in Ontario', Paper Presented to the 4th Annual CAMPUT Regulatory Educational Conference, Lake Louise, Alberta, 1990.

Hirst, Eric, 'Electric utility DSM programs through the year 2000', *Public Utilities Fortnightly* 130(4) 1992, pp. 11–14.

Hodgkinson, Ann, 'Structural changes in the world aluminium industry and implications for Australia', *Journal of Australian Political Economy* 14 (1983), pp. 34–58.

Holloway, Steven Kendall, *The Aluminium Multinationals and the Bauxite Cartel*, Macmillan, London, 1988.

Hood, Christopher, *The Limits of Administration*, Wiley, London, 1976.

Hooker, C.A., R. MacDonald, R. van Hulst and P. Victor, *Energy and the Quality of Life: Understanding Energy Policy*, University of Toronto Press, Toronto, 1981.

Hughes, Thomas P., *Networks of Power: Electrification in Western Society 1880–1930*, Johns Hopkins University Press, Baltimore, 1983.

Hutton, L.B., and F.N. Stace (eds), *The Engineering History of Electric Supply in New Zealand*, Electric Supply Authority Engineer's Institute of New Zealand, Wellington, 1958.

ICF Incorporated, *The Economic Costs of an Electricity Supply–Demand Imbalance*, Report Prepared for British Columbia Hydro and Power Authority, February 1982.

Jenkins, Glenn P., 'Public utility finance and economic waste', *Canadian Journal of Economics* 18 (1985), pp. 484–98.

Johansson, Thomas B., Brigit Bodlund and Robert H. Williams (eds), *Electricity: Efficient End-use and New Generation Technologies and Their Planning Implications*, Lund University Press, Lund, 1989.

Johnson, Michael, and Stephen Rix (eds), *Powering the Future: The Electricity Industry and Australia's Energy Future*, Pluto Press, Sydney, 1991.

Joskow, Paul L. and Richard Schmalensee, *Markets for Power: An Analysis of Electric Utility Deregulation*, MIT Press, Cambridge, MA, 1983.

Kaufman, Alvin, 'Electric power: Regulation of a monopoly' in Robert J. Kalter and William A. Vogely (eds), *Energy Supply and Government Policy*, Cornell University Press, Ithaca, NY, 1976.

Kaufman, Herbert, *The Forest Ranger*, Johns Hopkins University Press, Baltimore, 1960.

Kellow, Aynsley, 'Political science and political theory', *Politics* 16 (1981), pp. 33–45.

Kellow, Aynsley, *Making Policies and Prescribing Placebos: Pollution Control in New Zealand*, New Zealand Institute of Public Administration, Public Sector Research Papers IV (3), Wellington, 1983.

Kellow, Aynsley, 'Public project evaluation in an Australian state: Tasmania's dam controversy', *Australian Quarterly* 55(3) 1983, pp. 263–77.

Kellow, Aynsley, 'A neglected option in Tasmania's power debate', *Search* 14 1983–84, pp. 306–8.

Kellow, Aynsley, 'The policy roles of bureaucrats and politicians in New Zealand', *Politics* 19 (1984), pp. 43–53.

Kellow, Aynsley, 'Electricity planning in Tasmania and New Zealand: Political processes and the technological imperative', *Australian Journal of Public Administration*, 45 (1986), pp. 2–17.

Kellow, Aynsley, 'Federalism, development and the environment', *Regional Journal of Social Issues* 18 (1986), pp. 75–84.

Kellow, Aynsley, 'Promoting elegance in policy theory: Simplifying Lowi's arenas of power', *Policy Studies Journal* 16 (1988), pp. 713–24.

Kellow, Aynsley, 'Australian federalism: The need for New Zealand (as well as Canadian) comparisons', *Australian–Canadian Studies* 6 (1988), pp. 59–72.

Kellow, Aynsley, 'The dispute over the Franklin River and south-west wilderness area in Tasmania, Australia', *Natural Resources Journal* 29(1) 1989, pp. 129–46.

Kellow, A., 'Institutional arrangements for responsive electricity planning under uncertainty', Paper presented at the National Conference 'Improving Public Sector Management', Centre for Australian Public Sector Management, Griffith University, Brisbane, 5–7 July 1990.

Kennaway, Richard, 'International aspects of New Zealand's energy resources', Paper presented at the 1982 Australasian Political Studies Association Conference, Perth.

Kennedy, James Lehr, 'The role of regulators in electric utility strategic planning' in J.L. Plummer, E. Oatman and P.K. Gupta (eds), *Strategic Management and Planning for Electric Utilities*, Prentice-Hall, Englewood Cliffs, NJ, 1985.

Knight, A.W., 'The development of hydro-electric power in Tasmania' in H.G. Raggatt (ed.), *Fuel and Power in Australia*, Cheshire, Melbourne, 1969.

Kolsen, H.M., 'The economics of electricity pricing in New South Wales', *Economic Record* 42 (1966), pp. 555–71.

Laros, Michael A., and Brian J. Daly, 'Demand-side management: Surviving in the '90s', *Public Utilities Fortnightly* 130(3) 1992, pp. 16–18.

Lijphart, Arendt, 'Comparative politics and the comparative method', *American Political Science Review* 65 (1971), pp. 682–93.

Lindblom, Charles E., 'The science of "muddling through"', *Public Administration Review* 19 (1959), pp. 79–88.

Lindblom, Charles E., 'Still muddling, not yet through', *Public Administration Review* 39 (1979), pp. 517–26.

Longfield, C.M., *The Past, Present and Future of Australian Power Supplies*, Economic Society of Australia and New Zealand, Melbourne, 1947.

Lowe, Doug, *The Price of Power*, Macmillan, Melbourne, 1984.

Lowi, T.J., 'American business, public policy, case studies, and political theory', *World Politics* 16 (1964), pp. 677–715.

Lowi, T.J., 'Decision making vs policy making: Towards an antidote for technocracy', *Public Administration Review* 30 (1970), pp. 314–25.

Lowi, T.J., 'Four systems of policy, politics and choice', *Public Administration Review* 33 (1972), pp. 298–310.

Lowi, Theodore J., 'The state in politics: The relation between policy and administration' in Roger G. Noll (ed.), *Regulatory Policy and the Social Sciences*, University of California Press, Berkeley, 1985.

McColl, G.D., *The Economics of the Electricity Supply Industry in Australia*, Melbourne University Press, Melbourne, 1976.

McCraw, Thomas K., *TVA and the Power Fight 1933–39*, J.B. Lippincott, Philadelphia, 1971.

McKay, P., *Electric Empire: The Inside Story of Ontario Hydro*, Between the Lines, Toronto, 1983.

Magnusson, Warren, William K. Carroll, Charles Doyle, Monika Langer and R.B.J. Walker (eds), *The New Reality: The Politics of Restraint in British Columbia*, New Star Books, Vancouver, 1984.

Maguire, G., 'Instability in the development of the electricity supply industry in New South Wales', *Australian Quarterly* 38 (1966), pp. 9–25.

Marchak, Patricia, *Green Gold: The Forest Industry in British Columbia*, University of British Columbia Press, Vancouver, 1983.

Marcuse, Herbert, *One Dimensional Man*, Beacon Press, Boston, 1964.

Marsh, W.D., *Economics of Electric Utility Power Generation*, Oxford University Press, Oxford, 1980.

Mathews, R., *Public Investment in Australia: Study of Australian Public Authority Investment and Development*, Cheshire, Melbourne, 1967.

Mathiesen, Thomas, 'Civil disobedience at 70° north', *Contemporary Crises* 7 (1983), pp. 1–11.

Mavor, James, *Niagara in Politics: A Critical Account of the Ontario Hydro-Electric Commission*, E.P. Dutton, New York, 1925.

Mazmanian, Daniel A. and Jeanne Nienaber, *Can Organizations Change? Environmental Protection, Citizen Participation and the Army Corps of Engineers*, Brookings Institution, Washington, DC, 1979.

Meier, A.K., and J. Whittier, 'Consumer discount rates implied by consumer purchases of energy-efficient refrigerators', *Energy* 8 (1983), pp. 957–62.

Messing, Marc, H. Paul Friesma and David Morell, *Centralized Power: The Politics of Scale in Electricity Generation*, Oelgeschlager, Gunn & Hain, Cambridge, MA, 1979.

Mills, Stephen, *The New Machine Men*, Penguin, Melbourne, 1986.

Mitchell, David J., *W.A.C. Bennett and the Rise of British Columbia*, Douglas & McIntyre, Vancouver, 1983.

Morinière, Olivier de la, 'Energy service companies: The French experience' in T. Johansson, B. Bodlund and R. Williamson (eds), *Electricity: Efficient End-use and New Generation Technologies and Their Planning Implications*, Lund University Press, Lund, 1989.

Morley, J. Terence, Norman J. Ruff, Neil A. Swainson, R. Jeremy Wilson and Walter D. Young, *The Reins of Power: Governing British Columbia*, Douglas & McIntyre, Vancouver, 1983.

Motlagh, Cyrus K., *Structuring Uncertainties in Long-range Power Planning*, Michigan State University Public Utilities Papers, East Lansing, 1976.

Muirden, Bruce, *When Power Went Public: A Study in Expediency: The Nationalistion of the Adelaide Electric Supply Co.*, APSA Monograph 21, Adelaide, 1978.

Muller, R.A. and P.J. George, 'Northern hydroelectric development in an optimal expansion program for Ontario Hydro', *Canadian Public Policy* 11 (1985), pp. 522–32.

Murphy, Frederic, and Allen L. Soyster, *Economic Behavior of Electric Utilities*, Prentice-Hall, Englewood Cliffs, NJ, 1983.

Nelles, H.V., *The Politics of Development: Forests, Mines and Hydro-electric Power in Ontario 1849–1941*, Macmillan, Toronto, 1974.

Nelles, H.V., 'Public ownership of electrical utilites in Manitoba and Ontario 1906–30', *Canadian Historical Review* 57 (1976), pp. 461–85.

Newbery, David, 'Energy policy in Britain' in Peter Pearson (ed.), *Energy Policy in an Uncertain World*, Macmillan, London, 1989.

Newman, Terry, 'Tasmanian referenda since federation', Appendix T of the *Report of the Royal Commission into the Constitution Act 1934*, Government Printer, Hobart, 1982.

Noble, David F., *America by Design*, Alfred A. Knopf, New York, 1977.

Noonan, Rosslyn, *By Design*, Ministry of Works and Development, Wellington, 1975.

Oatman, E. and J.L. Plummer, 'The meaning of strategic planning in regulated and unregulated firms' in J.L. Plummer, E. Oatman and P.K. Gupta (eds), *Strategic Management and Planning for Electric Utilities*, Prentice-Hall, Englewood Cliffs, NJ, 1985.

Olley, R.E., 'Economic regulation of Crown-owned utilities', Paper Presented to the 4th Annual CAMPUT Regulatory Educational Conference, Lake Louise, Alberta, 1990.

Paehlke, Robert C., *Environmentalism and the Future of Progressive Politics*, Yale University Press, New Haven, CT, 1989.

Pearson, Peter (ed.), *Energy Policies in an Uncertain World*, Macmillan, London, 1989.

Peck, Merton J. (ed.), *The World Aluminium Industry in a Changing Energy Era*, Resources for the Future, Washington, DC, 1988.

Phillips, Charles F. Jr, *The Regulation of Public Utilities: Theory and Practice*, Public Utilities Reports, Arlington, VA, 1988.

Plewman, W.R., *Adam Beck and the Ontario Hydro*, Ryerson Press, Toronto, 1947.

Plummer, J.L., E. Oatman and P.K. Gupta (eds), *Strategic Management and Planning for Electric Utilities*, Prentice-Hall, Englewood Cliffs, NJ, 1985.

Powell, Paul, *Who Killed the Clutha?*, John McIndoe, Dunedin, 1979.

Prest, W., 'The electricity supply industry' in A. Hunter (ed.), *The Economics of Australian Industry: Studies in Environment and Structure*, Melbourne University Press, Melbourne, 1963.

Price, Don K., *The Scientific Estate*, Harvard University Press, Cambridge, MA, 1965.

Prichard, J. Robert S. (ed.), *Crown Corporations in Canada: The Calculus of Instrument Choice*, Butterworths, Toronto, 1983.

Pringle, Peter, and James Spigelman, *The Nuclear Barons*, Michael Joseph, London, 1982.

Puiseux, Louis, 'The ups and downs of electricity forecasting in France: Technocratic elitism' in T. Baumgartner and A. Midttun (eds), *The Politics of Energy Forecasting*, Clarendon Press, Oxford, 1987.

Pusey, Michael, *Economic Rationalism in Canberra: A Nation-building State Changes its Mind*, Cambridge University Press, Melbourne, 1991.

Ramsey, W., *Unpaid Costs of Electrical Energy*, Johns Hopkins University Press, Baltimore, 1979.

Read, P., *The Organisation of Electricity Supply in Tasmania*, University of Tasmania, Hobart, 1986.

Reeves, W. Pember, *State Experiments in Australia and New Zealand*, Macmillan, Melbourne, 1969.

Riley, Richard B., 'Public policy and the electric power industry in Canada: A comparative political analysis of power development in three western provinces', unpublished PhD dissertation, Duke University, 1975.

Roberts, Jane, David Elliott and Trevor Houghton, *Privatising Electricity: The Politics of Power*, Belhaven Press, London, 1991.

Roberts, Marc J., and Jeremy Bluhm, *The Choices of Power: Utilities Face the Environmental Challenge*, Harvard University Press, Cambridge, MA, 1981.

Robertson, E.J., 'Regulating Crown as opposed to investor-owned utilities: Some comments', Paper Presented to the 4th Annual CAMPUT Regulatory Educational Conference, Lake Louise, Alberta, 1990.

Robinson, J.B., 'Bottom-up methods and low-down results: Changes in the estimation of future energy demands', *Energy* 7 (1982), pp. 627–35.

Robinson, J.B., 'Backing into the future: On the methodological and institutional biases embedded in energy supply and demand forecasting', *Technological Forecasting and Social Change* 21 (1982), pp. 229–40.

Robinson, J.B., 'Energy backcasting: A proposed method of policy analysis', *Energy Policy* 10 (1982), pp. 337–44.

Rosenthal, S., and P. Russ, *The Politics of Power: Inside Australia's Electric Utilities*, Melbourne University Press, Melbourne, 1988.

Rowse, John, 'Toward optimal capacity expansion for an electric utility: The case of Saskatchewan Power', *Canadian Journal of Economics* 11 (1978), pp. 447–69.

Rowse, John, 'Economic benefits of co-operative power supply expansion', *Journal of Regional Science* 21 (1981), pp. 389–402.

Russell, Milton (ed.), *Perspectives in Public Regulation: Essays on Political Economy*, Southern Illinois University Press, Carbondale, IL, 1972.

Sabatier, Paul, 'Social movements and regulatory agencies: Toward a more adequate and less pessimistic theory of clientele capture', *Policy Science* 6 (1975), pp. 301–42.

Sanghvi, A., and D. Limaye, 'Planning for electrical generation capacity in the Pacific northwest: A decision analysis of the costs of over- and under-building', *Energy Policy* 7 (1979), pp. 102–16.

Sayre, Kenneth M. et al., *Regulation, Values and the Public Interest*, The Philosophic Institute of University of Notre Dame, Notre Dame, IN, 1980.

Schon, Donald A., *Beyond the Stable State*, Penguin, London, 1971.

Searle, J.N.L., *The New Zealand Electricity Industry: Its Organisation and Financial Structure*. Society of Accountants, Wellington, NZ, 1975.

Selznick, Philip, *TVA and the Grass Roots: A Study in the Sociology of Formal Organization*, University of California Press, Berkeley, 1949.

Sewell, W.R. Derrick, 'Energy in British Columbia', *British Columbia: Its Resources and Its People*, University of Victoria, Department of Geography (Western Geographical Series Vol. 24), Victoria, BC, 1986.

Shaffer, Marvin, 'Electricity planning under conditions of uncertainty', Seminar Paper, Department of Economics, Latrobe University, 3 May 1985.

Shaffer, Marvin, 'The benefits and costs of two BC Hydro construction projects', in Robert C. Allen and Gideon Rosenbluth (eds), *Restraining the Economy*, Economic Policy Institute, Vancouver, BC, 1986.

Shanks, Bernard, 'Dams and disasters: The social problems of water development policies' in J. Baden and R. Stroup (eds), *Bureaucracy vs Environment: The Environmental Costs of Bureaucratic Governance*, University of Michigan Press, Ann Arbor, 1981.

Shapiro, David, *Generating Failure: Public Power Policy in the Northwest*, University Press of America, Lanham, 1989.

Sichel, Werner, *Salvaging Public Utility Regulation*, Lexington Books, Lexington, MA, 1976.

Smith, G., 'The Tasmanian House of Assembly elections, 1982', *Politics* 17 (1982), pp. 81–8.

Smith, P., *Brinco: The Story of Churchill Falls*, McClelland & Stewart, Toronto, 1975.

Soloman, Lawrence, *Energy Shock*, Doubleday, Toronto, 1980.

Soloman, Lawrence, *Power at What Cost?*, Energy Probe Research Foundation, Toronto, 1984.

Sporn, P., *The Social Organization of Electric Power Supply in Modern Societies*, MIT Press, Cambridge, MA, 1971.

Stanley, J.K., and V.J. Martin, *Aluminium Smelting: A Cost-benefit Analysis*, Premier's Department, Victoria (Discussion Paper No. 4), September 1979; Postscript January 1980.

Stern, P.C. and E. Aronson (eds), *Energy Use: The Human Dimension*, W.H. Freeman, New York, 1984.

Stevenson, Garth, 'Mineral resources and Australian federalism', Research Monograph No. 17, Centre for Research on Federal Financial Relations, ANU, Canberra, 1976.

Stevenson, Garth, 'Federalism and the political economy of the Canadian state' in Leo Panitch (ed.), *The Canadian State*, University of Toronto Press, Toronto, 1977.

Stevenson, Garth, *Rail Transport and Australian Federalism* (Research Monograph No. 48), Centre for Research on Federal Financial Relations, Australian National University, Canberra, 1987.

Sullivan, Frank C., *Crisis of Confidence: Utilities, Public Relations and Credibility*, Phoenix, Canaan, NH, 1977.

Sultan, Ralph G.M., *Pricing in the Electrical Oligopoly (vols 1 & 2)*, Harvard University Press, Cambridge, MA, 1974 & 1975.

Swainson, N.A., *Conflict Over the Columbia: The Background of an Historic Treaty*, McGill-Queens University Press, Montreal, 1979.

Swan, Peter L., 'The economics of QANGOs: SECV and ELCOM' in *The Economics of Bureaucracy and Statutory Authorities*, CIS Policy Forums No. 1, 1983.

Taylor, Serge, *Making Bureaucracies Think: The Environmental Impact Statement Strategy of Administrative Reform*, Stanford University Press, Stanford, CA, 1984.

Technology Future Inc. and Scientific Foresight Inc., *Principles for Electric Power Policy*, Quorum Books, Westport, CT, 1984.

Thompson, Peter, *Power in Tasmania*, Australian Conservation Foundation, Melbourne, 1981.

Tighe, P. J., 'Hydroindustrialisation and conservation policy in Tasmania' in K.J. Walker (ed.), *Australian Environmental Policy*, University of New South Wales Press, Kensington, 1992.

Townsley, W.A., *The Government of Tasmania*, University of Queensland Press, St Lucia, 1976.

Trethowan, J.C., 'Public enterprise', *Australian Journal of Public Administration* 36 (1977), pp. 44–51.

Uslaner, Eric M., 'Energy, issue agendas, and policy typologies' in Helen M. Ingram and R. Kenneth Godwin (eds), *Public Policy and the Natural Environment*, JAI Press, Greenwich, CT, 1985.

Veblein, Thorstein, *Engineers and the Price System*, A.M. Kelly, New York, 1921.

Victoria, Parliament, Natural Resources and Environment Committee, *Electricity Supply and Demand Beyond the Mid 1990s*, April 1988.

Vining, A., 'Provincial hydro utilities' in Allan Tupper and G. Bruce Doern (eds), *Public Corporations and Public Policy*, Institute for Research on Public Policy, Montreal, 1981.

White, Clinton O., *Power for a Province: A History of Saskatchewan Power*, University of Regina, Regina, 1976.

Wildavsky, Aaron, *Dixon-Yates: A Study in Power Politics*, Yale University Press, New Haven, CT, 1962.

Wildavsky, Aaron, 'If planning is everything, maybe it is nothing', *Policy Sciences* 4(1973), pp. 127–53.

Wildavsky, Aaron, and Mary Douglas, *Risk and Culture*, University of California Press, Berkeley, 1981.

Williams, Robert H., 'Innovative approaches to marketing electric efficiency' in Thomas B. Johansson, Brigit Bodlund and Robert H. Williams (eds), *Electricity: Efficient End-use and New Generation Technologies and Their Planning Implications*, Lund University Press, Lund, 1989.

Winner, Langdon, *Autonomous Technology: Technics-out-of-control as a Theme in Political Thought*, MIT Press, Cambridge, MA, 1977.

Wittfogel, K.A., *Oriental Despotism: A Comparative Study of Total Power*, Yale University Press, New Haven, CT, 1957.

World Bank, *The World Bank's Role in the Electric Power Sector: Policies for Effective Institutional, Regulatory, and Financial Reform*, World Bank, Washington, DC, 1993.

Young, Oran, *Natural Resources and the State*, University of California Press, Berkeley, 1981.

Zinberg, Dorothy S. (ed.), *Uncertain Power: The Struggle for a National Energy Policy*, Pergamon Press, New York, 1983.

Zucker, Richard C. and Glenn P. Jenkins, *Blue Gold: Hydro-electric Rent in Canada*, Economic Council of Canada, Ottawa, 1984.

Index